ALDRIDGE CRICKET
1853 - 2003

RB Publishing

First published in 2005 by RB Publishing
116, Aldridge Road
Little Aston
Aldridge
WALSALL
WS9 0PF

For
Aldridge Cricket Club

The Stick & Wicket Pavilion
The Cricket Ground,
The Green
Aldridge
WALSALL
WS9 8NH

© **Copyright 2005** Aldridge Cricket Club & RB Publishing

All rights reserved. No part of this publication may be reproduced, stored in a retrieval system or transmitted, in any form or by any means, electronic, mechanical, photocopying, recording or otherwise, without prior permission in writing from either RB Publishing or Aldridge Cricket Club.

ISBN 0 - 9521381 - 3 - 1

Design & Layout by **Robin G A Bolton**
Typeset in 10pt Book Antiqua by
RB Publishing, Little Aston, Aldridge, Walsall

Printed and bound in Great Britain by
Warwick Printing Company Limited
Caswell Road, Leamington Spa, Warwickshire, CV31 1QD

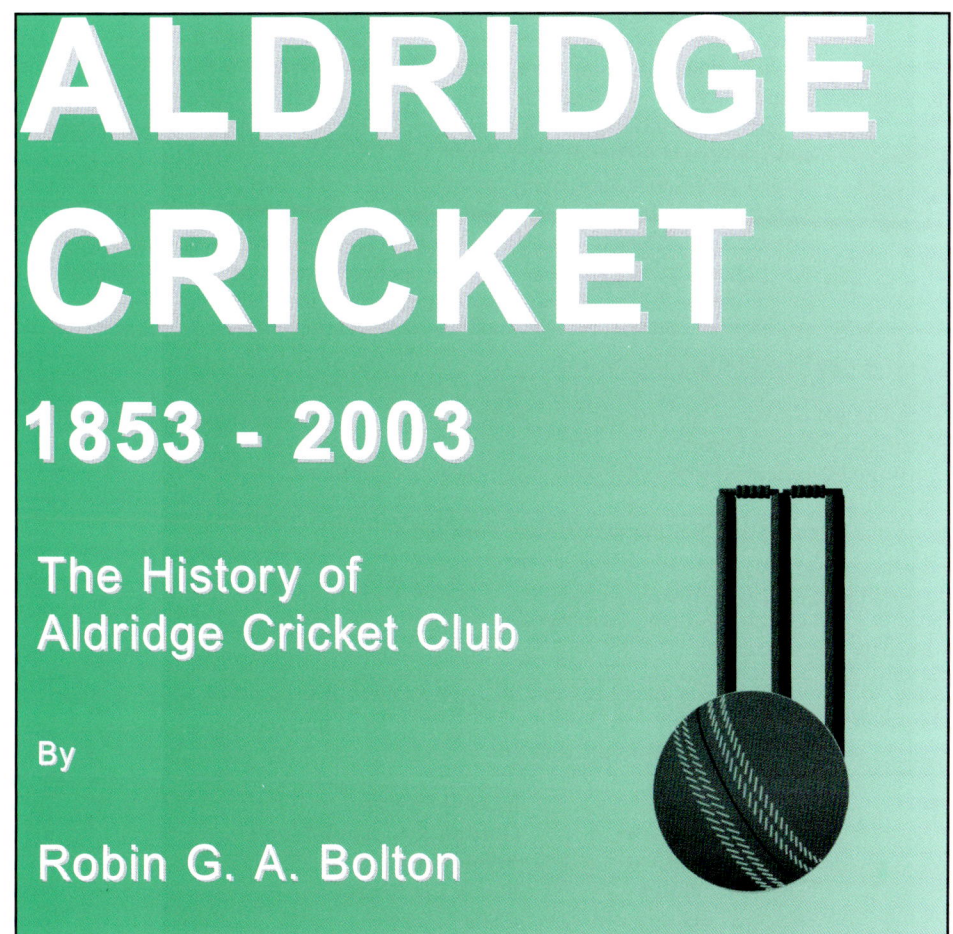

The Author
Robin G. A. Bolton

Rob's qualifications for writing and producing Aldridge Cricket stem initially from the fact that he has spent most of his life in the environs of Aldridge and Walsall. In producing this book, his love of historical research, especially of Local History and Historical Geography, has been combined with being an avid follower of the game of Cricket at national level. It has also provided a unique opportunity to explore just how the game is rooted in the social and physical fabric of his local area.

Early retirement from the teaching profession, has afforded Rob the time to research, write and produce books and magazine articles. Publications to date have mainly been focused upon the branch of youth work which particularly interests him - that of the Brigade Movement (Boys' Brigade etc.) and aspects of related social history, especially from the nineteenth century. A special interest is that of photographs of those brigades from the late 19th and early 20th centuries. After spending many years energetically involved with The Boys' Brigade, Youth Marching Bands, and Community Circus, he still retains some links with his past. He is involved with the Church Lads' & Church Girls' Brigade as well as The Boys' Brigade, in various national projects, preservation of archives and competition judging. Any 'spare' time is given over to working in the garden or walking in the countryside.

Acknowledgements

Paul Bailey & Bloxwich Cricket Club.
Stan Brookhouse Aldridge Historical Society
Donald Heitzman Aldridge Historical Society
Janet Hopley Aldridge Parish Church.
Brian Lund 'Reflections of a Bygone Age' Nottingham (Comic Postcards)
John Sale Aldridge Historical Society
Walsall Local History Centre, Essex St. Walsall.
Birmingham Local Studies Dept., Central Library, Birmingham.
Lichfield Record Office, The Friary, Lichfield.

> The author would like to thank all officials, members and former members of the Cricket Club for their enthusiasm, assistance and support throughout the months of preparation. In particular, thanks are due to:

Keith & Sally Buller	Sam Harvey	Russell Pickston
John Burton	Frank C. Hastilow	Gordon & Barbara Popple
Phil Butler	Dr Mearns Milne	Bryan Popple
Keith Davies	David Partridge	Bob & Liz Riggs
Bob Dyer	Stephen Peak	Chris Talbot
Jonathan Franks	Mike Pemberton	Alan Waldron
Jim Hartley	Arthur Pheasant	Ian Whittock

Sam Harvey

Sources

Newspapers from the Walsall Local History Collection: In particular: Walsall Observer & Walsall Advertiser. (Microfilm)
Newspapers from the Birmingham Local Studies Dept. Central Library, Birmigham. (Microfilm)
Score Books and Minute Books 1905 - 2004 Aldridge Cricket Club. Some deposited at the Walsall Local History Centre.
The Complete History of the Walsall Cricket Club. Evans, Benjamin. Privately published, 1909.
Aldridge Cricket. Matthews, Jack. Aldridge Cricket Club, 1948
Aldridge, Rushall and Pelsall Yesterdays. Woodall, Richard D. Norman A. Tector Ltd., undated: c.1952
Men of Aldridge. Gould, Jim. Alan Sutton, (First Published 1957) 2nd Edition, 1983.
Town & Westminster, A Political History of Walsall. Dean, Kenneth J. Walsall County Borough, 1972
The Wisdom of Aldridge Cricket Club. Pemberton, Mike. Privately published, 1978.
Arlott on Cricket. Allen, David Rayvern (Ed). Fontana/Collins, 1984.
Cricket On The Air. Allen, David Rayvern. BBC, 1985.
The History of Bloxwich Cricket Club. Jenkinson, T. H.. Bloxwich Cricket Club, 1986.
Aldridge History Trail. Fox, Betty. Walsall Local History Centre, 1990.
Aldridge in Old Photographs. Farrow, Jan. Alan Sutton, 1991.
Heraldry for the Local Historian & Genealogist. Friar, Stephen, Sutton Publishing, 1992.
The Daily Telegraph Chronicle of Cricket. Barrett, Norman (Ed). Guinness Publishing, 1994.
Street Names of Aldridge, Rushall, Streetly & Pheasey. Fox, Betty. Walsall Local History Centre, 1996.
The Midland Counties Combined League Handbook, MCCL, 1996.
Aldridge Revisited. Farrow, Jan. Sutton Publishing, 1998.
Aldridge Village Memories. Brookhouse, Stan & Sale, John. Privately published, 2001.
150 Years of Aldridge Cricket Club, Official Commemorative Brochure. Whinyates, David (Ed). Aldridge C.C. 2003.
The Aldridge Cricket Club Website. www.aldridgecricketclub.co.uk

Foreword

It is indeed a privilege and an honour to be writing this brief Foreword to what is the third, and certainly the most comprehensive, book chronicling the history of Aldridge Cricket.

I have been associated with the Club for almost a third of its existence and from the outset was impressed by the traditions it expounded. In my early days at Aldridge I was fortunate enough to be given a very rare item - a copy of Jack Matthews' book 'Aldridge Cricket'. Its pages have always seemed to epitomise the care and commitment given so willingly by successive men and women over the generations. I trust that in some small way those of us such as myself, Jonathan Franks, Gordon Popple, Alan Waldron and many others who follow in his footsteps, will continue in that tradition.

Our Club facilities today rival any to be found in the midlands and I have no doubt our forebears would have been justly proud of them. This book records in detail the tremendous progress made by Aldridge Cricket over 150 years.

We are indebted to Robin Bolton for all the hard work and commitment he has given to this project. Robin, a former teaching colleague, could not have guessed that a chance meeting in Aldridge, and a tentative enquiry as to whether he would be interested in doing it, would have led to him being engrossed for two years. Thanks to his thorough and painstaking work we now have a comprehensive knowledge of not only the 20th century history but also extensive information relating to the first fifty years, a period previously unknown.

This publication will appeal not only to current and former members of Aldridge Cricket Club and those associated with it, but also to those interested in the history of the locality. I particularly recommend this book to our younger 'Academy' members in the hope that they may grow to understand and value their heritage and all it stands for.

I trust that the reader will be rewarded with as much information, and experience as much enjoyment, as Robin, myself and the others who have contributed to its production.

Russell Pickston

Hon. Secretary, Aldridge Cricket Club

Contents

	PAGES
Introduction	1 - 2
'Jack'	3 - 4
The 1860s & 70s	5 - 8
The 1880s & 90s	9 - 14
Playing Statistics/Records 1853 - 1904	14
The 1900s & 10s	15 - 25
The Club Crest	26
The 1920s & 30s	27 - 33
Trophies	34
The 1940s & 50s	35 - 42
The 1960s & 70s	43 - 52
The 1980s - 2003	53 - 59
The Ladies	60
Groundsmen, Grounds and Pavilions	61 - 77
Club Officials	78
Club Presidents	79 - 83
Playing Statistics/Records 1905 - 2004	84 - 85
On Tour	86 - 90
Benefit Games	91 - 95
The Davies Family	96 - 97
Colts/Juniors/Youth Academy	98 - 100
The Social Side	101 - 106

Introduction

A record of happiness...

Aldridge Cricket Club 1853 - 2003

When Jack Matthews was penning his little review 'Aldridge Cricket' just after the Second World War, he naturally, possessed the massive advantage of meeting regularly with, and in many cases knowing as close friends, people connected with Aldridge Cricket Club since the early years of the century. Having an unsurpassed and intimate knowledge of the workings of the Club from his own experience over more than forty years was clearly very helpful. For Jack it was a labour of love but not one without some inherent sadness, for he was unable to chronicle the period before his arrival in Aldridge. A small snippet of information from fragments of an old newspaper served only to provide a tantalising glimpse into a nineteenth century world, which he assumed would forever remain cloaked in mystery. Jack was, of course, unable to utilise the information resources and technology that are today taken for granted. The Walsall Local History Centre with its microfilms of old newspapers along with the ability many of us now have to communicate via computer are two that readily come to mind. Jack's detailed and erudite testimony ended in 1948, the baton being taken up again some thirty years later by Club member Mike Pemberton in his book 'The Wisdom of Aldridge Cricket'. Mike's work differed from that of Jack in that it was very much focused upon the records of players. Both his effort and achievement in assembling 'Wisdom' was colossal, and it remains the Club's definitive statistical analysis. Using the minutes of the Club meetings, Jack's book, writing columns for the local paper and many years of Club experience, Mike was also well positioned to summarise the history to 1978. There is no doubt in my mind that the task of producing this book, particularly as one who is an 'outsider' so to speak - who has never played for the Club, has been made very much smoother by having these two exceptional volumes to hand.

Following months of intensive document and newspaper research, some forty years of previously unknown Club history, prior to 1905, has now been revealed. This new information includes matches, players and Presidents, although sadly, not that elusive precise foundation date. Remarkably, whilst delving deeply into the Walsall Local History Centre Newspaper Archive, I came across the date of 1812 for the formation of Walsall Cricket Club, certainly the oldest club in the area, and a fact previously unknown to that institution! The last fifty years of cricket at Aldridge have now been explored and detailed with numerous photographs employed to both assist and enhance the narrative. Jack's book 'Aldridge Cricket' featured only eight photographs and 'The Wisdom of Aldridge Cricket' used no illustrations, so I make no apology at this juncture, for fully exploiting the visual medium.

Jack Matthews wrote in 1948...

'Some few years ago, the brothers Bert and Walter Myring (now both deceased), were engaged in the demolition of a Wesleyan Church in Birmingham, and under the foundation stone found, amongst other papers, a "Birmingham Post" dated June 23, 1874, in which is given in detail an account of a match which took place at Aldridge between the home team and a club known as "Walsall Albion".

As one may expect, the record of a century and a half of Aldridge cricket includes heroes and famous players. It is, however, mainly and most importantly about those folk who just want to enjoy their sport and participate in a game they love. There are unfortunately many, not mentioned in this record, who have helped to shape Aldridge C.C. and for whom the Club has been a big part of their life. I have no wish to exclude anyone, but there are just too many to name them all due to the very size and longevity of the Club. The sense of total commitment to and involvement in the Club, is one aspect of membership that has, perhaps, changed more than ever over the years. Fifty or more years ago, a player's time was not only given up for games but also a rich local social life and circle of friends where everything was Club-related. As a village 'institution' the Club was paramount and all pervasive as it had been for much of the previous century. Today, players frequently come from outside the Aldridge area, they turn up, play and then return home, perhaps many miles away. There are still some, however, whose whole family life 'cradle to grave' has centred round the Club. Brought to the ground in pushchairs by their young parents to watch Grandad playing, they later followed the fortunes of Dad as he got into the First XI. Whilst still at primary school they made new friends whilst visiting the Club and before they knew it they had spent their whole youth there. Marriages were often the result of meetings at the Club. Now, as players, they bring their own children to watch or to play. It is this continuity which makes a cricket book such a pleasure to write and hopefully to

Aldridge Cricket Club 1853 - 2003

read. John Arlott, that great broadcaster and commentator on the game, writing a foreword for a cricket club centenary book in 1975 summed up cricket books as follows:

'Above all, though, they evoke nostalgic memories, recall each local generation's heroes - and provide a record of happiness the game gives. A cricket club is a nucleus such as no other sport possesses in comparable numbers; a boy may grow up in its shadow, to play in his manhood, and watch in his old age in a continuity he could hardly expect of other games. That, surely, is why cricket histories abound - and why it will be a sad day for cricket when they cease to be written.'

Although Cricket is a sport played well by young fit and healthy men and women, it is, of course, also a game requiring the development of a considerable range of skills. For most, these skills are quite often only honed to perfection just as the body starts to feel the onset of 'age'. At Aldridge there have been many players who have worked their way through the Junior sides and into the 3rd, 2nd, and eventually the 1st XI, played there for maybe ten years and then retired willingly to the 2nds and 3rds in later life. This sometimes means a playing career well in excess of 40 years! Association with the Club, of course, often continues well after a lengthy playing career has finished. Many Aldridge players have, with great distinction, continued to be involved with the Club by coaching, serving on a cricket committee, umpiring or perhaps helping with the 'Stick and Wicket'.

Given the fact that over the years the close association between Club and Village has diminished, a distinct feature of the Club has always been its ties with Aldridge people. In researching this history it has sometimes been impossible to separate one from the other - the Club has been part of the local scene, part of its history, frequently near the centre of it. The story of cricket and community has been strongly inter-woven, bound together with complex strings of everyday life. Originally, the team comprised landed gentry, farmers, factory owners and even military folk. Rectors and Curates of Aldridge who had, before 1853, travelled to Walsall for their cricket, were, upon the formation of the Club, able to get involved locally with playing and administration. Church organists, Choirmasters, Vergers and even Grave-diggers were also part of the Club. The decorative names over Shops and Public houses along the High Street, the likes of Baker, Wincer, Hilditch, and Swann frequently mirrored the Cricket Club Team List - regularly posted in the windows of those self-same establishments. Famous village doctors such as Cooke, and Milne, solicitors like Potter, and Partridge, teachers, saddlers, builders, decorators, garage mechanics, printers, workers at the coal mines and brick-works formed the backbone of the team for many years. More recently, factory and office workers from the new local Industrial estates and many from further afield have joined the Club. When there was a Parish Council,

and later an Urban District Council, members of the Club such as Sam Bonner, Howard Walton and Jessie Buckley were active participants. Friendly Societies, social clubs and other sports clubs in the village were often run and supported by members of the Club, notably of course, the Hockey Club which has shared a ground for a century and now partners the Club in running the 'Stick & Wicket'.

Village cricket has changed. It is, of course, as John Arlott put it, still 'a serious matter'. In July 1955 C. Gordon Glover in a Radio broadcast called 'The Truth About Village Cricket' talked with disdain of some of the 'wishful mush' which had been written about village cricket in the past ...

'The brown boots, waistcoats, and braces of other days have gone. Village cricket is mighty respectable these days. Even grey flannels can raise a frown. The hard-hitting blacksmith - if ever he existed- is now replaced by the wiry technician from Pest Control. The country parson is a rare bird upon the field today. And the wicket itself rarely displays the picturesque and hazardous evidence of cattle which have paused in passing. And these things are probably all to the good, if it is a game of cricket and not a comic charade which is required. Nevertheless, let us be honest about the matter. Village cricket seldom was, seldom is, and seldom will be the nursery of Test cricketers. It is a law - and a pretty astringent one- unto itself. Picturesque possibly, hot-tempered certainly, but a piece of sacrosanct, buttercuppy mumbo-jumbo, not at all!'

Aldridge C.C. in 1955, could still 'boast' a reasonable quantity of the 'hazardous evidence of cattle' as well as a country parson, although no doubt, the latter would have objected strongly-and perhaps irreverently, to being grouped on the field with the former. Certainly, whilst hardly ever a comedy, it did take the Club decades to shake off the image of being trapped in a bygone rustic world. Cricket today is a much more complicated professional business than it was in the 1950s. More leagues, more teams, more travelling, more weeknight games, more semi-professional players, more changeable sides, Youth Academy, electronic scoreboard etc. All this along with a ground and its facilities experiencing infinitely more uses than could have been dreamt of half a century ago.

It is the sincere hope of the author that the reader will derive as much pleasure from the perusal of this record of one hundred and fifty years of happiness as he has found in compiling it.

'Jack'

Aldridge Cricket Club 1853 · 2003

John H. Matthews Aldridge Cricket Club 1902 - 1960

The Midlands Club Cricket Conference Year Book for 1950 in its 'Cricketers of the Year' feature, aptly summed up 'Jack Matthews' by stating that his name and that of Aldridge Cricket Club were synonymous. He was appointed to the village school in 1902 and perhaps because of his love of sport, particularly football and cricket, or because the Headmaster Mr Frank Stephens was Club Captain, Jack became immediately associated with the club. Initially as a playing member, he was according to Howard Walton 'a bowler of no mean ability', but from 1913 as Hon. Secretary and Treasurer. In his own likeable and amiable way he piloted the club through rough and smooth waters along with stalwarts such as Alf Buckley, Howard Walton and Bill Groves. A confirmed Bachelor, he lived with Mr & Mrs Alf Buckley at Druids Heath.

Jack was a strong believer in the good influence games have on character and he was untiring in his efforts to create a keen spirit amongst his lads in their school sports. Many distinguished Aldridge cricketers received their early training under him at school and were guided into to the club through his efforts. Arthur Pheasant, Frank Hastilow, Sam Harvey, et al. Some of his pupils went on to achieve honours in a wide variety of sporting fields. Charlie Holland, as well as playing for Jack's football team, played Cricket and Hockey for the Aldridge Clubs as well as starring in two Olympic Games as part of the British Cycling Team. C. H. Ward the eminent Ryder Cup player and 1949 champion golfer, was introduced to sport in one of Jack's football teams. Stan Brookhouse, the Aldridge Historian and one-time scorer for the club remembers him well... *'We liked him as a teacher, we were all keen on sports'*. On Mondays and Wednesdays he ran a boys' club at the Assembly Rooms, which according to Arthur Pheasant, always seemed to include games.

In 1937 & 1938, along with Dr Victor Milne, he organised and conducted enjoyable and successful cricket tours of Scotland with the 'Staffordshire Knots' recruited mainly from Aldridge players but supplemented by neighbouring clubs such as Bloxwich. If anything was being organised for Aldridge Cricket Club then Jack was behind it, fund-raising Whist Drives in the Assembly Rooms, in Rookery Lane, being his speciality. Jack was proud of his county and often wore a blazer sporting a splendid Staffordshire Knot badge.

Retirement from teaching only served to increase Jack's devotion to furthering the welfare of the club. Sam Harvey remembers that he was a common sight in the vil-

lage driving around in his car with registration No. 'BRE 352' In January 1949, his famous volume 'Aldridge Cricket', appeared. It was written in October of the previous year. A most entertaining book, far more than a mere history, it received an enthusiastic welcome from all past and present members of the club and could be obtained for 10/6d at Aldridge Post Office or direct from the author. Although produced at great personal cost, Jack obviously enjoyed its compilation, he inscribed a number of copies thus:

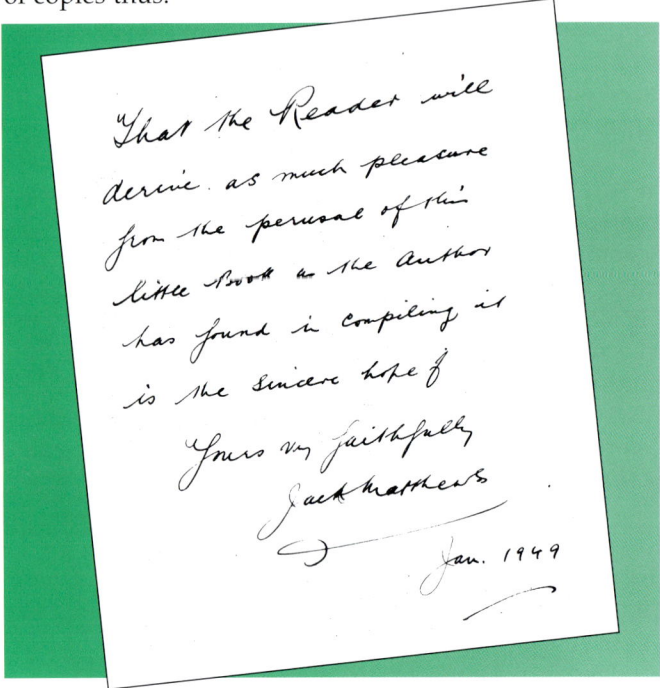

'That the Reader will derive as much pleasure from the perusal of this little Book as the Author has found in Compiling it, is the sincere hope of Yours Very faithfully, Jack Matthews'

ALDRIDGE CRICKET CLUB

ALDRIDGE,
January, 1949.

To Cricketers and all others interested.

We wish to bring to your notice the Book "Aldridge Cricket," written by our Hon. Secretary, Mr. J. Matthews.

Those who have so far seen and read it, acknowledge that here is the book all have long been waiting for.

It is written in a most entertaining and interesting style, and besides being a very complete and up-to-date history, deals with practically every aspect of the Club's activities.

The fine photographs and handsome binding make it a book worthy of the splendid traditions of this old established Club—in fact, a book you will be proud to own.

Mr. Matthews, we know, has been under great personal expense in producing the book, but he is hoping that sufficient copies will be sold to enable him to hand over a profit to the New Pavilion Fund.

We trust all members will purchase a copy, and do their utmost to make the book a financial success.

A. BUCKLEY, *President*
H. WALTON, *Chairman*
W. GROVES, *Captain*

Aldridge Cricket Club.

Some personal tributes to Jack's book appeared with the order form. Dr Milne wrote four paragraphs, opening with:
'As a general rule, Cricket histories with their recurring lists of names, dates, scores, etc., make rather drab reading, but in this work the writer has dealt with necessary facts and figures in a way that will cause no boredom to the reader.'

Ivor Wincer stated: *'...Has brought back to me many happy memories, some still fresh in my mind, notably my first century for Aldridge,'*. The 'Walsall Observer' of January 1st 1949 reported: *'A book that will be warmly welcomed by many followers of local cricket, even outside Aldridge ...The Author is able to write from personal knowledge of the Club for 46 years...introduces many personal touches about players, and recalls many amusing incidents.'*

Jack's 'Little Book' is now a treasured possession of a select group of Aldridge Cricket folk and copies are unobtainable on the open market. It tells the story of most of the middle third of the Club's 150 year history, a time when it grew from being just an ordinary village side into one of the premier clubs of the Midlands. To paraphrase the words of Howard Walton in his Foreword *'For fifty eight years Jack Matthews **was** the Aldridge Cricket Club'*.

In 1953 as part of the Club's Centenary celebrations a plaque was installed in the pavilion in celebration of Jack's 40 yrs service.

I make no apology for re-using much of Jack's information and text in this volume. Where I have quoted him verbatim the text is printed in green.

The 1860s & '70s

Aldridge Cricket Club 1853 - 2003

A summer's day 1861. The lark sings high in the sky and the incense of wild flowers and fresh mown grass fills the air. Farmer Joseph Proffitt's field in the Staffordshire village of Aldridge, although not exactly flat, on this day sports two sets of stumps out in the middle. A small tent has been erected near the boundary hedge to serve as a pavilion and changing room, and the excited tones of mens voices can be heard through its canvas walls. All is set for a special holiday game, not just any game, the game - of cricket. It was Monday August 19th and the Aldridge eleven, a mixture of village gentlemen, farmers, shopkeepers etc. some of whom had played since the early days of the club some eight or nine years before, were looking forward to a fine game. In this scene, replicated no doubt throughout much of the kingdom, they were hosting their local friends but arch cricketing rivals, who hailed from nearby Walsall Wood.

The umpires took their places and the Aldridge men arranged themselves in the field. Walsall Wood was to bat first, with openers Cresswell and Jackson striding purposefully to the wicket for what would be a much shorter stay than they might have wished. Mr T. C. Bagnall, Aldridge's star player, was rapidly into action dismissing Cresswell for only two runs. Stumps began to fly as the irregular and unfamiliar Aldridge track proved disastrous for the visitors, only six batsman scoring and none achieving more than four runs; even with byes the Walsall Wood total was only 21. Such a score, however, was not untypical on a makeshift wicket and the Walsall Wood players were not too downhearted. Next, it was the turn of the home side to show what they were made of. Playing at number three T. C. Bagnall, not satisfied with his five-wicket haul, top scored with a splendid 15 runs inspiring team-mates Davenhill and Eglington to reach double figures. By the time the visiting bowlers, notably Smith and Cresswell, had struggled to see off all the Aldridge men, the total had climbed to a mighty 74 runs, quite a feat! Being a day match the men of Walsall Wood attempted to regain their pride in the second innings, but again fell victim to the village bowlers, managing to scrape together only 17 runs in total. Aldridge finished as convincing winners, by an innings and thirty-six runs. No doubt the celebrations, in the Swan, Anchor and Elms Inns in the High Street went on well into the evening.

We have to thank the Walsall Free Press & Advertiser for the record of this 1861 game, the earliest which could be found. The details published are shown below:

WALSALL WOOD

	1st			2nd	
G. Cresswell	b. Bagnall	2	b. Bagnall		2
H. Jackson	b. H. Jackson	4	s. H. Jackson		2
D. Smith	s. Bagnall	3	s. H. Jackson		3
T. Cresswell	s. Bagnall	0	l.b.w.		1
T. Lowbridghe	b. Bagnall	0	b. H. Jackson		0
W.S. Joberns	b. Bagnall	0	b. H. Jackson		0
- Cooper	c. Elliott	0	l.b.w.		0
S. Nutting	c. Elliott	3	s. H. Jackson		2
T. Langford	b. Bagnall	4	not out		4
T. Adkins	b. Bagnall	0	b. Bagnall		0
P. Jilks	not out	1	b. Bagnall		1
	Byes &c	4	Byes &c		2
		21			17

ALDRIDGE

	1st	
W. Bate	b. G. Cresswell	6
H. Jackson	b. G. Cresswell	8
T. C. Bagnall	c. G. Cresswell	15
G. Merrall	c. G. Cresswell	0
H. Davenhill	c. Cooper	12
W. Davenhill	c. Cooper	2
- Horseley	b. Smith	0
W. Eglington	b. Smith	11
T. Matthews	b. Smith	9
W. Elliott	b. Cresswell	4
V. Reynolds,	not out	2
	Byes &c	5
		74

Note: Farmer Joseph Proffitt lived in Lea House very close to the present cricket field, and owned land called Bithams and Druid Field.

The Swan Inn c.1860

White's Directory of 1851 and Kelly's Post Office Directory 1868 give us a deeper insight into the make - up of the Aldridge team at the time. At least three of the players were farmers, William Bate, Henry Davenhill and William McKenzie Eglington. Eglington, from Bourne Vale, and his rustic friends were establishing a tradition of farmers playing in, and being associated with, the Aldridge Club. Such associations would last for some seventy years and include Samuel Bonner of Manor House Farm and the legendary Howard Walton who for a time farmed part of Manor House Farm (the Bithams) and later the Bull's Head Farm, Barr Common. T. C. Bagnall was probably Mr Thomas Bagnall resident at 'The Red House' Great Barr, or at least one of that family. Thomas Matthews was a prominent Aldridge resident and Vincent Reynolds the village butcher.

Aldridge Cricket Club 1853 - 2003

In the 1860s, interest in the game of cricket increased dramatically. Three weeks after the Aldridge v Walsall Wood match, just a few miles away at Aston Park in Birmingham and following a game of 'North v South' the first England team to tour Australia was chosen. This England team, whilst not truly representative since at least ten players refused the terms of free passage out and home and £150 per man, set out from England aboard the S. S. Gt. Britain on the 18th October 1861. The tour was said to be a great success at home and in Australia. Perhaps cricket could really call itself the National Game. The reasons for growing popularity were numerous, but one was certainly that more and more people were able to read the results and follow the exploits of the major players and teams. In local newspapers, few other sports were given coverage to the same extent as cricket.

In a game versus Wednesbury Old Park Club on Monday 23rd June 1862 a few new names appear in the Aldridge team; T. Sutton, W. Green, G. Bury and Rev. J. Huntsman. Rev. Huntsman opened the batting and was the highest individual scorer on either side with the grand, not out, total of 21. Like many games at this time, there was a set 'finishing time' and Wednesbury were judged to have won the game because the score was 'in their favour'.

For Aldridge, an added inducement for cricket to take off as a sport was the village's close cultural connection with the town of Walsall of which it now forms a part. The Walsall journals which were available regularly reported Cricket and Quoits games, it was only in the 1880s that Football, Bicycling and Paper-chasing were in competition with cricket for column space. Walsall's Town Cricket team had been formed in 1812 and a certain class of young men of the district, were inspired by the possibilities of playing the game. William Gatus Watson, in his book of 1924 'Staffordshire Cricket', talks about numerous clubs springing into existence in the 1850s. This was, according

to Watson, partly the result of the first 'All England XI', under the direction of William Clarke, visiting Staffordshire and thus providing inspiration. School teams introduced boys to the game, gave them every opportunity to see it played at a high level and developed their individual skills. All the local Schools such as the Beech Tree House and Aldridge Grammar-Manor House, fielded teams which were training grounds for the club cricketers of the future.

Players, in the 1860s, used very little in the way of specialist clothing, but by 1863, equipment could be obtained by taking a trip to Walsall. There, at J. R. Robinson's shop, in the centre of town, on The Bridge, they could buy Bats, Balls, Wickets, Gloves and Leggings. According to the advert in The 'Walsall Advertiser' Clubs could be supplied at 'Makers' Prices' and for all those eager youngsters…'Youths' Bats, Balls and Stumps'. In 1866, J. T. King of 64, Stafford Street Walsall advertised 'Cricket Goods - Match Bats 4s to 21s Boys Bats 6d to 5s .'

NB. There were twenty shillings (s) to the pound and twelve pennies (d) to the shilling.

J. R. Robinson was a well-known Stationer who, in 1856, published E. L. Glew's 'History of the Borough and Foreign of Walsall' the first such work. Not surprisingly he just happened to be very closely involved with Walsall Cricket Club. In fact, Robinson, in the 1840s, was a player in the same Walsall side as Mr Frank James, Walsall Cricket Club President 1847 - 49, who would, twenty years later, be an Aldridge resident and Aldridge Club President. Robinson also acted, in the 1860s, as Walsall's Secretary and regular Scorer. Was it just a coincidence that Robinson's was the local supplier for the British & Foreign Bible Society and the cricketing Rev. Huntsman the local agent?

Transport between Walsall and Aldridge was made much easier in the 1860s. A trip to Walsall from Aldridge could be made aboard the horse-drawn omnibus leaving the village from its terminus outside the Elms Inn in the High Street. Before there was a village team, Walsall had been the only place locally for Aldridge cricketing men, who could afford to travel, to indulge their sport. In 1833, there is a record of Rev. H. Harding, then Rector of Aldridge, playing for Walsall and presenting them with a scorebook; in those days there was always a great cricketing tradition amongst the clergy.

The Lichfield Advertizer reported upon a match which took place on Monday July 24th 1865 between a combined Aldridge-Little Aston Team and Willenhall. The match took place in the *'beautiful park of the Hon. E. S. Parker-Jervis'* which was the attractive grounds surrounding Little Aston Hall. (The Cricket Ground is today the site of the BUPA Hospital) Although Rev. Huntsman was Priest in Charge in Walsall Wood, his prowess as a batsman was available to all who would give him a game. No doubt, the very thought of playing with the 'gentry' at Little Aston Hall would have been irresistible to this well known and well connected intrepid cricketing clergyman!

The scores were as follows:

Aldridge

	1st		2nd	
Rev. H. J. Huntsman	b. Iliffe	8	not out	33
G. Brawn	b. Iliffe	15	b. Ray	4
J. Shorter	b. Joint	2	b. Iliffe	5
M. Barton	b. Hutchinson	2	b. Iliffe	2
W. Davenhill	b. Winser	10	run out	5
J. Reynolds	b.Iliffe	4		0
Colonel Brown	b. Winser	9	b. Ray	0
A. C. Jervis Esq.	not out	10	run out	10
G. Bonham	c. Iliffe	6		-
G. Pearce	b. Winser	14	run out	5
Byes 6 Wide Balls 12		18	Byes 5 Wide Balls 5	10
Total 91			Total 77	

Willenhall

Gnosill	c Huntsman	0
Webster	run out	0
Joint	Stumped G. Brawn	0
Iliffe	hit wicket	5
Winser	b. Col Brown	4
Hutchinson	run out	3
Heath	c. G. Brawn	4
Moss	hit wicket	0
Ray	Stumped G. Brawn	7
Barnes	not out	1
Hand	b. Col Brown	0
Byes 1 Wide Balls 15		16
Total 40		

Rev. Huntsman certainly justified his inclusion in the side but the result was not in doubt. The Willenhall side were very careless at the crease, with two run outs, two hit wickets and two stumpings they stumbled towards a grand total of 40. The Advertizer reported:

'When "time" was called the Aldridge party had not finished their second innings, the game, therefore, was decided by the first innings, in which the Aldridge men had a majority of 51 runs over their opponents.'

Mr G. Brawn the wicket-keeper on this occasion is said to have been related to the Joberns family and A. C. Jervis Esq., was probably from the Hall.

In 1868, Mr Proffitt sold off much of his farmland and some of the land, known as 'The Bithams', was incorporated into Manor House Farm. It is possible that it was at this time the Cricket club had to look to Edward Tongue Esq., for permission to use one of his fields on Manor Farm. Manor Farm was adjacent to Mr Proffitt's land, and a field near the top of Frank James' Hill to the rear of the Moot House was made available. The support of Mr Frank James, a cricket enthusiast and recent arrival in Aldridge was no doubt important in securing a suitable field, and the start of a long association with the club.

Aldridge Cricket Club 1853 - 2003

Matches in the 1860s and 1870s frequently involved teams being dismissed for very low scores, partly the result of less than perfect wickets but also due to the efforts, of 'star' players, in many ways similar to the position today. Frequently, teams without a particular star being available, or where one or two of the best players got themselves out were doomed to fail. In July 1876, a home game v The Butts Institute from Walsall resulted in Aldridge being all out for the not so grand total of seven runs, certainly the lowest Aldridge score ever recorded! Players were not always local and those with talent who were, knew how to make the game profitable. For instance, according to a letter published in the Walsall Observer on June 24th 1871 the charges 'demanded by the talent of Bloxwich for playing and officiating in matches' was: Umpire 1s 6d, Bowler 2d per wicket Batsman fid per run. Bowling was often a mixture of 'round arm' and under-arm, although under-arm bowling, used widely in the first quarter of the nineteenth century, was less common. Round arm bowling was the first step toward 'Over-Arm' bowling as we know it today. Over arm was legalised in 1864 but it would be the late 1870s before it was seen to any great extent in England. Transport to and from matches was a good deal slower than it is today but the number of teams in the locality meant that there was always a team willing to take on 'The Village' at home or away. In the 1860s & 70s there is a record of Aldridge playing Walsall Wood, Wednesbury, Walsall Albion, Walsall Victoria, Rycroft Rosebud, Butts Institute, Norton Canes, Essington, Bott Lane Mission, Walsall Drapers, Walsall 2nd XI, Walsall Exchange and Oscott Unity. Unfortunately, it has not been possible to work out all the figures and averages for individual players, particularly as many of the names as printed in the local paper were often not correct. In the 1870s an appeal was printed in the Walsall Observer requesting more accurate details from match correspondents:

'We shall be glad at all times to receive accounts of matches from our cricketing friends of every class, and to give insertion to them but we must ask those who forward them to write plainly, (particularly names) on one side of the paper, and to let us have them as early as possible after they are played. Ed.'

The allusion to 'every class' indicates that by the 1870s cricket was not just a game for the 'knobs'. The Aldridge team in the 1870s however, included representatives from the principal families of the village who were involved in a leadership role in the local community by virtue of their status as landowners, and prominent businessmen. The population of the village in 1871 is recorded as only 1, 417. Amongst the most notable were the sons of Mr Frank James JP who, in 1865, had built his home, 'Portland House' in the village. Frank James owned a large Foundry business in Walsall, and had married twice; marriages which produced no fewer than eight sons, most of whom would eventually turn out for Aldridge C.C. in the coming years.

Portland House/Aldridge Court

One player, in an home game against Walsall Albion on June 13th 1874, was Mr J. Myring whose daughter was destined to marry Mr Alf Buckley and eventually become herself, Club President some eighty-five years later! In that match v. Walsall Albion however, we are told that Mr J. Myring bowled his deadly 'under-arm' ball but his 'grubhunters' obviously held no terror for the Albion because they managed to knock up 108 compared with Aldridge's paltry 20; not the kind of 'comeback' Aldridge had been hoping for. A week earlier, at their 'Malt Shovel' Ground, the Albion had scored what the Walsall Free Press & Advertiser called an 'easy victory' over Aldridge. The Walsall Albion were regular opponents, the ground being just off the Birmingham Road (A34) near what is now its junction with The Broadway. This ground was the home ground, for many years, of long standing opponents the 'Walsall YMF'. An Hotel and a housing development called 'Cricket Close' now occupy the site of the former ground and 'Malt Shovel' Pub.

The first record of a match involving one of the 'James boys' is in August 1875 v Walsall Albion, the whole side were out for 19 runs being thoroughly beaten, yet again by Albion who made 69. Other notable names which appear in the 1870s are; Millward brothers, G. G. Potter, Chapman, Bird, Selvey, Davies, Holland and Sales. Perhaps the nature of the games in the 1870s determined the make up of the sides. There were no leagues or knock-out competitions, matches were all 'friendly' fixtures. A team was assembled for each match from available players, registration, insurance and even regular practice were not pre-requisites! Of fourteen games reported during the 1870s Aldridge won only three the highest Aldridge total being 96 and the lowest ... that miserable 7 v The Butts Institute. Since the losers in local derbys had, it seems, to pay for a new ball, the 1870s was an expensive decade.

The 1880s & '90s

Aldridge Cricket Club 1853 - 2003

The 1880s would turn out to be a decade of change for the cricket club, particularly in respect of the ground. Aldridge entertained Oscott Unity in May 1880 and although accumulating only 58 runs due to the bowling of Arkinstall, were able to keep Unity down to 41 runs thanks to the accuracy with the ball of Rev. W. Bedford and Frank Holland James. Rev. Bedford, like Rev. Huntsman more than a decade previously, played for a number of local teams, particularly Sutton Coldfield, and was keen to be called in to bolster the village team. Frank H. James, virtually a regular by this time was making a name for himself as a bowler, even getting some games with Walsall 1st XI. James Chapman, as wicket-keeper, found that his services were in demand locally, turning out for Little Aston when available. On June 27th, versus Walsall Athletic at home, Aldridge knocked up a score of 102, the first century total on record; two James' brothers scoring more than half of the runs. During the 1880 season names such as J. Myring, F. Hopley, J. Bird, C. Everall, R. Batchelor, W. Price feature, along with F. H. James, C. H. James, G. P. James, H. B. James, H. H. James & H. V. James. Often, nearly all the James brothers would play in the same match, that really would put pressure on the scorer. People in future years would look back on the early 1880s and admit that, for a while, the James' were Aldridge Cricket Club! In August 1880, eleven of Walsall played twenty two of Town as a benefit match for Mr Hawke (Walsall Professional) The Police Band Played and the whole event was well attended, F. H. James played for Walsall & G.P. & H. James played for Town!

In 1881, the population of the village was recorded as 1,889 only about four hundred more than at the start of the previous decade but representing an increase of well over 25%. In terms of cricket players however the choice seemed to remain limited. Mr J. H. Warrin from Walsall, a brilliant all-rounder was called in to boost the team for the season. In his opening match, on May 21st, he scored 52 not out to secure an impressive victory over local rivals Shenstone. Supported by R. Thomas and W. Price he went all through that summer, setting the pace. Warrin's 41 against Hill Top on June 25th contributed to an Aldridge total of 138, Hill Top only managing 29 in two innings, after he had taken six of their wickets. Warrin's enthusiasm and skill seemed to inspire the team and the numbers rose to the point at which it was possible to field a second team of youngsters, at least for a few matches against Queen Mary's School in Walsall. The season ended with a meeting to ratify the change of ground. Capt. Tongue was thanked for his kindness in letting the team use his field (part of Manor House Farm,) and the offer of Mr George G. Potter to use his field in the coming season was accepted. Mr Potter's field could have been just off Hobshole lane. Moot House, Mr Potter's residence at the time, was then called 'Moss House'. Potter was only the occupier of Moot House, not the owner although he had interests in many areas in and around the village. There was, this year, a move, within the membership of the cricket club, to form a football club which would be 'beneficial to the village' but it was decided to leave the matter for further consideration.

The Walsall Observer in March 1882 carried a long report called 'Cricket and the Coming Season'. It was devoted to the so called decline of cricket in the Walsall area. Walsall's one professional player (Mr Hawke), it was stated, should be spending time with the Grammar School Club, possibly a few hours weekly. In a rather harsh statement it said:

'Go to any cricket ground in the district-or at all events, to most of them-you never see anyone fielding; the men are either batting or bowling or lounging behind the net smoking and talking…..The Australians were good examples to us and it would not be to much to say that they won many of their matches by their extraordinary cuteness in the field.'

Certainly, the England Team had not performed well down under, playing four matches but winning none, managing at best to draw in two of the games. We can presume that Aldridge were not guilty of the sort of extreme slackness alluded to in the article, particularly as the 1882 season turned out to be one of the better years. A highlight of 1882 was the August Bank Holiday Tour to Llandudno, the first recorded 'Tour' in the club's history. As is often the case with tours, all the regular side were not available but a representative side included Messrs Warrin and Bullows. Mr Bullows had played for Aldridge in 1881 and was now a regular in the Walsall XI. Victory for Aldridge was secured after a good first innings total of 89. Llandudno were bowled out twice with Aldridge not losing any wickets in their second innings; a very successful tour. Ominously, there was no report of the celebrations, hopefully the North Wales pubs were only 'dry' after the weekend and not during it!

At the end of the season two matches were played versus Mr W. G. Allen's XI, resulting in honours being equally divided. A strong Aldridge team included G. G. Potter, R. Thomas, J. H. Warrin, C. James, E. Tongue, J. Chapman, W. T. Holland, and T. Minors. Mr W. G. Allen's side included E. B. Dent, E. J. Newman and F. T. Cozens.

Mr A. T. Bullows was back in the 1883 side alongside J. H. Warrin. In the Whit Monday game in May v Walsall 2nds Warrin took 8 wickets in the first innings. Mixed fortunes followed the team with some great wins over Wednesfield and Aston Lower Grounds but some disappointing results such as that v. Sutton Coldfield when opening bat and wicket keeper, James Chapman, was the only one to score double figures. Mr A. Parker-Jervis of Little Aston Hall was playing for Sutton; earlier in the season he had been in the Little Aston Side which managed a draw against Aldridge. The Second XI played matches against

Walsall Grammar School and Walsall Locomotive. In a match v Walsall 2nd XI at Chuckery, James Chapman carried his bat scoring 80 in a winning total of 121.

In April 1884 the big pre-season event was the Club Concert staged in Mr G. G. Potter's newly opened Anti-Botch Association Rooms in Rookery Lane. Mr Potter, the Club President, was establishing a long tradition of Cricket Club events in the building, later to become known as the 'Assembly Rooms'. The Club funds were further swelled by another entertainment in the hall a month later.

The 2nd XI featured again in 1884 with matches against Walsall Locomotive & Butts St Mark's. It is perhaps interesting to note that on May 31st two teams were fielded as follows: 1st XI: J. Chapman, W. Price, W. Hampson, H. Stone, T. Hunter, J. H. Warrin, R. Colston, W. Princep, T. Whitehouse, J. Hudson & T. Stone. 2nd XI: H. Myring, H. Wright, W. Myring, W. Brown, W. Lote, T. Ellison, W. Wright, J. Hastilow, J. Brown, B. Price & T. Hopley. Before the end of the season lots of other names appear; S. Dibble, T. Cooper, R. Reynolds, W. Webster, A. Bate, H. Crumpton, T. Sales, L. Hood, H. H. James, R. Thomas, E. Holland & R. Batchelor. Not a settled side by any means and certainly not a successful one… after losing to Gt. Barr in August two of their players, T. Poppleton & H. Dyoss were recruited for some matches but to no avail. Only four games were won out of the eleven recorded.

The 1885 season started in the same calamitous way as the 1884 season had finished. On May 11th Aldridge played Walsall 2nd XI at home but could only make 36 runs in two innings compared with Walsall's 89. The comment in the 'Observer' said it all *'Aldridge had a hard task set them to get 89 but no one was prepared for the utter collapse of the whole team.'* However, the season improved - it couldn't get worse - and particularly when some of the James boys were available, a few good wins were posted before the close.

It was probably either in 1884 or 1885 that the Club moved to the present field courtesy of Dr William Cooke the new tenant of Manor Farm. Mr. S. C. Cashmore joined the 1st XI in 1886. Samuel Charles Cashmore was to become one of the great stalwarts of Aldridge cricket. He was Headmaster of Aldridge School, Church organist and Choirmaster. Links between cricket club, school and the church would be greatly enhanced as the direct result of his interests. Another churchman, none other than the new Rector Rev. James Slade f.f. Chamberlain MA would also make his mark during the 1887 season along with his colleague Rev. Oliphant. In his first recorded match, v YMFS, Rev. Chamberlain scored 23, the second highest score and a great help to a famous victory by 40 runs. He would go on to top score in other matches during the season. 1887 was turning into a vintage year for newcomers. A young player by the name of Ted Milner appeared in June in a game v St. George's 2nds and was bowled for 2 runs. Then, when Aldridge played the newly formed Walsall Town Unity in July, another youngster - Ted Joberns was batting No 3, but unfortunately he did not trouble the scorer. A few years would have to go by before the true worth of these gentlemen would come to fruition. No games at this time were played on Sundays.

A rather unusual match took place on a wet Wednesday in July 1888. It was an all day game at home v 3rd Battalion N. Staffs. Regt. The reason for the game was that a certain 'Lt' James was a member of the Staffs. Regt. team. The result was an easy victory for Aldridge by an innings and 37 runs. The bowling of H. H. James and the batting of Rev. Chamberlain (44) secured victory. In what was nationally the wettest season on record, the Walsall Observer reported on an all too familiar scene:

'Weather was most unfavourable for cricket, rain falling during the early part of the game and a bitter north-west wind blowing, making it very unpleasant for fielding. F. James Esq. With his usual hospitality, invited the teams to luncheon at Portland House.'

There is a full report from the 1888 Annual Dinner which was printed in the Walsall Observer of Dec 1st. In this we get an excellent snapshot of the way in which the club functioned at the time. The earliest report of its type, the

Aldridge Cricket Club 1853 - 2003

function is reported as taking place at the Elms Inn, presumably the favoured watering hole of the day. In the absence of the President, Mr G. G. Potter, the chair was taken by Mr Frank James supported by the Rector Rev. J. Chamberlain. The proceedings provide interesting reading:

A toast to Her most gracious Majesty the Queen was followed by the singing of 'God Save the Queen'. This was followed by another toast to the Prince & Princess of Wales and other members of the Royal Family. 'The Bishop and clergy of the Diocese' was a toast coupled with the Rector, Rev. Chamberlain who *'could leave his study occasionally and enter into the amusements of his parishoners'*. In his response Rev. Chamberlain said that he knew some people said clergymen were better off the field than on it, but he did not endorse that opinion because a clergyman would often come into contact with persons on the cricket ground that he would not otherwise have a chance of meeting. He added that looking back on the past season he was pleased to say that he had not heard any language used on the ground by the Aldridge cricketers which could be taken exception to. Mr James then submitted the toast of the evening 'The success of Aldridge Cricket Club'. The cash in hand was £2. 3s 5d, not so large as last year due to the cricket field having to be levelled. He then followed with some friendly criticism of the club before proceeding with the prize distribution.

1888 Prizes:
Mr Sam Cashmore (Bat) 181 runs in 16 innings, Ave 12.6,
Mr Chapman (Bat) 89 runs in 11 innings.
Mr C. Hurst (Bat) 76 runs in three innings.
Rev. James Slade f. f. Chamberlain MA, 8 innings, Ave, 15.2.
C. H. James 11 innings, Ave 8.
H. H. James 13 innings, Ave 7.3
50 and over in an innings:
Mr. J. Chapman: 50
Mr C. Hurst: 51
Mr. S. Cashmore 55 (Highest Scorer, pair of pads)

A toast was given enthusiastically to Mr Potter in his absence. Mr James received a toast to thank him for stepping in to the position of Chairman at the last minute. Mr James stated that he thought the club was deeply indebted to Dr. Cooke for allowing the use of the ground for the matches, as it was not every gentleman who would have allowed his ground to be interfered with for such purposes. Mr Joel Cooke, (son of Dr Cooke) who was present, said it afforded the family great pleasure for the ground to be put to such a purpose. During the evening some 'capital' songs were given, ably accompanied on the piano by Mr Cashmore.

The year 1889 is famous in cricketing history for, amongst other things, the official abolition of the four-ball over in favour of five. However, it is quite probable that Aldridge like many teams nationally, had been using six-ball overs for some years. 1889 for Aldridge was the first year that a regular 2nd XI was fielded including such names as J. Cooke, Simmonds, Bridgett, Hudson and Milner. The first XI was much stronger than in previous years, due to the performances of S. Cashmore, Rev. Chamberlain, and notably, the fine all rounder W. Brawn. Mr W. Brawn in particular used his skill with both bat & ball to turn most games in favour of Aldridge. On the odd occasion that he did not play the team seemed to collapse, for instance on Sat. Sept 21st Aldridge played YMFS at home but were bowled out for 30, YMFS scored 133 for 6. This game is remarkable in that there were no less than five members of the clergy playing: Rev's Chamberlain & Oliphant for Aldridge and Rev's Hodgson, Heale & Boyle for YMFS, perhaps both sides could claim to have God on their side!

The team in the 1890s was no more settled than it had been in the 1880s. Regular opponents such as YMFS, Gt. Barr, Bloxwich, Sutton & Walsall 2nds were still providing stiff competition, perhaps too many matches just tipping the wrong way in the first few years. A number of key players left the scene early in the decade but they were replaced. Later in the '90s much improved home grown talent would take to an equally upgraded cricket field with a real vengeance.

Aldridge Cricket Club 1853 - 2003

An 'easy' win over Walsall Town Unity, in May 1890, was perhaps indicative of weaker competition rather than Aldridge strength. Brown, Milner, Price, Whitehouse, W. Myring, J. S. Hudson, H. Myring, J. Hudson, Green, Willock and Broomhall making up the winning 1st XI. S.

Cashmore, Rev. Chamberlain, Millington, Joberns, A. C. Cooke, J. G. Cooke & Bridgett were other regulars. Bridgett played for both Bloxwich and Aldridge at this time, later only Bloxwich. The 2nd team had quite a good year indicating some good prospects for the years to come. In fact, the club faced the 1890s with much confidence. The field was now, literally in better shape and there was a smart new pavilion adorning the side of the ground, albeit a touch on the small side. The Pavilion plans had been drawn up by a certain Mr Edward Joberns. Home team and visitors could now change on site.

It is likely that Dr William Harry Cooke MD JP, the club President, who let the field, came to watch his sons Joel, John-George & Adrian becoming an important part of the team. By the end of 1890 Adrian Cooke had become quite a reasonable bowler and a fair all-rounder as well as occupying the esteemed position of Club Captain. Match reports of 1891 often included 'bowled A. C. Cooke', occasionally four or five in a match; by the end of the year he was sharing the bowling honours with a certain 'E. Milner'. In winning a match against Burntwood Asylum in June, all the wickets were shared by messrs Cooke & Milner but the real winning blow was delivered by Milner with an innings of 58 runs more than the combined opposition score. On Lady Day 1891, Dr Cooke surrendered his leases on the Farm. The Cooke 'Lads' however, continued to play for the club for the next three or four years.

1892 was the first year that Mr J. Dilks played in the team, a name which by the end of the decade would be synonymous with Aldridge Cricket. It is not certain, but I believe Aldridge Cricket Club's Mr Dilks to be the No. 2 Plant Colliery Manager Mr John Dilks. Mr Charles Holland James was playing in his final season before getting married in December and leaving the village. There would, of course, still be plenty of other James's to play for Aldridge. It has often been the case that many generations of the same family have played cricket for Aldridge and this family association over many years can be found in many other clubs. However, in the nineteenth century, families were often quite large in comparison to modern times, and population movement less, so it was common to find teams with three or four brothers or cousins. For instance Bloxwich had the Thomas and Wootton families, the Beebee's played for Walsall Centenary, and the Meacham's for Hamstead. Sometimes the names of players may have caused some slight amusement in the ranks of the Victorian onlookers. 'Wisdom' followed 'Wise' in to bat for Walsall Town Unity and when we played Burntwood Asylum there were two 'Dafts' playing for the team! Followers of Nottinghamshire cricket, of course, will know that the name 'Daft' (Richard) indicates one of the all time great names of the early game in that county and indeed, English cricket, the Burntwood Daft was no mean cricketer. An Aldridge Junior side played in 1892 in a game versus Vicarage Walk from Walsall. At the end of 1892, Mr A. C. Cooke stepped down as Club Captain but remained as Secretary. Mr W. Brown was given the 'Best Bowling' award for the 1892 Season and Mr Dilks the 'Best Batting' award.

The familiar face of Rev. J. S. ff. Chamberlain, Rector of Aldridge, Chairman of the Club and regular 1st Team batsman, was not seen at the crease in the 1893 season. By the time his official farewell presentation took place on Friday 16th June he had already moved to take up a new living at Staplehurst in Kent. Rev. Chamberlain had been held in high esteem in the Cricket Team as he was in the village. After an outside tea at his leaving event, there was an evening party at Dr Cooke's public Hall. The organisers must have put on a good spread since the remains of the tea, cakes etc., were given to the schoolchildren on the Saturday morning under the superintendence of Mr Cashmore, Miss Potts and Miss Hume. Mr E. Joberns read an illuminated address, which was then presented to Rev. Chamberlain at the event. Ted Joberns, made the presentation as churchwarden, at the time he had just taken over the job as Cricket Club Treasurer from Mr Harrison. There was, in the 1890s, a very close relationship between club and church socially as well as being physically adjacent. Samuel Charles Cashmore, for instance, besides being Headmaster of the Free Grammar (Church) school,

Aldridge Cricket Club 1853 - 2003

church Organist and Choirmaster, was also a regular fine batsman in the 1st XI. According to Jack Matthews, Mr Cashmore was wont to give his boys plenty of exercise with the big roller after school hours and even during the lunch interval, always with the special injunction, 'Tread flatfooted, boys!'

A Junior side turned out again in 1893 for a return match against Vicarage Walk from Caldmore, Walsall, opponents from the previous year. On Saturday July 1st the Juniors were well beaten but later in the month, through tenacity, managed to come out on top in the return match. The match on July 1st is interesting because it included a very young player by the name of 'Buckley' who 'on debut' as we say today, came in at No 10 and was bowled out for 0. In the 1st XI, Dilks and Brown continued in their winning ways with the ball. In a match versus Ward End on June 10th Dilks took 5 for 18 and Brown 5 for 19. At the end of 1893 it was time for another familiar figure to bow out of his multi-faceted rôle in Aldridge Society. Sam Cashmore retired as Head of the school and a special presentation of a tea service was made to wish him well. On Tuesday December 12th a special 'choir supper' was held at his home in order for all to say goodbye. The Rector presented him with a 'splendid' pipe. He also finished with the Cricket Club at the same time, so the question being asked by everyone was; could the versatile Sam Cashmore be replaced? The answer turned out to be a resounding 'yes', and what's more, the most worthy successor actually attended Sam's special leaving supper!

1894 was the year that Mr Frank Weaver Stephens, Sam Cashmore's successor, made his mark upon village life, including the Cricket Club. The void left in the team following the exit of the two stalwarts Rev. Chamberlain and Sam Cashmore in the same season was to be more than adequately filled by this one man. F. W. Stephens, A. R. C. O., was appointed Head of the Endowed (Boys) School, and church organist and choirmaster, positions for which he was well qualified. But what about the cricket team? All worries were soon dispelled when it was announced that F. W. S. had been a regular player with the famous West Bromwich 'Dartmouth' Club but would now be available to turn out for Aldridge. He settled-in quickly and was joint highest scorer in his first recorded game with the club on Monday May 14th 1894 against North Walsall. By the end of the season he regularly occupied top spot in the batting and was a useful addition to the bowling of Brown and Milner. (Dilks didn't play in the 1894 season). Although playing the occasional game for Walsall when they were short, F. W. S. would continue to represent Aldridge for many years, eventually becoming Club Captain. Brown continued his success of the previous years, on May 14th taking 7 wickets for 15 runs. A month later, against West Bromwich Victoria, Brown scored 19 and took 4 wickets including a hat trick, followed in August with 5 for 9 runs v. Sutton Town. Other notable players in 1894 included Messrs: Tonks (Wicket Keeper), Hastilow, Rowbotham, Beasley, Gilbert, Fletcher, & Kimble.

The 1895 season was perhaps the first when Teddy Milner came into his own. Against Darlaston 2nds he took six wickets for 27. Aldridge batting strength was looking up too. Stephens, Tonks, and Milner all scoring over 50 on more than one occasion during the summer. For 1896, success continued where 1895 finished. The 2nd team turned out much more frequently including a game v the YMCA 2nd Team at Walsall when Aldridge won easily aided by a young Alf Buckley who stumped two and caught another, although it may have perhaps been difficult sometimes to find two complete teams given the names of some of the players. The name 'Bonner' occurs on the teamlist for the 2nd team match on July 18th, presumably this was Mr Sam. Bonner the farmer responsible for the cricket field probably being 'roped-in' just for that one match. Sam was certainly not a regular cricketer and would have been much happier had he been asked to play football.

By 1897, Buckley had been selected for the 1st XI and Mr J, Dilks returned to the village side halfway through the season after a few seasons with Pelsall. The 2nd team continued to turn out in '97 much as they had in previous years as a 'scratch' side. We cannot be certain, but it seems

Mr J. Dilks   Club Captain 1898 - 1900   Photo: Bloxwich C.C.

Aldridge Cricket Club 1853 - 2003

likely that the Mr Lynch who turned out for the 2nds in 1897 & 98 was the Landlord of the Swan Inn, if so then it was obviously only right that when he was bowled for 0 against YMFS 2nds on May 14th 1898 he was bowled by 'W. Swann'.

In 1898, one of the greatest supporters of the team, Mr Frank James JP, moved out of his specially built residence, Portland House, to live near Stafford for the duration of his retirement. Fortunately, his connections with the village, and in particular the Cricket Club, would still be maintained. However, the link with those pre and post match entertainments at his home or in the grounds, which had been a feature of many early years of the club was finally broken.

The 1899 season can be ranked as one of the best in the Club's history. The record was: Played 16 games, won 9 lost 2 and drew 5. Although, as usual the victories were a team effort, the record of Teddy Milner with both bat and ball meant that frequently Aldridge C. C. played only a supporting rôle to the 'Claynup Roadshow' …this is why: With the bat: 65 v Bloxwich out of 138, 72 v Burntwood Asylum out of 215, 35 v Bloxwich Wesley out of 71, 42 v Burntwood Asylum out of 102. With the ball: 5 wkts for 15 runs v Nechells, 7 wkts for 21 runs v Sutton Town , 8 wkts for 7 runs v Bloxwich Wesley (In 46 mins!) 5 wkts for 3 runs v West Bromwich Victoria, 5 wkts for 14 runs v Pelsall Albion , 5 wkts for 16 runs v Sutton Town. Under the captaincy of Mr J. Dilks the team went from strength to strength into the twentieth century. Unfortunately, Mr Dilks left Aldridge and we know that he joined the Bloxwich team in 1902. Dilks played for Bloxwich 1st & 2nd XI's with much success and the photo of him reproduced here is from the end of his first year with the Bloxwich team.

Playing Statistics & Records 1853 - 1904

CLUB RECORDS

Highest Aldridge totals:

215 v Burntwood Asylum. 15/6/1899 Away
204 v Springhill Baptists. 14/9/1901 Home
191 v Walsall 2nd XI. 22/6/1889 Home

Lowest Aldridge totals:

7 v Butts Institute. 29/7/1876
10 v Walsall 2nd XI. 9/5/1885

First recorded total score of 100 or more:

129 v Walsall Albion 2nd XI. 19/6/1880 Home

Highest Winning margin:

141 (162 v 21) v St. George s 2nd XI. 11/6/1887

Highest Losing margin:

188 (49 v 237) v Shannon s. 8/8/1903 Away

PERSONAL MILESTONES - PERFORMANCES

Greatest all- round performance:

Ted Milner: 92 (in 70 mins - including 18 boundaries) and taking 6 wickets for 25 v Burntwood 15/6/1901

Batting:

First recorded 50 for Club:

J. H. Warrin. 52 v Shenstone 21/5/1881

Highest Totals:

Ted Milner: 92 (As described above)
W. Simmons: 83 not out v S. Coldfield 2ndXI15/6/1895 Home
H. Skidmore: 83 v Bilston 30/7/1904 Home
W. Brawn: 82 not out v Walsall 2nd XI 22/6/1889 Home
James Chapman: 80 not out v Walsall 2nd XI 18/8/1883 Away
Ted Milner: 72 v Burntwood Asylum 17/6/1899 Away
Sam. C. Cashmore: 62 v Burntwood Asylum 15/6/1889 Away

Bowling:

1st recorded Hat - Trick:
Mr Brown v West Bromwich Victoria 7/7/1894 Home

2nd recorded Hat - Trick:
Ted Milner v Sutton Coldfield 11/5/1901 Home

Ted Milner had a hand in taking all 9 wickets
v YMF 25/7/1903 Home
Bowled 6, Caught & Bowled 1, Caught 1, Stumped 1.

The 1900s & '10s

Aldridge Cricket Club 1853 - 2003

In May 1900, the six-ball over officially replaced the five ball over in England. Although the club score-books for this time have been lost, we can assume that, like most English teams six-ball overs at Aldridge were in fact commonplace by then. A more serious concern for the club however was the loss of Mr Dilks at the end of the 1900 season. Standards in the club had been generally high under Mr Dilks and in the early months of the season Aldridge were undefeated. In fact the record was very good, even including 2nd team matches.

One interesting match which took place on July 7th 1900 was an invitational match when Mr Dilks captained his invited XI to play against Aldridge.
The details are as follows:

Aldridge
E. Milner c S. Beebee b Evans	6
Stackhouse c Newman b Breeze	4
Stephens b Danks	22
Simmons c Beeze b J. Dilks	8
Westwood b Breeze	2
Silver b Breeze	5
Beasley c A Breeze b G. Breeze	1
Myring c J. Dilks b Breeze	4
Buckley b E. Dilks	18
H. Milner c A. Breeze b J. Dilks	5
Hudson not out	26
Extras	10
Total	106

Mr Dilks's XI
F. Dilks c Buckley b Simmons	2
A. Breeze b Simmons	0
G. Breeze b Stackhouse	3
S. Beebee c Milner b Simmons	10
Evans run out	12
E. Dilks c H. Milner b E. Milner	2
J. Dilks run out	9
Mills c Simmons b Stackhouse	0
Wolf c Simmons b Stackhouse	11
Danks c Myring b Simmons	8
Newman not out	3
Extras	3
Total	63

The 'Walsall Observer' in reporting the match stated: 'Mr Dilks, the Captain playing against Aldridge caused much rivalry and excitement. Aldridge were 14 runs short with only 2 wickets in hand but the last member made the score reassuring by putting on 26 runs for the last wicket. Aldridge won by 43 runs.'

The members present in the Anchor Hotel for the Annual Dinner of 1901 on Wednesday 24th April, looked back on a successful 1900 season but with a degree of trepidation regarding the season soon to be upon them. Mr Victor James, former playing member and Aldridge District Councillor, presided at the event in the absence of Dr. Cooke. Dr. Cooke seemed to have relinquished most of his few 'social' responsibilities by 1900, perhaps due to his ill health. In 1891, the cricket field which had formerly been the responsibility of Dr. Cooke had been, seemingly returned directly to the Trustees of the late Randall Francis Tongue Croxall Esq. JP acting as Lord of the Manor. It was of some concern that the annual ground rent had, for the coming year of 1901, been doubled. About fifty members attended the dinner, including J. Elkin Treasurer and A. Buckley Secretary. The proceedings started with loyal toasts being given, firstly to the King - for the first time, Cricket Club, H. M. Forces, and the Patrons. The chairman said that he had been connected with club for about thirty years, his family much longer than that. The Club, in his view, was still fairly flourishing but wanted more members and, in an obvious reference to the vacant position of Captain, *'wanted a good man with the game at heart to lick them into shape and to insist on their practising'*. He went on to say that there used to be both a first and second eleven and the competition used to be very keen for places in the first. Lamentably there was no second team at all now and it *'appeared to be a hard job to get players at all'*. He thought that there was as good cricketing talent in the village now as in the past, and it seemed a pity that they could not work up enough enthusiasm for the club to persuade them to join. In the straightforward way, no doubt inherited from his father, he stated that although they had an excellent subscription list, money was useless without men. Mr Buckley responded on behalf of the club stating that during the past season the 1st XI had played 18 matches, had won 13, lost 3 and drawn 2. Not at all, in his view, a bad record. The Second Team had not been a success however, out of 14 fixtures arranged only 4 had been kept, and no matches had been arranged for the coming season. With a subscription of only 2s 6d, he felt that more ought to join. The fixtures for the present cricketing season, he said, had been arranged with far stronger teams than usual, and he urged all members of the club to practice regularly and earnestly and not simply turn up on Saturday afternoons to take their places in a match. Financially the club was sound and had a balance in hand from last year of 5s despite the second team losing the club £3.

The Annual Dinner proceeded with prizes presented by the Chairman. There was a gold medal for best batting average, won by Mr F. W. Stephens and a pair of boots as 2nd Prize for the best bowling average won by Mr James Simmons. The 3rd prize, also a pair of boots, was won by Mr Milner as the player who had scored 50 runs in a single match: *'but the boots were not finished, and could not be presented.'* Mr J. Stackhouse won a prize of 5s for being the best fielder, Mr James Simmons won another prize, this time of 10s 6d presented by Mr J. Myring for his making

The local Jessop

the largest number of catches. A prize of 10s 6d was given by Mr Nicholls for the third best batting average and was won by Mr Tonks. The last prize was one of 5s given by Dr Wolverson for the best catch of the season and was won by Mr Westwood. Mr Stephens stood up to propose a toast to the 'Patrons' saying that the club provided a healthy and innocent occupation for the young men of the village on evenings and Saturday afternoons. Patrons, he said were found in two types, those who gave money and the spectators…the latter were very important. But he would like to remind them that there were always two sides playing:

'…Some of our spectators do not show visiting teams that consideration which they had a right to expect. If the other side were giving a better show than the home team let them show that it was appreciated, if only for the sake of their own good name'.

Mr Wincer replied for Patrons. (Thomas Wincer was the Landlord of the 'Elms' Inn on the other side of the High Street, the regular 'HQ' of the Club.) Mr J. Myring thanked the Chairman and commented that the name of James had always been connected with the Cricket Club, he could remember when the James' were the Aldridge Cricket Club. The family, he said, had formed the club, and brought it to perfection. He would couple with the toast the names of the Chairman's father, wife and son.

Teddy Milner 'Claynup' as he was known to his friends, was a fine athlete who in his younger days had made quite a name for himself as a sprinter and a footballer and was very proud of the medals and prizes he had gained. For the 1901 season he took on the role of Club Captain in what turned out to be a very successful year, one of many in this era. Teams such as YMF, Sutton Coldfield, Perry Barr, Walsall Town Unity, Burntwood, , Shannon's and Cannock & Rugeley were punished. Some very interesting games being reported in the local press. On Sat. May 11th v Sutton Coldfield, Aldridge knocked up 120 for five before sending all of the Sutton team back to the pavilion for 18. Ted Milner top scored with 35 bowled a hat trick taking 5 wickets for 6 runs. J. Stackhouse took 5 for 8 runs. The Observer reporter noted the Aldridge fielding as being *'exceptionally smart all round'*. It would certainly have been true to say that Ted Milner was becoming the 'local Jessop', Gilbert Jessop being England's No. 1 all-rounder at the time. Against Burntwood in June Ted hit 92 runs in 70 mins as well as taking 6 wickets for 25 runs. His innings was described as 'Perfect' particularly his driving, 18 boundaries coming off his bat. It would be easy to get the impression that Teddy Milner, the 'pocket rocket' of the day, was the only star on the field; but in that year of 1901 there was a veritable firmament! Take the game against Spring Hill Baptists in September, for instance; Simmons took 6 wickets for 2 runs, Stackhouse 4 wickets for 7 runs, and Silver knocked 53 out of a superb total of 204. Teddy Milner put himself in to bat at No 11 and didn't take a single wicket! Spring Hill were dismissed for only 11 runs, a winning margin of 193 runs and a club record, certainly one which was still intact in 1978. One problem of not fielding a 2nd XI in 1901 was that not everyone could get a game. On more than one occasion we see the name of 'Myring' coming in at No 10 or 11 to make up a short-staffed opposition.

1902 was the year F. W. 'Gaffer' Stephens took over the captaincy of the club. He made quite an impression upon a young schoolteacher by the name of Jack Matthews who also arrived in Aldridge that year.

'He was a forceful left hand batsman and made some capital scores for Aldridge. As captain, he was a strict disciplinarian on the field, and though his 'martinet' manner did not always 'go down' well with some, yet he must, in the writer's opinion, be classed as one of the best captains the club has ever had.'

Jack went on to recall some of his first games with the club:

'Strange it is, how trivial little incidents frequently remain fixed in the memory, even when more important happenings are forgotten. Such is the case in the writer's first two games for Aldridge. In his initial match, the 2nd XI met the Grammar

School Old Boys on a ground lying between the Mellish Road and Rushall Hall. The Old Boys had some very useful players, one of whom was Billy Wistance, later to become one of Walsall's regular players until the 1914 war, when he with many other gallant lads fell in action. Billy made a good score, hitting hard all round the wicket, and enabled his side to give Aldridge a good trouncing. Three or four wickets fell to the new member of the team, and right proud he was on making quite a favourable impression with his bowling. One of the Aldridge players was Jack Elkin, - never a good cricketer - but one who was always at hand to make up when the team was short.

Jack usually managed, during the course of a game, to meet with some sort of trouble, and in this particular match, in order to retrieve the ball after one of Billy's powerful drives, he took a flying leap to clear a ditch. However, as usual, he made a mess of things, this time quite literally, as he landed very disconsolately in a sitting posture, right in the muddiest part of the ditch. One can imagine the awful discomfort the poor chap suffered for the rest of the game.

The next match was played at Walsall Wood. Here the pitch was hardly up to 'Lords' standard, and a fairly fast ball from the writer 'got up' and struck one of the home batsmen a severe blow in the eye, causing a nasty gash and evoking loud cries of 'Take him Off' from the few spectators who looked on with seething displeasure at the sanguinary onslaught. The offending bowler was duly relegated to the outfield where he had no further opportunity of 'murderous' attacks, but was submitted to constant threats as to what his fate would be if he tried any more of 'that stuff'. One of the Aldridge players in this game was Frank Dawson, who, to this day, often recounts the incident.

Financial worries dominated the early years of the century and on March 15th 1902 the Walsall Observer carried the following story:

'*The Committee of the Aldridge Cricket Club found they had an adverse balance so it was thought advisable to try and clear it off before commencing the coming season. Circulars were sent out announcing their intention of holding a dance for the purpose of clearing the debt. This was held on Thursday 27th in the Public Hall which was generously lent for the occasion by the Aldridge Conservative & Unionist Club. Great credit is due to the M.C. Mr A. Gough of Walsall for the able and genial way in which he performed his duties. The music was supplied by Mr E. Moore's Band who gave as big a treat as usual to both dancers and onlookers. The Committee would take this opportunity of thanking all who attended for their hearty and unanimous support. Mr Wincer of the Elms Hotel was responsible for the refreshment, being put on in his usual well-known style.*'

In the seasons 1902 and 1903 1st & 2nd teams were fielded against the likes of: Birmingham YMCA, Darlaston, Deakin & Francis Birmingham, Walsall Brotherhood (v 2nd XI), Sutton Grammar School (v 2nd XI), Walsall Brotherhood 1sts, Tamworth, Cannock & Rugeley, YMF 2nds (v 2nd XI), Bournville, Old Hill, Bilston, Burntwood, YMF, Brierley Hill, Shannon's and Perry Barr. Generally, this was a slightly tougher class of team than Aldridge had become acquainted with in previous years. It was natural that 'star' players such as Teddy Milner would make an impression on the young Jack Matthews:

'Teddy's hitting was prodigious, driving and hooking being his specialities. Seldom nowadays do we see a ball lifted over the Rectory wall, but he often accomplished this feat, and "Gossy Hill" at the other end of the field also came in for attacks. His advice to us youngsters was, "Get to it," and "Hit 'em hard." He was terribly severe on any leg ball a trifle short of a length, hooking it with all his might. Where the present tea pavilion now stands, a fairly large tree once flourished, and the writer clearly remembers one of Teddy's specials landing right in the midst of its branches. His bowling too was of the greatest value to his side. He generally "opened" and could bowl all through without showing any signs of fatigue or slackness. His accurate length and direction forced any batsman to be always on the alert. Ted was a glutton for work, and when bowling at the nets one could always be sure of some good practice. What a mistake many bowlers make by not taking their practice seriously!

He could not be considered mercenary, but it was surprising what an extra amount of energy would be forthcoming when a batsman at practice adorned the top of the middle stump with a sixpence or a shilling. The odds were on Teddy getting the coin.

On one occasion, however, he met more than his match. There was no separate practice pitch in his day, so the nets were set up at the end of the "square". Well - one evening, the little door in the Rectory wall was opened, and out strode a young gent all togged up in immaculate cricket flannels with blazer complete and carrying a "posh" cricket bag. He reached the little knot of players congregated round the nets and asked if he might join in and have a "knock". His request was readily granted and Teddy prepared to hurl down a few of his extra specials. His first delivery, however, had no terrors for the batsman. A perfectly executed drive sent the ball whizzing down to the corner stile - the next landed in the neighbourhood of "Gossy Hill", and the newcomer treated all attacks with levity or distain. Ted tried all his wiles, but nothing worried the batsman. After a sparkling ten minutes' batting, the like of which had seldom been witnessed by most of those present, the Cambridge "Blue," as later he was found to be, made way for the next waiting batsman. Teddy's only comment was, "By gum, we could do with him!"'

Teddy Milner
Photo taken in the 1920s

The Cricket Club Annual Dance was by now a regular fixture and prime fund-raising event. The 1903 event was held on Thursday March 26th. The Observer reported that it was held in 'the Hall' Aldridge and those attending were: '*Cllr. John, Mrs and the Misses Williams, Mr & Mrs D.*

Aldridge Cricket Club 1853 - 2003

J. Smith, Mr & Mrs J. Bell, Mr & Mrs Cook, Mr E. Power, Miss Aston, Mr Miller and the Misses Miller. Mr J. Parkes, Mr T. Parkes, Miss White, Mr G. Wincer, Miss Bannister. Mr & Mrs Letts, Miss Chapman, Miss Rhead, Mr G. Wilks, Mr F & Miss Smith, Mr Bates, Miss Lester, &Co. In the absence of Mr A. Gough, who was unable to attend through illness, Mr F. W. Stephens ably officiated as M.C. assisted by the following Stewards: Mr A. G. Smith. Mr Westwood, Mr J. Elkin, and Mr J. Aston. The dancing which commenced at 8 o'clock to the strains of Mr E. Moore's Band was kept up till about 2.30. Refreshments were supplied by Mr T. Wincer of the Elms Hotel in his usual manner.'

Cricket, although a team sport, can be influenced by either having good individual players on your side or absent from it. The year 1903, showed that even with the trojan Teddy Milner, still being likened to Jessop, it was virtually impossible to produce regular wins playing against top flight sides when the rest of the team failed to perform with the bat, particularly early in the season. Unfortunately, Frank Stephens was unavailable for most of this season. Frequently Milner scored half of the runs, for instance; 41 out of 81 v Burntwood, 26 out of 40 v YMF. However, on 2nd June v Brierley Hill Teddy knocked 52 out of 104 which gave the team its first victory of the season by just one run. The Walsall Observer reporter commented:

'Milner appeared to be a 2nd Jessop, and in less than half an hour had made 52 runs out of a total of 61 for one wicket. His hits comprised ten 4s four 2s and four singles.'

Although this fine performance was a turning point in the season Aldridge were still to fall victim to other teams before the year was out. Reinforcements in the form of the somewhat peripatetic S. & H. Beebee a well known cricketing duo who had recently played for Bloxwich were brought in to boost the team. Chasing an excellent total of 237 knocked by Shannon's on August 8th Aldridge could only manage 49 all out, even with a very good effort by 'new boy' Buckley who got a 'three for'.

Alf Buckley and other prominent members of the Club were becoming aquainted with Jack Matthews in his first few years in the village. Jack remembered those days when, some forty five years later, he wrote:

'One of the prominent players then was Alf. Buckley - a good all-rounder, but recognised chiefly as the Club's best fast bowler. His height enabled him to make the ball "rise" alarmingly and on many occasions he ran quickly through a timid side. Through him the writer came into contact with the Myring family- all keen workers for the Club. Mr J. Myring's name has already figured in these notes, and all his family were connected in one way or another with Aldridge cricket. Mr Myring was one of the stalwarts of the early days, and during his lifetime occupied at various times practically all the important offices - Captain, Secretary, and member of the committee,

being for a lengthy period, Chairman. Both sons, Frank & Bert, played in their early days and also served the Club faithfully as Committeemen. Many will remember Bert for his pertinacity and strong persuasive manner with the collecting box on the ground. Few escaped his vigilant eye. The lady members of the family were especially active when social functions took place, and when the youngest married Alf. Buckley, who was then Secretary, their interest and activities were even more intensified.'

In May 1904 we find the Beebee's playing for the YMF against an Aldridge team consisting of F. Stephens, F. Milner, A. Buckley, J. Simmons, J. Myring, F. Smith, L. Mills, E. Smith, B. Myring, J. Matthews & L. Fisher. By the end of the season H. Perry and W. Bednall had been added to the list. Jack recalls that:

'Howard Perry and Billy Bednall came from Walsall and played with Aldridge for many seasons. Quick running between the wickets was their speciality, and when they were together, the bewildered fielders were kept on tenterhooks. Little Billy Bednall, he of the twinkling eyes, was also one of the smartest fielders ever seen on the Aldridge ground, and woe betide any batsman who took liberties when he was at "cover"'.

The Club minute books survive from 1905 onwards and were available to Jack Matthews as they have been to those of us who follow in his literary wake.

In 1905, Mr. Edward R. T. Croxall was re-elected President, Frank Stephens remained Club Captain and Alf. Buckley Hon. Secretary. The groundsmen were J. Hastilow and E. Milner. The meetings were, at this time, often held in the Boys School with the Chairman of the Annual Meeting being the Rector, Rev. W. J. Newbold. Mr J. Myring was Chairman for other meetings. The Club 'Headquarters' was stated to be The Elms, hardly surprising since Mr Thomas Wincer, the landlord was a big supporter of the club, his youngest son, Ivor, was to eventually become one of the 'celebrities' of Aldridge cricket.

Items such as repair of the large roller, re-painting of figures for the scoreboard and new rope for the flagpole were all items considered worthy of debate in these early years of the 20th century. Finances were often in a rather precarious state.

Johnny or 'Jack' Sales, as he was often known, was a player who impressed Jack Matthews:

'Jack Sales was one of the fastest bowlers Aldridge has ever had. For a short man, he could certainly "whip" them down, and on a poor wicket the batsmen had a rather anxious time. He later removed to Kingsbury and often played against us for the strong Colliery team there.'

Johnny Sales' reputation was well known locally, as was

Aldridge C.C.. In 1906, the Walsall Wood Wesley Cricket Club published a review of their year - in poetry. There were twenty-nine verses of good old fashioned doggerel which made much of the fact that they actually got a game with Aldridge and won it! Indisputably, as these few stanzas show, their cricket was better than their verse...

*"For matches he wrote to Buckley Alf.
He called in Captain Stephens.
They placed our letter on the shelf
And said we had lost our reasons.*

*Just keep your eye on Johnny Sales!
Old Teddy's not so fast.
If Buckley comes then watch your bails!
Now, 'Win', is all I ask."*

Perhaps Teddy was not quite as fast by 1906, but he remained at the very hub of the team, in more ways than one. According to the Club minutes he was engaged as 'bag carrier' at the rate of 1/- per match away and 6d at home.

Howard Walton

In 1907, Mr Alf. Buckley took on the captaincy of the club for the first time, a position he would hold initially for two years and again in the years before and after the 1st World War.

1908 turned out to be a memorable year for the Club, for it was at this time that a young Howard Walton appeared in the Aldridge area. Howard came from Walsall to work at Manor Farm under the auspices of Mr Sam Bonner. It is said that as a lad he was seldom seen without a bat in his hand, in fact he was something of a cricketing prodigy. It was not long before the whole village was agog at this young cricket wonderboy. Aldridge Cricket Club had struck lucky! Although things on the playing side were settling down well, in 1909, there were concerns about the state of the pitch and the pavilion...even the rectory wall required whitewashing. There seemed to be very little cash in the funds to attend to all the jobs. A letter was sent to the Hockey Club asking them to pay extra for the use of the roller: *'we cannot let them have pavilion and roller for same price.'* Estimates for painting the pavilion were obtained and the whole project was shelved until next year.

The first decade of the twentieth century had seen firmly established at the centre of the team a number of young men who would have an influence lasting for many years to come. Some had begun their playing careers in the previous century others were just starting out. Names such as Mr J. Dilks, Teddy Milner, Frank W. Stephens, Alf. Buckley, Jack Sales, Howard Walton, Ivor Wincer, and Jack Matthews becoming almost legendary in the annals of Aldridge Cricket.

Cricket clubs are not simply about grounds, pavilions, statistics, emblems or traditions, they are about people. Aldridge C.C., as we have already seen, in the first decade of the twentieth century, had been blessed with a fine cohort of players and administrators. The oldest team photograph which we have, dates from 1912, it is here we see, for the first time the faces behind the names; the real 'Club'. The village cricket club, and Aldridge is no exception, was as much about the village as it was the game of cricket. In the first part of the twentieth century, when Aldridge really was a village, and not a particularly large one at that, the leading characters of the club were also well known 'players' in the game of village life. Village institutions were interwoven and inter-dependent. This tradition of social inclusion went back to the start of the Club with the involvement of the Rector and names such as Dr. William Cooke, G. G. Potter, Sam. Bonner, Ed. Joberns and Frank James.

Mr Jim Myring, the minutes record, as one of the leading members of the Club - Chairman in 1910, was given the task of attending to the pavilion. What they don't record is that this was because of his 'day job' as a builder. The Myring family over the years has had very close connections with the club and Aldridge Society in general. Sons Frank and Bert both played for the club and served as committeemen for years. Mr J. Myring had a strong association with the Ancient Order of Foresters, friendly society, the Aldridge 'branch' was known as the Court 'Captain Cook' 4159 which met at the Swan Inn. Mr E. R. T. Croxall, Club President at the time, had the local branch of another friendly society, the Royal Antidiluvian Order Of Buffaloes actually named after him. Mr Myring was

Aldridge Cricket Club 1853 - 2003

1912

F. Dawson (Umpire). T. Pendry, A. Bell, G. Hall, N. Maiden, G. Hudson, R. Bachelor, E. Smith, J. Hodgetts, J. Beards,
J. Lees, W. Glaze, H. Walton, A. Buckley, J. Matthews, I. Wincer, S. Davies,
C. Glaze.

also a keen 'Buff' and it was 'Brother Myring' who had ceremonially handed Mr E. R. T. Croxall the silver trowel when the foundation stone for the new R. A. O. B. orphanage had been laid in 1903. Myring's was the building contractor for the Orphanage, a familiar village institution and landmark for more than half of the twentieth century. J. Myring was also, for years, chairman of the Conservative Club. Alf Buckley, whilst Club Secretary married one of the family, a young Jessie Myring, and reinforced what became little short of a dynasty, since years later both Alf and Jessie occupied the position of esteemed Club President. The minutes of the Annual Meetings at the end of the 1900s and into the 1910s indicate that there were problems with the appointment of the position of Club Secretary, probably the most important official. Frankly, no one wanted to do the job. In 1909, Ted Smith and George Hudson agreed to act as joint-secretary for the club, but this arrangement was short-lived when in 1910 Jack Aston volunteered to take over. Although Jack worked hard for two years, by 1912 he felt compelled to resign because he found living away from the village to be a serious handicap. George Hall was prevailed upon to accept office, upon the understanding that it would be for 12 months only. This legacy of short-term secretaryship became a thing of the past when a certain young school teacher, who had been with the club for eleven years, was asked if he would undertake, if only temporarily, the work of Secretary. Jack Matthews, in his own words rather reluctantly, consented to do the job, one which he was still proud to perform more than forty years later.

Jack Matthews saw that there was a need to raise the standard and efficiency of the club and set to work to do just that. More members, improved ground conditions, a more attractive fixture list and wider publicity were all given his earnest attention, with a great measure of success. Writing in 1948, Jack recalls a typical trip to an away fixture:

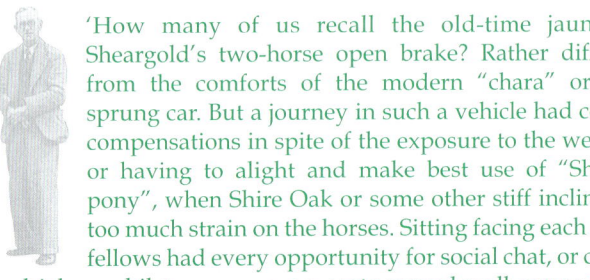

'How many of us recall the old-time jaunts in Sheargold's two-horse open brake? Rather different from the comforts of the modern "chara" or well sprung car. But a journey in such a vehicle had certain compensations in spite of the exposure to the weather, or having to alight and make best use of "Shanks' pony", when Shire Oak or some other stiff incline put too much strain on the horses. Sitting facing each other, fellows had every opportunity for social chat, or croaks and jokes, whilst rugs or even coats spread well across knees formed a fairly serviceable, if not ideal, card table. Certainly such journeys took a longish time, but on the homeward ride following a well fought game, no one grudged the steeds their well

Aldridge Cricket Club 1853 - 2003

**The 'Elms' Inn, High Street c.1912.
The 'HQ' of the Club for many years of the early 20th century.
Thomas Wincer, Landlord.**

earned rests, especially as these breaks, by a strange coincidence, always took place at a welcome spot, where the needs of man and beast could be blissfully met.

"Summer Time" not being in operation in those days, the concluding stage of the journey homeward was generally made in semi or complete darkness, so what could be better than a lively "spot" of harmony? Often a mouth-organ would be produced and topical choruses rousingly sung, interspersed with "Sweet Genervieve", "The Anchor's Weighed" or some such old favourites. The vociferous rendering of "Hearts of Oak" was always well timed so that the final lines, "We'll fight and we'll conquer again and again!" announced our return, as the weary horses were pulled up to a halt outside the Club headquarters. Some groping for, and grabbing of bags, a few cheery and hearty "Good nights" and another cricket "outing" was over.

The Elms, used as 'HQ' by the Club in the late nineteenth and much of the first quarter of the twentieth century, was kept by Thomas Wincer until just before WWI. Thomas, a great supporter of the Club also occasionally chaired Club meetings. Ivor Wincer, Thomas's youngest son, was one of Aldridge Cricket's star players. In 1910, he had been presented with a silk scarf for his *'splendid batting performances'* In 1911, he made a brilliant century at Burntwood, his 115 not out being the first recorded century for the Club. It was Howard Walton, however, who topped the averages that year and for the following two years, 1912 and 1913.

'Of all the "away" matches in the early days perhaps the fixture with the Mental Institution at Burntwood was the most popular. The pitch and ground was about the best on which we then played and we were always sure of a good game against a very capable side. The Medical Officer in charge was very keen on cricket and many of the attendants were well seasoned players, while often one or two of the more normal patients were given a place in the team. The patients, both men and women, took an extremely lively interest in the game, as visiting fieldsmen, especially those near the boundary, would audibly discover, whilst a few of the more dependable ones were often found minor jobs during the course of the match. One would be put in charge of the score-board, whilst others were allowed just inside the fence in order to retrieve and return balls from any boundary hits.

On one occasion, while Aldridge were batting, one of these border patrols saw what he thought was a fine chance to get free. He had managed to squirm through the long grass right up to the hedge in the next field before his snake-like movements were discerned. At once a "hue and cry" was raised. The fielders hurriedly forsook their cricket and made off after the fleeing one. He probably would have delayed the game even longer but for the fact that the new boots he was wearing were severely slowing down his progress, so down he sat and removed them, thus giving his pursuers a decided advantage. As it was, he gave them a good run, but was eventually brought back and hurried off to "quarters". "All in the day's work!" as one of the attendents was afterwards heard to remark.

Aldridge Cricket Club 1853 - 2003

One of the privileged patients was a regular giant of a man. The bat in his huge hands looked like a mere child's plaything and if he hit the ball, a boundary was almost sure to result. Very little running would he do - it was a four or nothing, and seldom would he speak - only grunt. In one match, the writer clearly remembers getting this smiter "plumb" in font, and the umpire without hesitation gave the fatal signal. But Goliath refused to budge - appeals to him wrere of no avail. The l.b.w. rule was clearly not in his book of rules, and rather than risk an awkward scene, our Captain let him stay. The next ball, however, scattered his stumps and off he went, grunting and grumbling all the way.'

Then there was the outing to Wimblebury, not much of a ground, but there we met a grand sporting crowd. The team at one time was composed of the "Harveys" plus a few others. First came Farmer Harvey, who would often pause before his stroke to enquire of Farmer Walton how his roots were, or the prospect of the wheat or barley crop. Then came Bert, his round-arm "swingers" coming straight at you from "down the hill". Uncle Fred, Nephew Harry, Cousin Bill and serveral other blood relations followed. And how those chaps could throw! Pioneers of jet propulsion they were.

After the match, the "Lamb and Flag" would have a hectic time, but the repeated and urgent calls for bread and cheese and pickles or even ham and eggs never caught "Violet" napping. Several of the homesters, eager for a drink and a "confab" would come sidling in. Games, past and present would be discussed, and it was then that Jim Stephens, the "Wisden" of Wimblebury, that master of facts and figures, would get his chance to "air his views" or clear up doubts.

Oft repeated calls from the ever patient driver would eventually be effective in getting all aboard and gaily homeward bound.'

No team can operate successfully without a good supply of young players. Howard Walton may have dominated the club averages but a wider playing base was sought by the Club. In December 1910, a meeting was held in the school to try to raise membership and even run a second eleven in the coming season. Mr Bonner presided over the meeting but it was poorly attended. However, the mood was upbeat with the minutes recording that there was *'every hope of our end being accomplished'*. By the AGM in April there was to be a 2nd eleven captained by Mr J. Hodgetts.

'The 1912 season saw the arrival of two other youngsters, Arnie Bell and Bill. Glaze. Arnie, a fine forcing left-hand batsman and left-arm bowler must be classed as one of the finest all-rounders the Club has had, whilst Billy Glaze made some very useful scores. In 1913 Arnie Bell finished the season at the head of the bowling, capturing 22 wickets for 74 runs in 53 overs - a remarkable performance. Other players coming into prominence during this period were Percy Stephens and Sam Davies, whilst occasionally in 1913 and 1914, the Club had the assistance of Archie Tucker, a stylish batsman and a very brilliant fielder.

We older members and contemporaries of H. A. Tucker have watched with interest his rapid rise in the legal profession, and are pleased to note that at the present time he occupies such an eminent position as County Court Judge.'

The fact that the years leading up to the fateful summer of 1914 were not the best of years for the pitch did not seem to deter the Aldridge batting duo of Ivor Wincer and Howard Walton. Ivor topped the batting averages for 1914 including another fine century. 1914 was the year that the Clubs's playing strength was boosted still further by the arrival of Wal. Stone and Billy Jinks, former Walsall players.

It was reported in the Club Minutes of the AGM, on April 3rd 1914, that Mrs Tongue, the widow of Captain Tongue, resident of the Manor House and a supporter of the club, had died and that it was a *'Loss to the Club'*. Her son, Edward R. Tongue-Croxall had been Club President. The Club would soon have to steel itself to similar news on a much more regular basis, although it would not suffer as badly as some.

World War gave the members of Aldridge much more to think about than cricket. However, some 'normal' business provided a distraction from the conflict. For instance, early in 1913 the new Landlord of the Elms, Mr Chapman, complained that the club was catering on the field and thus boycotting his house. It was minuted that he hoped that in the next season he would be allowed to cater on the field. Chapman could not have predicted that it was to be a long wait - more than five years. The losses of the Davies family are detailed elsewhere but many other players were affected in some way by the conflict.

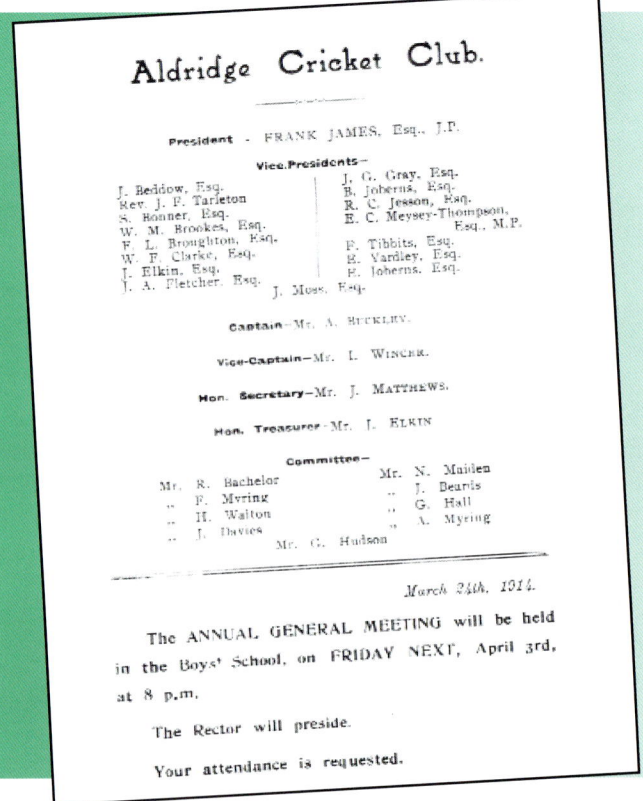

Aldridge Cricket Club 1853 - 2003

R. Bachelor.	W. Glaze?	F. P. Stephens.	?	A. Bell.	J. T. Davies.	?
H. Walton.	J. Matthews.	W. Jinks.	A. Buckley.	E. Smith.	W. Stone.	
		?	C. Glaze?	?		

Photograph taken in front of the original pavilion

1st XI c.1919

'Our players served in many theatres of the war. Alf. Buckley and Arthur Hilditch were in Russia, one in the north, the other in the south. Ted Joberns was a prisoner of war for a long period. Ivor Wincer served in Egypt and in fact, when hostilities ceased, chose to remain in the Service and reached one of the highest ranks.'

[In fact, Ivor Wincer became 'Air Commodore Wincer C.B.E.' He died in 1965]

The Manor House, now vacant due to the death of Mrs Tongue, was taken over as an Auxiliary hospital. Convalescent soldiers, wounded at the front were cared for in quite large numbers. The Club's facilities, just a few hundred yards away, were put at the disposal of the soldiers and were much appreciated.

Interestingly, the General Meeting of March 1915 seemed quite optimistic. Mr Bonner, the farmer, allowed the use of the field free of rent for the duration of the war. Every Saturday and in the evenings the pitch was to be used for 'recreation' games. Membership of the club actually increased from 73 - 91! It was clear, however, that the general feeling was for a short war, with phrases in the minutes such as: '...and on resuming in 1916 would still be at liberty to play...' In fact, nothing of Aldridge C.C. was 'resumed' in 1916, 1917 or 1918.

Club officials eventually convened another official meeting on 7th February 1919. The mood was now one of wishing to put the war behind them:

'the general feeling throughout the country was to forget, as far as possible, the war, and try and get back to former times.' All present were in favour of reviving the game, agreeing that it, '...would be a good thing to have a Club in the village again.'

It might be assumed that deciding to revive the team and actually getting the players together immediately post-war would be difficult. However, even with captain Alf Buckley still in the frozen wastes of northern Russia until late in the season, and Ivor Wincer lost to Aldridge cricket, everything went well under the captaincy of Wal.

Outside the Manor House Auxiliary Hospital during the First World War.

Aldridge Cricket Club 1853

MEMBERS, 1919.

Many of the following amounts include Donations in addition to usual Subscriptions.

Name	£ s. d.	Name	£ s. d.	Name	£ s. d.
Mr. E. Joberns	1 10 6	Mr. A. Hilditch	0 5 0	Mr. E. Smith	0 2 6
,, F. B. Clark	1 10 0	,, F. Homer	0 5 0	,, B. S. Smith	0 2 6
Anon. (per J. P. W.)	1 10 0	,, J. Hastilow	0 5 0	,, L. Watson	0 2 6
Dr. Jones	1 1 0	,, W. Jinks	0 5 0	,, J. Walls	0 2 6
Mr. W. Glaze	1 0 0	,, J. Lees	0 5 0	,, N. Winlock	0 2 6
,, J. P. Wynne	1 0 0	,, E. N. Mills	0 5 0	,, B. Wyler	0 2 6
,, J. F. Myatt	1 0 0	,, J. Matthews	0 5 0	,, W. P. Young	0 2 6
,, R. Bonnett	0 10 6	,, J. McGaw	0 5 0	,, T. Wincer	0 2 6
,, W. M. Brookes	0 10 6	,, E. Milner	0 5 0	**Junior Members.**	
,, A. Buckley	0 10 6	,, H. Milner	0 5 0		
,, P. B. Cooke	0 10 6	,, F. Myring, sen.	1 5 0	W. Purslow	0 2 6
,, F. W. Dewsbury	0 10 6	Dr. Moodie	0 5 0	E. Pritchard	0 2 6
,, J. Elkin	0 10 6	Mr. J. B. Marriott	0 5 0	F. Baker	0 2 6
,, J. A. Fletcher	0 10 6	,, P. Neale	0 5 0	S. Beardmore	0 2 6
,, J. C. Gray	0 10 6	,, J. Power	0 5 0	W. Holland	0 2 6
,, B. Joberns	0 10 6	,, F. S. Rogers	0 5 0	F. Myring	0 2 6
,, E. J. Joberns	0 10 6	,, G. Shutt	0 5 0	W. Groves	0 2 6
,, L. N. Mills	0 10 6	,, P. Stephens	0 5 0	J. Baker	0 2 6
,, F. W. Stephens	0 10 6	,, W. Stone	0 5 0	R. Pritchard	0 2 6
Capt. I. L. Wincer	0 10 6	,, J. Sales	0 5 0	F. Faulkner	0 2 6
Mr. E. Yardley	0 10 6	,, T. Tibbits	0 5 0	F. Foster	0 2 6
,, J. Beards	0 10 0	,, F. Thomas	0 5 0	H. Orton	0 2 6
,, J. Beddow	0 10 0	,, S. Turner	0 5 0	J. Parkes	0 2 6
,, E. Bickley	0 10 0	,, J. C. Tibbits	0 5 0	R. Moodie	0 2 6
,, W. P. Clark	0 10 0	,, R. Underhill	0 5 0	J. Brown	0 2 6
,, F. Dolman	0 10 0	,, H. Williams	0 5 0	H. Walton	0 2 6
,, C. Glaze	0 10 0	,, H. Whitehouse	0 5 0	P. Beardmore	0 2 6
,, G. Hall	0 10 0	,, S. Wilson	0 5 0	J. Taylor	0 2 6
The late Mr. S. Henley	0 10 0	,, B. Newell	0 4 0	S. Bickley	0 2 6
Mr. F. James	0 10 0	Miss Cooke	0 2 6	W. Durkin	0 2 6
,, P. Lloyd	0 10 0	Miss Hepburn	0 2 6	H. Bednall	0 2 6
,, E. E. Skett	0 10 0	Mrs. J. Myring	0 2 6	J. Beddows	0 2 6
,, F. Tibbits	0 10 0	Mrs. F. Myring	0 2 6	H. Foster	0 2 6
Sir T. C. Warner, M.P.	0 10 0	Mr. J. Booth	0 2 6	J. Cooper	0 2 6
Mr. H. Walton	0 10 0	,, E. Bennett	0 2 6	E. Skett	0 2 6
,, S. Aston	0 5 0	,, John Brown	0 2 6	C. Holland	0 2 6
,, J. Aston	0 5 0	,, W. Beasley	0 2 6	R. Clare	0 2 6
,, J. Barnett	0 5 0	,, T. Cunnington	0 2 6	H. Myring	0 2 6
,, W. Bednall	0 5 0	,, H. Crumpton	0 2 6	J. Myring	0 2 6
Mrs. A. Buckley	0 5 0	,, J. Connop	0 2 6	Mr. S. Bonner—Use of Boys' pitch in lieu of Subscription.	
Mr. W. Buck	0 5 0	,, J. T. Davies	0 2 6		
,, A. Beardmore	0 5 0	,, R. Davis	0 2 0		
,, R. Batchelor	0 5 0	,, J. Ditchfield	0 2 6	**SUMMARY**	
,, A. Bell	0 5 0	,, Felthouse	0 2 6	£ s. d.	£ s. d.
,, J. C. Booth	0 5 0	,, C. W. Gretton	0 2 6	1 at 1 10 6 =	1 10 6
,, W. Coston	0 5 0	S. E. H.	0 2 6	2 at 1 10 0 =	3 0 0
,, W. H. Clarke	0 5 0	Mr. G. Holden	0 2 6	1 at 1 1 0 =	1 1 0
,, W. Clare	0 5 0	,, F. Myring, jun.	0 2 6	5 at 1 0 0 =	5 0 0
,, W. Davenhill	0 5 0	,, A. R. Myring	0 2 6	14 at 0 10 6 =	7 7 0
,, J. Davies	0 5 0	,, T. H. Mold	0 2 6	14 at 0 10 0 =	7 0 0
,, H. Edwards	0 5 0	,, J. Phelps	0 2 6	49 at 0 5 0 =	12 5 0
,, J. Ellis	0 5 0	,, T. Pendry	0 2 6	1 at 0 4 0 =	0 4 0
,, W. Godridge	0 5 0	,, H. Pointon	0 2 6	64 at 0 2 6 =	8 0 0
,, G. Hudson	0 5 0	,, E. A. Poulton	0 2 6		
,, J. Hodgetts	0 5 0	,, A. F. Phillipson	0 2 6		£43 7 6
,, J. Hilditch	0 5 0	,, A. G. Smith	0 2 6		

Stone. The Club won 15 of the 21 matches played and lost only 3. Wal. Stone, who contributed another fine century was ably supported by Howard Walton, Arnie Bell, Billy Jinks and Billy Glaze who scored over 1,500 runs between them. Arnie, Billy Jinks and Howard being responsible for over 160 wickets. Post - war continuity was achieved through the likes of Mr F. P. 'Percy' Stephens, son of former Captain Frank W. Stephens and a real Club stalwart of the time. Percy was one of those who fits the axiom 'like father like son' very well indeed. He had replaced his father in the team in 1913 although his expertise was with the ball rather than with the bat. In other respects Percy's whole career would mirror that of his father even more precisely. Like his dad, Percy was a schoolmaster by profession and politically active in the Conservative party becoming a member of Aldridge Urban District Council and secretary of Aldridge Conservative Club... just as his father had before him. Later, he would serve the Club as umpire.

Membership in 1919 rose to over 150 bringing in more than £43 in subscriptions. 1919 was also the year that Teas were first provided on the ground for the players. Although a 'new' pavilion was in the process of being erected the willing ladies who 'managed' the Teas, co-ordinated by Mrs Buckley managed to overcome all difficulties including raising sufficient funds to set up the Club with crocks and kitchen utensils. But what of the Landlord of 'The Elms', the Club 'HQ', who had waited since 1914 for cricket to continue ? Needless to say a very

Aldridge Cricket Club 1853 - 2003

Outside the Rectory c.1919 - 1920

sharp letter of protest was received about the trade being diverted from his house. It had been the custom, pre-war, for players to seek refreshment from glasses rather than cups during the interval between innings, or even before if their side was batting. It was, apparently, common for someone to be sent to 'round up' the stragglers so that the game was not held up. Seemingly the Club was never fully forgiven for this loss of trade and that landlord left the Elms in 1922. By the end of the same year the Club was meeting at the 'Swan' a new era was beginning.

The 1919 season, the first since the war, would perhaps be better described at the start of a new chapter rather than the end of a decade, for in many ways that is what it was for the Club. Mr T. Pendry was appointed umpire and Mr S. Beardmore as scorer. In September a 'Testimonial' match was played for Ted Milner which raised the grand total of £11. The word 'testimonial' had been chosen carefully since, according to the committee, in those days, 'benefit' suggested charity and Ted was held in great respect.

A healthy credit of £17 by the end of 1919, was a tribute to the efficient running of the Club. The Hockey Club, for instance, had its charges for the use of the ground increased from 11/9d to one guinea.

> **By the way...**
> Some well-known Aldridge Cricket Club personalities are preserved in village street names.

> As a long and distinguished serving Councillor on the Aldridge Urban District Council, Howard Walton's name lives on today in the Street which was named after him. Howard served on the housing committee. Another prominent member of Aldridge C. C.- President from 1959 - 1969, Aldridge Councillor, Mrs Jessie Buckley, is said to have been the reason for 'Jessie Road' being so named. A section of Little Aston Road has always been known as 'Frank James Hill', Frank James being associated with the Club for many years as President. 'Bonner Grove' recognises the well-known Bonner family, Sam Bonner farmed Manor Farm from the 1880s having the Club as a tenant. His son, Charles Gus Bonner, was awarded the Victoria Cross in 1917.

The 1900s & '10s

Aldridge Cricket Club 1853 · 2003
The Club Crest

A Crest is a badge or armorial device, but not a coat of arms. Generally it has usually been used as a family personal device within which there is a hidden meaning. In heraldic terms such a device should not really exist without being part of a full Coat of Arms. However, in the 19th century in particular, many were 'issued' and are officially 'bogus' without being part of an official coat of arms or heraldic achievement.

The adopted club crest, that of a former President Frank James, can be seen today upon a wooden plaque, which has for years graced the wall of the Stick & Wicket. It was, no doubt, donated by Mr James - proud to have his family name associated with the Club. Members of the James' family featured in the team over many years. Typically, there are allusions within the elements of the crest to supposed attributes of the family.

The large beast depicted, is not a Lion as would be expected from the mane, but a 'Tyger' shown in heraldry as 'sejant erect' - sitting up. A mythical heraldic animal which has the body of a wolf with a thick mane and a lion's tail. He has massive powerful jaws and a pointed snout. The tyger comes from Hyrcania where he was famed for his swiftness by the Persians who called their arrows 'tygris' and who named their river after him. Females of the species were devoted mothers but could be tricked '*by those who rob the tygre of her young*' who placed looking glasses in her way '*whereat she useth to long to gaze…and so they escape the swiftness of her pursuit.*' Because of this fable, the female tyger is often depicted looking into a mirror.

Frank James was a large 'powerful' man, fit and strong as his great longevity testifies. In his youth he played cricket for Walsall and would have enjoyed being regarded as being 'swift'.

The Wreath or torse is a band of twisted strands of material worn about the medieval helmet as decoration and to conceal the base of the crest where it was bolted to the tournament helm (helmet). In armoury, the wreath is conventionally depicted as having six visible twists of alternate tinctures, that to the left, the dexter, always being of a metal; for example 'Or' (Gold or yellow). The James crest has a wreath of gold and red that is, 'Or and Gules'.

We now come to the stylised scallop shell held by the Tyger on the Dexter. It is known in heraldry as 'Escallop Gules' (Shell of Red). This feature is the most revealing of all the elements of the crest, because the shell signifies perhaps the most famous 'James' who ever lived. Pilgrims to the shrine of St. James used it as a badge. St. James was one of the Apostles of Jesus and is usually referred to as 'St. James the Greater'. He was killed in Jerusalem and his relics were conveyed to Santiago de Compostela in northwest Spain. There are many stories about the reason for the scallop shell originally being associated with James. It may have been the pilgrims using the shells as primitive cups and spoons, or perhaps it came from the earlier Roman Festival of the sea godess 'Salacia' celebrated on St. James' day (July 25th). Pilgrims to the shrine wore, and often still wear, a scallop shell on their clothing. In medieval times the Galicians, the people living around Santiago de Compostela, put scallop shells over their doors to indicate that they were willing to accept pilgrims into their homes. In French 'une coquille Saint-Jacques' - literally, a 'St James shell' - is the term for a 'scallop'. St. James eventually became the patron saint of all pilgrims. English children many years ago would collect old shells, bits of coloured pottery, flowers, leaves etc. and build a little 'grotto'. This activity harked back to the ritual of constructing shell grottoes on St. James's Day for the use of those who could not afford the pilgrimage to the shrine at Compostela.

Since the crest on the wooden plaque has a green background, in heraldry it could be said to be on a green 'field', although 'crests' would not normally be on any field. The heraldic description would run something like this:

'On a wreath Or and Gules, A male Tyger sejant erect Or and Holding an Escallop Gules. Depicted upon a field Vert'

From the 1950s and until quite recently, the club crest, always printed in black and white, had been used in slightly 'modified' form. The shell, being somewhat stylised, had critics pointing out that it was becoming rather similar to a cricket ball. In centenary year all the Club notepaper was reprinted with the crest in its correct colours and including the original red scallop shell.

The plaque depicting the James crest

The 1920s & '30s

Aldridge Cricket Club 1853 - 2003

Talk of a 'Golden Era' in the history of any cricket club is usually based upon the time when some of the club 'greats' were at their best. This glorious state of affairs certainly applies to Aldridge as it entered the 1920s and is one, few would argue, which extended well into the following decades. During this time the Club was really 'working'. Administration, mainly in the hands of the able Jack Matthews was extremely sound, pavilion facilities and the pitch were greatly improved and 'home-grown' Junior members emerged. Quality players in both 1st and 2nd XIs thrashed the opposition whilst supporting staff, such as the ladies, umpires, groundsman and scorers were some of the finest servants in the Club's history.

'The years 1920 to 1923 saw the arrival of several players who did grand service for the Club, amongst them being Jim Bird, Cecil Lowe, T. H. Partridge. B. W. Emery and Jim Holgate. One of these, Cecil Lowe, besides being a fine batsman, was perhaps the most consistent bowler since Milner's day, and seldom did he send down a bad over. He topped the bowling in 1922 and the two following years, and could generally be depended on to get runs when they were most needed. His death in 1928 at quite a comparatively early age came as a terrible blow to us all. A true sportsman in every sense of the word, he was a gentleman whose memory will always be respected and admired by all who had contact with him.'

In 1930 Howard Walton described Lowe as: *'the finest bowler Aldridge ever had...'*. Wal Stone and Bert Partridge opened the batting between 1920 -1924 and Bill Emery played right up to the 1939 war when he joined forces with the Y.M.F. team which carried on when Aldridge temporarily closed. Bill's well disguised off-spinners with the occasional 'wrong 'un' provided him with many wickets keeping him high in the bowling averages. Although he continued to play weekend cricket in Walsall after the war he would still turn out for his old team in mid-week matches.

A 'new' pavilion was open for use in the summer of 1920 and the clubs finances were stretched to meet the cost. A very able committee, which included new members such as Richard 'Dickie' Bonnett (Of 'Buxton & Bonnett' Walsall) took the expenditure in its stride. Big fund-raisers were the Whist Drive's and dances which continued throughout the year. Mr F. W. Stephens, former Club captain, stood down from his position as 'M.C.' in 1920 but remained as Chairman. Much of the work relating to the Whilst Drives was now being performed by Mrs Buckley and her 'team' an indication that the ladies were not to be satisfied with just providing 'teas'.

'Jimmy Holgate was a regular 'speed merchant' and his few years with the village team were productive of a good 'bag' of wickets. An aggregate of 160 wickets in three consecutive seasons shows what a powerful force his bowling was to the team.

1st XI c. 1920

| E. Milner (Umpire) | T.H. Partridge | A. Lowe | ? | | A. Buckley | W. Emery | ? | C. Holland (Scorer) |
| | | W. Stone | J. H. Matthews | H. Walton | ? | E. J. Joberns | | |

Aldridge Cricket Club 1853 - 2003

1922

C. Holland, A. Hilditch, C. Lowe, J. Holgate, B. W. Emery, J. McGaw, E. Milner,
W. Stone, J. Matthews, W. Bednall, H. Walton, A. Buckley, T. H. Partridge, W. Jinks.

While we much regretted his departure from Aldridge Cricket, we have been very pleased to follow his successful career since linking up with the Wolverhampton C.I.D.. At the end of the last war, he was appointed to a very important Government post in Greece, when that country was passing through a most turbulent period of its history.'

The Annual Dinner of 1920, held at the Elms Hotel was reported in the Walsall Observer. The chaiman was Mr. F. W. Stephens who looked back upon the year. The loss of Arnie Bell to Aston Unity was regretted but there was good news on the membership front; it had increased from 97 in 1912 to 170. The Junior members were doing splendidly. Mr Walton topped the batting and received a pipe in a case, for averaging 24 per innings. The winner of a pair of leg guards was Mr A. Bell who took 33 wickets at a cost of 6 runs each. In the 2nd Team Mr Howard Perry's batting Ave of 18 was the highest, he received a walking stick as a prize! The bowling prize, a cricket bat, was carried off by Mr Jack Hastilow, who was a comparatively recent acquisition by the club.

Later in the year there was a Presentation of a Gold Watch to Mr J. H. Matthews, in appreciation of his services.

By 1921 there were strong 1st XI and 2nd XI's and a 'Junior Section'. Howard Walton was 1st team Capt. with W. Bednall in charge of the 2nd XI. Jack Matthews remained as Secretary and T. H. Mold Treasurer. Due to the coal strike the Whist Drive was postponed. Club President, Mr Frank James, was sent a congratulatory telegram

1st XI 1920s

? ? ?   T.H. Partridge   A. Lowe   ?   ?   ?   ?   E. Milner
W. Stone   J. H. Matthews   H. Walton   ?   A. Buckley

on the occasion of his 100th birthday (Nov. 8th). Mr Cooke the landlord of The Swan in 1922 was approached regarding the annual Club Dinner since the landlord of the Elms was leaving and would not book up another dinner. Consequently, Club 'HQ' was officially changed to the Swan in March 1922. A regular sight on away match days was the Dawsons Charabanc parked on the High St. outside the Swan. In 1924, a price of 2s 9d per journey (about 13p in today's money!) was agreed. Dawsons provided the Club transport well into the 1960s.

Frank Myring Jr. 1928

In 1922, the policy of the Club encouraging Junior talent was beginning to bear fruit. Fred Baker, Bill Groves and Frank Myring, all products of the Junior Section, were regular 2nd XI players. Like Harold Ray, who came to the Club in 1923. They all eventually became elite club players. Fred Baker became one of the Club's best all-rounders, and Frank Myring (Jnr.) a grand fast bowler and powerful hitter of the ball. Frank gained a 'Sunday Mercury' prize bat in 1928 by knocking up a record score of 148 not out in 90 minutes on Saturday 19th May v Birmingham Battery at Selly Oak. At the Annual Dinner 1928, at the Swan Hotel, Frank received the ball used in the Selly Oak game, with a suitably inscribed silver plate.

Bill Groves, who became Club Captain and eventually President, was inspirational in his leadership and always regarded as a fine sportsman. Harold Ray became one of a list of fine wicket - keepers following on from Wal. Stone, and Joe Whyld. Harold was the epitome of good keepers, short but smart and a dab hand with the bat at times of crisis. He scored a famous 102 not out playing for the 2nd XI in 1926.

Eric Tatlow played for a few seasons in the 1920s having the distinction, in 1925, of scoring a record total of 625 runs, even breaking Howard Walton's record-breaking sequence!

At the Annual Meeting 1924, held at the Swan Hotel, Arnie Bell was welcomed back to the club and Messrs A.

R. Myring & R. Bonnett were thanked for their ground collections. The President, Mr E. Joberns, in a letter to the Sec. offered a prize of £2. 2s with a view to encouraging junior players, this would be called the 'Junior Efficiency Prize'. The Secretary reported that he had interviewed Dr. Victor Milne with a view to obtaining his support for the club, and the doctor had agreed, and said that he looked forward to many enjoyable games during the coming season. Dr. D. Moodie, his partner, had told him (the Secretary) that Dr. Milne was *'almost as good a cricketer as he was a footballer'* which drew considerable applause.

Dr. V. Milne c.1925

Dr. Victor Milne, who had moved down to the Aldridge area from his home town of Aberdeen in November 1923 to play for Aston Villa, played at Centre Half in the 1924 Cup Final which Newcastle United won 2-0. He came to the Club in the 1925 season soon establishing himself as a fine all-rounder, for many years being a powerful force in both batting and bowling. Whilst he finished playing with Villa in April 1929 his best days with Aldridge had only just begun. His 121 not out, in 1930 was his best score. Over the years he contributed much to Aldridge cricket, on and off the pitch. His son, Dr. Mearns Milne also an Aldridge player in his day, has been associated with the Club for many years. Ray Clare and Stan Whitehouse, both from the Junior Section, came into the team in 1926 and were still playing more than twenty years later.

Another sportsman who 'also' played cricket was Charles Holland, who graduated from the position of scorer. Charlie's main sport was cycling. He made frequent appearances for Aldridge in the seasons from 1925 to 1928. In the 1926 season, along with Ray Clare, he won a special prize as 'best junior', one guinea each, donated by Ted Joberns. Charlie represented Gt. Britain in two Olympic Games, at Los Angeles in 1932 and Berlin 1936. He won a bronze medal in 1932 for the 4000m team pursuit. A real cycling fanatic, Charlie could sometimes be seen pedalling round the village with his two brothers, Jack and Alf, on their three seater 'Tridom'. He held the distinction of being the first British rider to compete in the Tour de France. Standing up at the Annual Club Dinner in

1937, Mr Howard Walton proposed 'The Visitors' and after a few comments on the '*appallingly apathetic and spiritless cricket*' played by the English team in Australia,............ Congratulated Mr Charles Holland on his remarkable cycling successes in the previous year.

The Walsall Observer reported:

'*... Mr Holland replying, recalled some of the happy times he had had as a member of the club and the lessons he learnt from the good sportsmanship of the members.*'

'The year 1929 was highly successful. It was then that Howard Walton attained the wonderful average of 66.2 and this season also saw one of the best victories Aldridge has ever had - against the Y.M.F. team at Aldridge. Generally, matches between these clubs have been very even, but this particular game was so remarkable, the score sheet is worth giving in detail.'

(See bottom of page)

Howard Walton was contemporary with, and a big admirer of, the great Surrey and England batsman Jack Hobbs. Hobbs, dominated the batting for England through the 1910s well into the 1920s and could be relied upon to score runs no matter what the batting conditions. Hobbs, regarded as 'The Master' was a player with style as well as being a 'run-machine'. In many ways Howard Walton could be said to have epitomised much of the 'Hobbs Touch', a first class batsman who always looked to play text-book cricket, he would not have seemed out of place opening for England with Sutcliffe at the other end.

There is no doubt that Howard Walton was one of that select band of people who become legends in their own lifetime. His name was spoken of with a kind of quiet

Howard Walton signed himself Yours truly The Hobbs touch on this photo.

ALDRIDGE

H. Walton, not out	110
F. Baker, run out	98
W. Groves)	
Dr. Milne)	
A. Kendrick)	
R. Clare)	
F. Myring) Did not bat.	
A. Buckley)	
H. Simmons)	
B.W. Emery)	
H. Hands)	
Extras	14
Total (1 wkt.) 222	

Bowling: Emery 6 for 9.
                Dr. Milne 4 for 15.

Y.M.F.

K. Saunders, b. Dr. Milne	0
H. Mason, c. Simmons, b. Emery	10
L. Owen, b. Emery	4
C. Wright, c. Myring, b. Emery	8
G. Haynes, b. Emery	0
F. Cartwright, c. Myring, b. Emery	0
J. Thorpe, b. Emery	2
H. Taylor, b. Dr. Milne	2
B. Whitehouse, c. Baker, b. Dr. Milne	0
G. Robinson, not out	0
H. Wright, b. Dr. Milne	4
Extras	19
Total:	**49**

subservient reverence. This personal aura of authority can be easily demonstrated when at a Club meeting in February 1930 the minutes record: *'Walsall Knock out Comp. - left on table.'* Behind these few words we can see the real character of H. W. emerge. The story was that the Committee were agreed that the game needed more 'promotion'. Aldridge with its fine phalanx of players had been a little cushioned from the full effects of what was a national malady in the game, but was still constantly drawing upon the recources of it's 2ndXI to make up numbers. Perhaps it was the long run of England Test Match defeats and draws and the emergence of the likes of Don Bradman which were to blame. England did beat the Aussies in 1929, but the win was described as 'lucky'. England were not so lucky, however, when Australia came to England in 1930. The Knockout competition idea was put forward by the Walsall club, whereby there would be a time limit to the games. Howard Walton was not in agreement with it on the grounds that it did not promote skilful cricket. It would be twenty years before Aldridge would participate in the competition. One can only reflect on what his thoughts may have been about 'twenty20' if it had been suggested at the time! Howard was not one for negativity however, being positive about the future of the game. Immediately, suggestions were made to introduce professional coaching. At this point I feel obliged to reproduce the words of Jack Matthews who was Howard's good friend and collegue throughout his whole time at the Club. Jack, for once, waxed lyrical:

> '...And still he, the complete personification of cricket art, calmly but majestically continued his triumphant career. A whole volume would be required to relate all the brilliant achievements of Howard Walton. Right from his entry into Aldridge cricket, he had showed himself a master of batting technique, and throughout the long years he was the mainstay and inspiration of the team. Never did he let his side down, and we old players and his contemporaries knew that while Howard was at the crease, there was always hope, no matter how critical the position was. His runs were always obtained by 'correct' cricket, footwork, timing and stroke play being models of perfect batsmanship. Perhaps his greatest season was 1927 in which he scored 1270 runs for 20 completed innings - an average of 63.5. Heading the batting averages for 24 consecutive seasons, with the one exception already mentioned, he has created a record that will probably never be surpassed.

In 1930 he showed his interest in the welfare of the Club, by volunteering to lead the 2nd XI which had lost several of its leadin players, and here his influence did much to restore lost confidence. It was then that he had the unique distinction of gaining both batting and bowling averages for the 2nd XI, whilst the phenomenal average of 140.5 for the 7 innings he played with

1931

S. Whitehouse, H. Myring, B. W. Emery, Dr. Milne, G. Newell, T. S. Davies, J. Davies
H. Simmons, W. Groves, H. Walton, R. Clare, E. Joberns, (Umpire).
W. Pulham (Scorer).

Aldridge Cricket Club 1853 · 2003

Through the old pavilion railings steps Howard Walton, the colossus of Aldridge cricket. A young Arthur Pheasant follows him out.

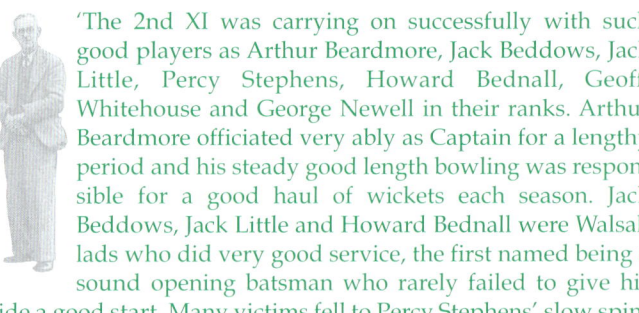

'The 2nd XI was carrying on successfully with such good players as Arthur Beardmore, Jack Beddows, Jack Little, Percy Stephens, Howard Bednall, Geoff. Whitehouse and George Newell in their ranks. Arthur Beardmore officiated very ably as Captain for a lengthy period and his steady good length bowling was responsible for a good haul of wickets each season. Jack Beddows, Jack Little and Howard Bednall were Walsall lads who did very good service, the first named being a sound opening batsman who rarely failed to give his side a good start. Many victims fell to Percy Stephens' slow spinners and his 58 wickets in 1925 created a 2nd XI record yet to be beaten. Geo. Newell is still making runs and taking wickets as a useful change bowler.'

Although a few of the older players dropped out, there was little change in playing personnel right up to 1939. Some younger players such as Harry Baker, Geoff. Hastilow, Len Davies, Arthur Pheasant and George Simmons started upon their careers in the senior teams. Generally the players were local lads who had been encouraged as youngsters by Jack Matthews. Families well-known in the village, such as Harry Baker of Bakers' the Stationers, Arthur Hilditch the Grocers and later Ironmongers in the High Street etc. Alf. Buckley, after a long and distinguished playing career, had taken over, in 1931, from Mr E. Joberns who due to ill health had stood down as Club President. In 1933, Howard Walton was presented with an illuminated address commemorating his 21 yrs association with the Club.

The Swan 'Hotel' remained as popular 'Club HQ' throughout the 1920s and 1930s. Annual Dinners were always held there during this time. A report on the 1931 dinner perhaps goes some way towards explaining the reason for its popularity... the Dinner was held in the:

'...good old fashioned deal-floored room with the usual slope, which precipitates the buxum waitresses at an alarming speed to the opposite end of the room. The formidable task of covering the capacious plates is accomplished very discreetly behind a clothes horse that refuses to be camouflaged by a spotless sheet and seems to conceal a never ending supply of roast beef, tender mutton, and succulent pork, to say nothing of vegetables.'

In 1936 Dr Milne put forward the idea of a Scottish Tour, the first real 'Tour' for the club since the Bank Holiday excursion to Llandudno in 1882. The tour, which took place in 1937 and repeated in 1938, is described elsewhere, and was very successful. Some matches were played well away from the immediate locality however, particularly at holiday times. Jack Matthews tells of the first match to be played at Coleshill:

'The old Whit Tuesday match at Coleshill was looked upon as a real holiday affair, and an occasion when wives and sweethearts were allowed to join the party. Our first match there was played when motor coaches were coming more generally into use, and so the journey was made by what must have been one of the earliest of its sort to be invented. And what a ride! After much

the 1st XI naturally placed him easily at the head of the list for the senior side.

Of course, a player of his ability came in for much 'Press' recognition, and invitations to play for Clubs considered to be in a much superior class than Aldridge were not few. There is not much doubt that could he have spared the time and also had the inclination, 'County' cricket would have gained a player whose fame would have spread far beyond the confines of the village of Aldridge. However, his choice lay with his beloved village club and its associates. Certainly he did play in some mid-week games with the Sutton Coldfield Club and he occasionally accepted invitations to play for his County of Staffordshire. At Edgbaston, his ability was recognised by his being chosen to lead the Warwickshire Club and Ground side on many occasions. But these often prolonged games meant too long an absence from his farm, and with Howard, though he loved his cricket, business came first.

From 1921 to 1939 he was the chosen Captain of the Club, and a fine skipper he made. In this capacity he was able to put into practice his detailed knowledge of the finer points of the game and while possessing a complete knowledge of his own team's capabilities and limitations, he was quick to discern those of his opponents. A slight alteration in the placing of the field, or a discreet change in the bowling has many times brought about the capture of a much wanted wicket, and what a galvanic effect that smart little clap of the hands, accompanied by the rallying call of 'Come on Aldridge,' would have on players becoming somewhat languid during a prolonged spell in the field! Yes, he was a great leader!'

Teams, of course are very much more than one man. Colossus though he was, Howard Walton could not have performed so well for so long without being surrounded by so many good players.

spluttering and backfiring it started off and was coaxed along with difficulty, shuddering and jerking until the steep hill in the middle of the town was reached. Here the contraption properly jibbed and started off backwards down the hill. One of the team, ignoring the maxim "women and children first" scrambled out and reached the ground in anything but an upright position, just as the driver succeeded in getting his brakes to act.

Play started at round about 12. In this match, one of the home players, for business reasons could not turn out at the appointed time, so a mutual agreement was reached whereby a sub. was allowed to field until this player's arrival. Aldridge made a very good start, only one wicket falling before luncheon interval was reached. The "Swan" as usual, put on a very good "spread" after which meal, all were feeling very perky and bright.

On resuming, however, this buoyant spirit was quickly dispelled. Playing a very unorthadox stroke, this same player who made such an inglorious exit from the coach, now fell backwards on to his wicket. Though he strongly maintained that he had completed his stroke, the umpire thought otherwise, so off he had to go - a bit of bad luck, but worse trouble was to follow. The pre-lunch absentee now made his presence known, by giving a display of some of the best fast bowling that Aldridge has ever had to encounter. Wickets tumbled and rattled with alarming rapidity, and in a short while, all were out for just over a hundred. Yes, Jack Nicholls was a real class speed bowler with as fine an action as it was possible to see. After a rather indifferent start, the town team gradually settled down and won the match by a fairly comfortable margin. If there were any sad feelings resulting from the defeat, these were quickly banished at the convivial gathering which followed the game. One of the party, however, refusing to be drawn into such undesirable haunts, chose other ways to soothe any sorrow he might have felt, and was indeed reported as "missing" when the return journey was due to begin. After search parties had scoured the neighbourhood, he was eventually discovered on his hands and knees, in the gathering gloom studying the epitaphs on the ancient tombstones in the nearby churchyard. So much for our first match at Coleshill.'

Merit Awards were introduced for the first time in the 1937 season and presented at the Annual Dinner at the Swan. These awards were introduced to replace those of 'best bowling' and 'best batting' etc. The first recipients were: S. Whitehouse 1st XI, G. Hastilow 2nd XI, both being presented with a blazer decorated with a handsome 'Merit' badge. Mr Buckley, it was reported, '... commented that it would be good if the Old Great Barr Park Club could be revived so that there would be a club in each of the Council's Wards now that the Rushall Club had a new ground.' Perhaps needless to say Alf Buckley was not long in reminding all present of the: '...beautiful Aldridge Ground from which five counties can be seen'.

Arthur Beardmore left the district at the end of 1937 and so the capable and efficient Arnold Ballinger took over as 2nd XI captain, a position he would still hold some ten years later. Perhaps surprisingly, war clouds loomed over Aldridge as early as 1937. At the Annual Dinner Mr Rowley appealed to members of the Club to enrol as street wardens, ambulance men or volunteer firemen under the Urban District Council's scheme for air-raid precautions.

1938 was again a most successful year with the 2nd XI being particularly strong, Cyril Beasley, Arthur Pheasant, Cliff Myring and George Simmons doing remarkably well. Mr E. Joberns, former President of the Club passed away and was remembered at the Annual Dinner in silent tribute. Howard Walton once more spoke out against the idea of 'Knockout Cricket' he launched into his attack by saying:

'To my mind it is nothing more than a burlesque and a travesty of a fine game,…' He went on to condemn the game further; 'The greatest crime about 'knock-out' is that some elementary schools have seen fit to regard knock-out cricket as a right and fitting means of competition among themselves.'

On the positive side, Mr Walton was in favour of the eight - ball over as used by the visiting Australians, in order to lessen the wasted time between overs. Howard Walton headed the batting averages yet again with Harry Crumpton the bowling. Dr Milne had the highest score with 112 and Arnold Ballinger headed the 2nd XI batting and George Simmons the bowling.

1939 started badly with the death of Bert Myring and Mr W. Baker both of whom had made a great contribution to the Club by collecting money on the field. By the end of the year things were to become far worse. However, the usual activities continued with plans for a verandah extension for the pavilion being agreed. On the field play continued:

'Two centuries in successive matches from Billy Groves' bat made 1939 a memorable season for him, and others who had good batting records were Ray Clare, Cyril Beasley, Geoff Hastilow, Geoff Walker and Cliff Myring, with Harry Crumpton and Ray Clare forming the spearheads of the attack. Owing to business, Howard Walton did not play in many matches and Billy Groves, with an average of 52.7, easily headed the list.'

Plans for the early 1940s were being made but the coming war was to change things. One example has been recounted by Sam Harvey. At the last Annual Dinner before the war, in the upstairs room of the Swan, Sam sat next to Gilbert Alsop, a well known former Walsall FC player, who was also an excellent cricketer. Gilbert was going to join the club for the following season but international events turned out to steer proceedings in a different direction. After the war Gilbert Alsop spent a few seasons with other local clubs and was for some time groundsman for the Walsall Phoenix Club at their ground on Sutton Road.

Aldridge Cricket Club 1853 - 2003 — Trophies

Walsall Observer Club Player of the Year

1991	A. Roberts
1992	
1993	C. Mc Nab
1994	W. Law
1995	W. Law
1996	W. Law
1997	J. Rowley
1998	W. Law
1999	R. Dyer
2000	A. Wylie
2001	N. James
2002	M. Higgins
2003	A. Wylie

Best Fielder Award

1978	T. J. Pendry
1979	G. Holland
1980	P. J. Williams
1981	R. Hemingfield
1982	D. J. Edge
1983	J. Davis
1984	D. Edge
1985 - 88	P. Hills
1989	G. Harrris
1990	C. Lee
1991	W. Hughes
1993	R. Capewell
1995	C. McNab
1996	S. A. Wolczek
1997	J. Rowley
1998	A. Cornick
1999	K. Sharpe
2000	G. Parkes
2001	G. Shelton
2002	G. Shelton
2003	A. Cornick

W. H. Bunn Cup.
For the most improved Junior of the Season (u.16s)

Year	Player	Year	Player
1964	M. J. Tyas	1984	D. Rowley
1965	No Award	1985	W. Hughes
1966	C. Allery	1986	A. D. N. Clews
1967	R. D. Lowe	1987	A. J. Clews
1968	M.D.G. Biddle	1988	?
1969	M. Dufty	1989	L. Mc Manus
1970	R. Hawkley	1990	M. Higgins
1971	A. Dancey	1991	M. Doyle
1972	P. Williams	1992	J. Hancox
1973	No Award	1993	G. Cornick
1974	F. Fitzpatrick	1994	R. Bleakley
1975	R. J. Dyer	1995	J. Hancox
1976	No Award	1996	S. Wolczek
1977	A. Harding	1997	G. Parkes
1978	N. Manwaring	1998	A. Cornick
1979	P. White	1999	G. Parkes
1980	A. Roberts	2000	A. Cornick
1981	G. Harris	2001	D. Shortland
1982	R. Barnes	2002	D. Shortland
1983	A. Hastilow	2003	I. Singh

Captain's Award
Originally 'Player of the year' award

Year	Player	Year	Player
1976	J. Milner	1991	R. Cutler
1977	T. M. Clews	1992	A. Waldron
1978	J. C. Heming	1993	B. Cornick
1979	M. Pinfold	1994	S. Peak
1980	A. G. Popple	1995	G. Popple
1981	A. Waldron	1996	H. Shippey
1982	M. D. Cooper	1997	B. Cornick
1983	K. D. Buller	1998	H. Shippey
1984	A. J. Franks	1999	R. Dyer
1985	S. Peak	1999	B. Popple
1986	A. J. Franks	2000	H. Shippey
1987	R. Biddle	2001	J. Hartley
1988	G. Popple	2002	J. Foster
1989	Don White	2003	Ladies Committee
1990	G. Popple		

Harry Crumpton 1st XI Bowling Trophy

1980	K. Parnell
1981	A. Roberts
1982	K. Parnell
1983	K. Parnell
1989	I. Manwaring
1990	A. Roberts
1991	K. Smith
1992	K. Smith
1993	R. Dyer
1994	R. Dyer
1995	R. Cattell
1996	K. Smith
1997	R. Kendal
1998	H. Shippey
1999	K. Sharpe
2000	K. Sharpe
2001	N. Steadman
2002	C. De - Witt
2003	M. Higgins

Portland Cup
H. Devey 1983
For outstanding performance

1983	D. Mc Kecknie
1985	I. Manwaring
1987	R. Eardley
1988	M. Pinfold
1989	R. Pickston
1990	I. Manwaring
1991	W. Hughes
1992	I. Manwaring
1993	N. Steadman
1994	C. Mc Nab
1997	G. Cornick
1998	W. Law
1999	W. Law
2000	S. Wood
2001	M. James
2002	J. Rowley
2003	S. Wood

Sally Johnson Memorial Cup
Most Improved Junior Player (o.16s)

1988	C. Mounford
1989	A. Clews
1990	M. Pedder
1991	G. Cornick
1992	G. Cornick
1993	J. Hancox
1994	G. Cornick
1995	J. Edge
1996	A. Cornick
1997	A. Cornick
1998	P. Sargent
1999	O. Quiney
2000	R. Shelton
2001	K. Fenwick
2002	A. Perkins
2003	J. Prior

The Wisdom Trophy
For Outstanding Performance

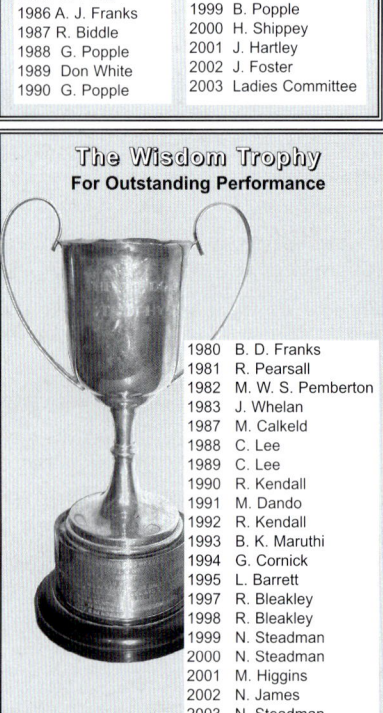

1980	B. D. Franks
1981	R. Pearsall
1982	M. W. S. Pemberton
1983	J. Whelan
1987	M. Calkeld
1988	C. Lee
1989	C. Lee
1990	R. Kendall
1991	M. Dando
1992	R. Kendall
1993	B. K. Maruthi
1994	G. Cornick
1995	L. Barrett
1997	R. Bleakley
1998	R. Bleakley
1999	N. Steadman
2000	N. Steadman
2001	M. Higgins
2002	N. James
2003	N. Steadman

3rd XI Captain's Award

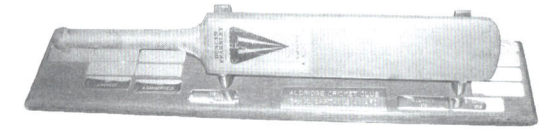

Year	Player	Year	Player
1982	S. Peak	1995	J. Braden
1983	S. Peak	1996	A. Dangerfield
1988	A. Dangerfield	1997	A. Dangerfield
1989	L. Barton	1998	B. Cornick
1990	M. Mann	1999	B. Cornick
1991	J. Hancox	2000	A. Walters
1992	L. Barton	2001	A. Lawrie
1993	T. Elphee	2002	Katie LLoyd
		2003	John Shortland

The 1940s & '50s
Aldridge Cricket Club 1853 - 2003

The Wartime Team

Standing: L-R Mearns Milne George Newell Dr Victor Milne   ?
Peter Wilson Stan Crowther Doug Redwood Jack Matthews
Sitting: L-R Ray Clare Billy Groves Alf Buckley Howard Walton Harold Ray
On ground: Stuart Joberns   Gordon Milne

Wartime conditions meant that during the winter period of 1939 - 40 there were no social functions and no income from Whist Drives and the like. National Service took away many of the Aldridge players and of course, much of the opposition. However, contrary to Jack Matthews' statement in his book that it was decided to: *'pack up for the duration'* initially he did all he could to keep things going. Firstly, even though official fixtures were cancelled, local clubs were written to in order to arrange games for the summer. Howard Walton represented Aldridge at a 'Wartime cricket' meeting of all the clubs in Walsall. It was agreed that local fixtures would be OK provided that only one team was required.

1940 was a grim year for the Treasurer, Jack Matthews having to report a deficit on the seasons working for the first time. Reasons of expense, shortage of players and lack of travelling facilities, it was thought, could all be overcome since most Clubs were trying to run one team. Mrs Buckley assisted by Mrs Hastilow continued to provide teas, evidently it would take much more than a World War to stop them!

After nearly eighteen months of war it was decided in February 1941 that play would not continue in the forthcoming season. Members were asked to contribute all or part of their subscriptions to enable the club to meet its financial obligations.

In early 1944 a meeting, at the New Elms Hotel, was called to discuss the resumption of play. A scratch game was arranged for May 13th. This was successful and the 1944 season was under way.

'Several new names appeared in the score book, chief amongst them being Douglas Redwood, Leslie Kenealey and Peter Wilson - all seasoned players with good reputations. Ray Clare and Bill. Groves proved as capable as ever and some really good cricket was provided. Enthusiasm reached a very high pitch, and when special appeals were being launched for funds for the Red Cross, a couple of very attractive matches were arranged for the cause. Aston Unity, the oldest club in the Birmingham League, visited us in the August Week, and after a very enjoyable game, the village XI proved victors by a good margin. Then in early September, Old Hill, one of the strongest League Clubs, brought over a very powerful XI, including Eric Hollies, the Warwickshire and England bowler, C. H. Palmer, the Worcestershire and England all-rounder, and several other county players. Aldridge put up a very good show, but found Eric's tricky bowling a bit too good for them. As a result of these two matches we were able to send a cheque for over £53 to augment this grand fund. Both these redoubtable teams were loud in their praise of Aldridge ground and Aldridge cricket in general. Certainly the pitch and ground never looked finer, a great credit being due to the voluntary work put in. We were favoured with two beautiful days, ideal cricket weather, while the splendid services of the W.V.S. with their Tea Canteens were highly appreciated by the large number of spectators. Unfortunately, illness prevented Howard Walton taking part in cricket in 1944. His ability would have proved invaluable in these important games.'

1945 was another good season for Ray Clare, topping both batting and bowling averages and with his 82 wickets creating a Club record. When another match was played to raise money for the Red Cross Fund, this time with Frank Bailey's Walsall XI, over £17 was achieved. A game with the R.A.F. realised well over £7 for their Benevolent Fund. In the latter game Ray Clare captured all 10 wickets a feat accomplished only once before, by Dr. V. Milne in 1926.

Ray Clare in 1947

At the Annual Dinner in March 1946 the Elms hotel rang out with applause as Mr & Mrs Buckley were presented with a Rose Bowl to commemorate more than 50 yrs service to the club. Mr Ray Clare was presented with the ball, mounted & inscribed, with which he took ten wickets for 14 runs in the match v the RAF in the previous August. The Club announced a record membership of 184. Two teams, it was hoped, would run for the coming season. An interesting aside was made by Jack Matthews who commented that they were once able to buy a ball for 5s 6d but now 29s 6d was the latest catalogue price!

Aldridge Cricket Club 1853 - 2003

It was perhaps the wettest season on record. Of the 21 matches in 1946 arranged for the 1st XI, 6 were abandoned without a ball being bowled and 9 others ended in draws. The team did not suffer defeat in any game. Many players were now back from war service and 1st and 2nd XI fixtures were resumed. Ray Clare was once again the most successful in batting and bowling for the 1st XI, whilst Jack Lloyd and Walter Pheasant did exceedingly well for the 2nd XI.

Cyril Beasley, Ray Clare and Geoff Walker had good aggregate scores in the 1947 season, with Arthur Pheasant and Ray Clare being very effective in the bowling department as usual.

Post war cricket was set to take Aldridge into a new era and the year 1947 would be one of decision and change. In many ways it turned out to be the most significant year in the history of the Club. The meeting on 27th October proved to be momentous for at least two reasons.

Firstly, gone it seems, were the days of the Secretary sorting out fixtures. The modern game required a 'League' structure and a number of these were being formed in the region. Early in the year Bill Groves and Ray Clare attended a meeting in Wolverhampton of the South Staffs League, but after much discussion over the next few months the members came out against entering it. At the September meeting a letter was read from the newly formed 'Midland Club Cricket Conference' League, inviting the Club to join. It was resolved that representatives should attend a meeting in Birmingham on 9th October and if they were impressed they were empowered to ask for the Club to be enrolled as members. Affiliation to the M.C.C.C. was considered to be of 'great benefit' and was approved at the meeting on Oct. 27th. The Secretary stated that he had forwarded the Guinea (21s) affiliation fee which cleared the Club until December 1948.

Secondly, the Manor farm, which included the Cricket Ground, had been put up for sale and Mr Buckley had attended the sale in Birmingham. The Chairman of the meeting, Mr Howard Walton, told the committee that Mr H. E. Swain had purchased the farm. He then said that he was going to make an announcement that was probably the most important ever made in the history of the Club - that Mr and Mrs Buckley had purchased the cricket field from Mr Swain. This meant that all the difficulties regarding security of tenure were now over. The whole meeting was gripped with excitement and the minutes record phrases such as 'wonderful gesture', 'magnificent gesture' and 'great incentive'.

At a special General Meeting called in December, Mr and Mrs Buckley were invited to become Life members of the Club.

Now the Club was more or less responsible for the ground Trustees were appointed, namely Howard Walton, Alf Buckley and Jack Matthews ... who else?

The 1948 season was the last to be recorded by Jack Matthews:

'The last season's cricket under review, 1948, started off in a blaze of triumph, outstanding victories being recorded and high scoring was the order of the day, especially in the 2nd XI where Cliff. Myring and Arnold Ballinger were the dominant figures in batting with George Simmons and John Pheasant doing most destruction with the ball.

The 1st XI was much strengthened by the return of Harry Crumpton, whose speed bowling was a decisive factor in many games. Cliff. Myring added two more centuries to the Club's Honours List, his 119 not out against the Gas Officials and a further 105 against Selly Oak being the season's highest individual efforts. A newcomer to the Club, Maurice Harraway, played several lively innings and Cyril Beasley, Arthur Pheasant, Stan Whitehouse and Leslie Kenealy all did grand work in their special spheres. Billy Groves, the popular Captain led a very happy team, but no doubt on many occasions longed for the services of that keen all-rounder, Ray Clare, who, owing to illness and much to everyone's regret, had to take but a passive part in the Club's affairs.

A pleasing feature of the last two seasons has been the good form shown by several of our 2nd XI youngsters. Sam Harvey, Leslie Marshall, Frank Hastilow and John Swann certainly possess ability and a right cricket temperament, and so long as the Club can find such good juniors, a successful future is ensured. May it be so!'

Jack finished his story with a poem:

'Walton, Buckley, Lowe and Bell,
Names that you remember well;
Milner, Sales and Tatlow too,
Hardly so well known to you,
Jinks and Holgate, Glaze and Stone
'Gainst all comers held their own,
Whitehouse, Clare and Groves and Ray,
Make our Club well-known to-day.
Now you youngsters, rally round
To our splendid cricket ground,
Where you'll find abundant pleasure
In your many hours of leisure;
And you'll get a cordial greeting
At your first and every meeting.'

So, in January 1949 Jack Matthews' long awaited, interesting, inspirational and informative book 'Aldridge Cricket' was published. Sadly, the joy associated with the book launch was somewhat subdued due to the announcement of the death, on Christmas Day, of club stalwart Ray Clare.

Jack was, no doubt, pleased with the years following the publication of his book. The 1948 season had brought in

Aldridge Cricket Club 1853 - 2003

1st XI 1948

F. P. Stephens (Umpire)
Stuart Joberns   Leslie Kenealy   Cyril Beasley   Harry Crumpton   Arthur Pheasant   C. Forrester   Jack T. Davies (Scorer)   Stan Whitehouse
Douglas Redwood   Harold Ray   Alf Buckley (President)   William Groves (Capt.)   Maurice Harraway

2nd XI 1948

J. Wright (Umpire)   John Pheasant   W. Onions   A. Johnson   Sam Harvey   David Partridge   L. Marshall   Jack Matthews (Hon. Sec.)
Geoff Walker   George. Simmons   Arnold D. Ballinger (Capt.)   Cliff Myring   Frank Hastilow

Aldridge Cricket Club 1853 - 2003

sixteen new senior members and twelve juniors with the standard of play continuing to rise as the population of the village began to increase rapidly. Transport to away matches in the late 1940s was sometimes aboard a converted builders lorry. Edgar Swain had two wooden benches, fitted facing each other, players travelling with their backs to the canvas sides. Bill Groves captained the 1st XI as well as performing duties such as towing the gang-mower behind his Rover. There were always comments about the roller, it seems, because it had a peculiar rattle. Bill reckoned that it was a coin trapped inside and there was speculation that it must be a large coin such as a half-crown (2s. 6d) but Bill would only say that the rattle had been there so long that if it had been a half crown it would now have worn to a 6d! Harold Ray skippered the 2nd XI for the 1949 season with an 'A' team led by John Pheasant. Harold Ray, who had been with the Club since the 1920s, became the regular First XI wicket Keeper and was well known for his habit of removing his false teeth at the start of the opposition's innings and handing them to an often somewhat bemused umpire for safe-keeping!

Local newspapers in the spring of 1950 carried the following notice:

'The cricket knock-out competition organised by the Walsall Cricket Club for a silver Trophy which was formerly run before the war is being revived and a welcome is cordially offered to all local cricket teams in the Walsall district.'

The revived competition, for the 'Mellor Cup', was too good an opportunity for Aldridge to miss. Here was the very thing to prove that the Club was pre-eminent amongst some sixteen clubs in the Walsall area. Bill Groves offered the use of the ground for some of the matches with the final being scheduled for Gorway, the home of Walsall Cricket Club. The night of the final, Monday 17th July, arrived with Aldridge pitched against arch-rivals Bloxwich. In the allotted 20 overs Bloxwich managed to knock up only 63 runs, not a severe challenge for Aldridge. However, by the last ball of the 14th over, Aldridge had scored 49 for the loss of five wickets and were having to struggle just a little, even given that they required only three runs per over to win. Facing Onions, Maurice Harraway touched a rising ball straight into Dunning the wicket keeper's hands, but in his anxiety, he snatched at the ball and dropped it. Four overs later Harroway cracked a four to the mid-wicket boundary to give Aldridge a well deserved victory. P. Cox took five wickets for 21 and A. Pheasant three for 41.

The superb Aldridge form continued throughout the 1950 season and was well demonstrated in a game versus Streetly. Streetly, playing at home, were dismissed for only 17 with Arthur Pheasant taking 6 wickets for one run and brother Walter finishing off the rest. Not one of the first seven Streetly batsmen were able to score. Aldridge scored 34 for one wicket before rain brought the Streetly humiliation to a premature close.

Presentation of the Walsall Knock-Out Cup to Aldridge. 17th July 1950

Left to right: S. Joberns, A. Ballinger, J. Pheasant, M. Harraway, W. Groves (Capt.), H. W. Shipley (Walsall Chairman), P. Cox, Ald. W. R. Wheway (Mayor of Walsall), A. Pheasant, W. Pheasant, D. Redwood, C. Beasley, J. Matthews (Hon. Secretary), C. Myring.

A year later and Aldridge, after three qualifying matches, against Little Aston, Rushall and Bloxwich, were back in the Knockout final, this time versus the F. H. Lloyd's XI. Lloyds failed to prevent Aldridge getting off to a good start with runs flowing from the bats of Arnold Ballinger and Cliff Myring. Even Lloyd's star player Gilbert Alsop with two for 28 and 32 not out with the bat, made no difference to the final outcome. Harry Crumpton bowled accurately taking five wickets for 31 to secure a second competition win. Both sides received commemorative takards given by the Walsall Festival of Britain Committee.

1951 turned out to be another good year for the Club with Arthur Pheasant and David Partridge receiving prize bats for leading the new 'points' scheme. Every year in the 1950s there was a fixture when the Cricket Club played a representative Church Team. The Rector, Rev Cartmel, was always very keen on these games… appropriately dubbed 'Saints v Sinners'. It is not known whether or not Rev. Cartmel called upon divine intervention to change the score, but when he looked to the heavens whilst out on the pitch he was not necessarily appealing to the umpire or to the Lord… as a keen 'ufologist' he was possibly looking for flying saucers preparing to descend on Gossy Knob!

One could easily be forgiven for concentrating upon the 1st XI when relating the triumphs of the early 1950s, but in fact all the Aldridge teams were strong during this period. Whilst the likes of Harry Crumpton and Arthur

George Simmons in 1996 holding the ball with which he took four wickets off consecutive balls in 1951

Pheasant were skittling out 1st Team opposition regular 2nd XI players such as George Simmons demolished all-comers in similar style, occasionally showing touches of real brilliance. One such game being on 28th July 1951 v Rushall 2nd's when George Simmons took four wickets off consecutive balls.

It was common during the 1950s for visitors and guests at the various Club Dinners to refer, with some degree of

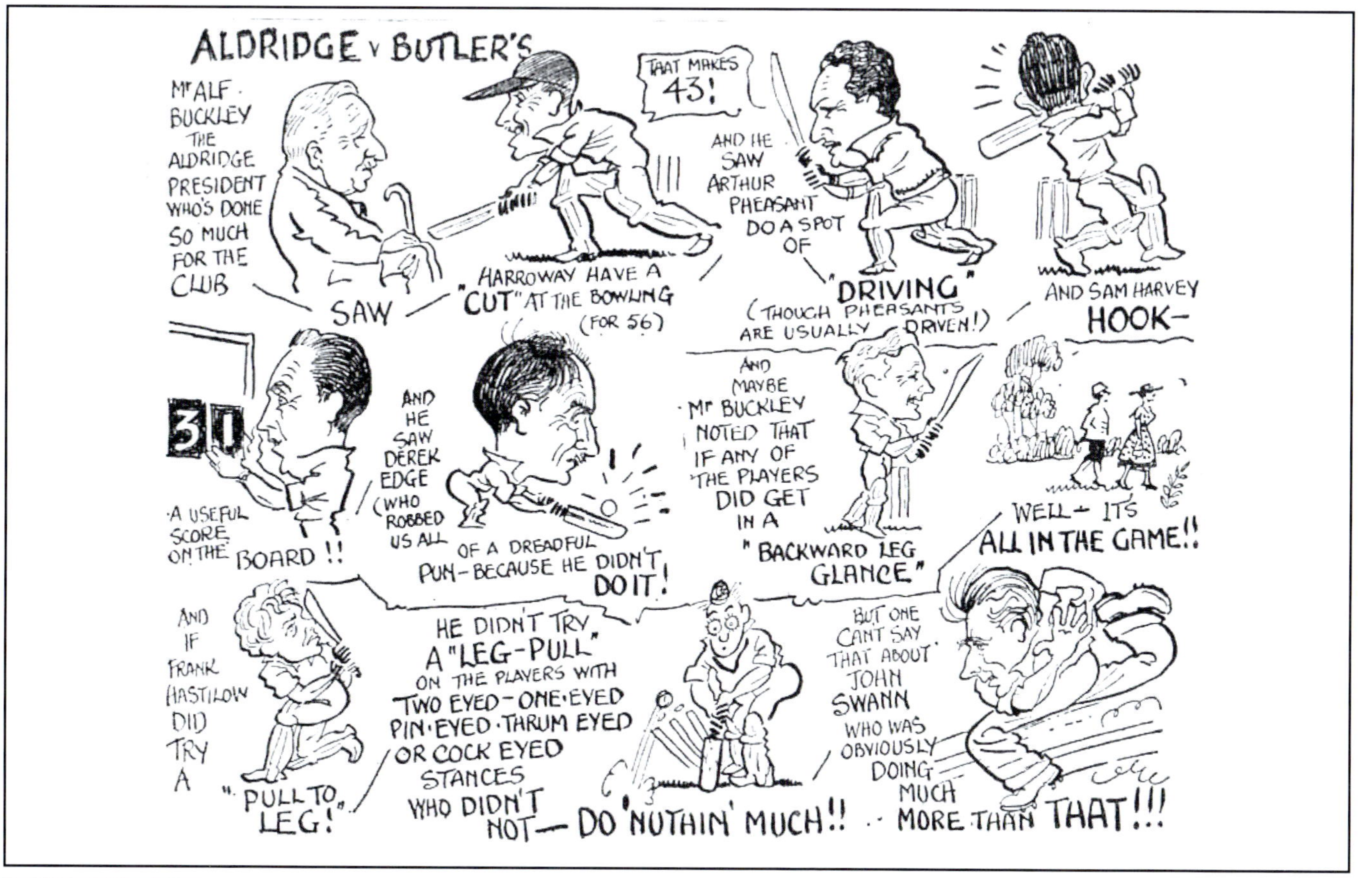

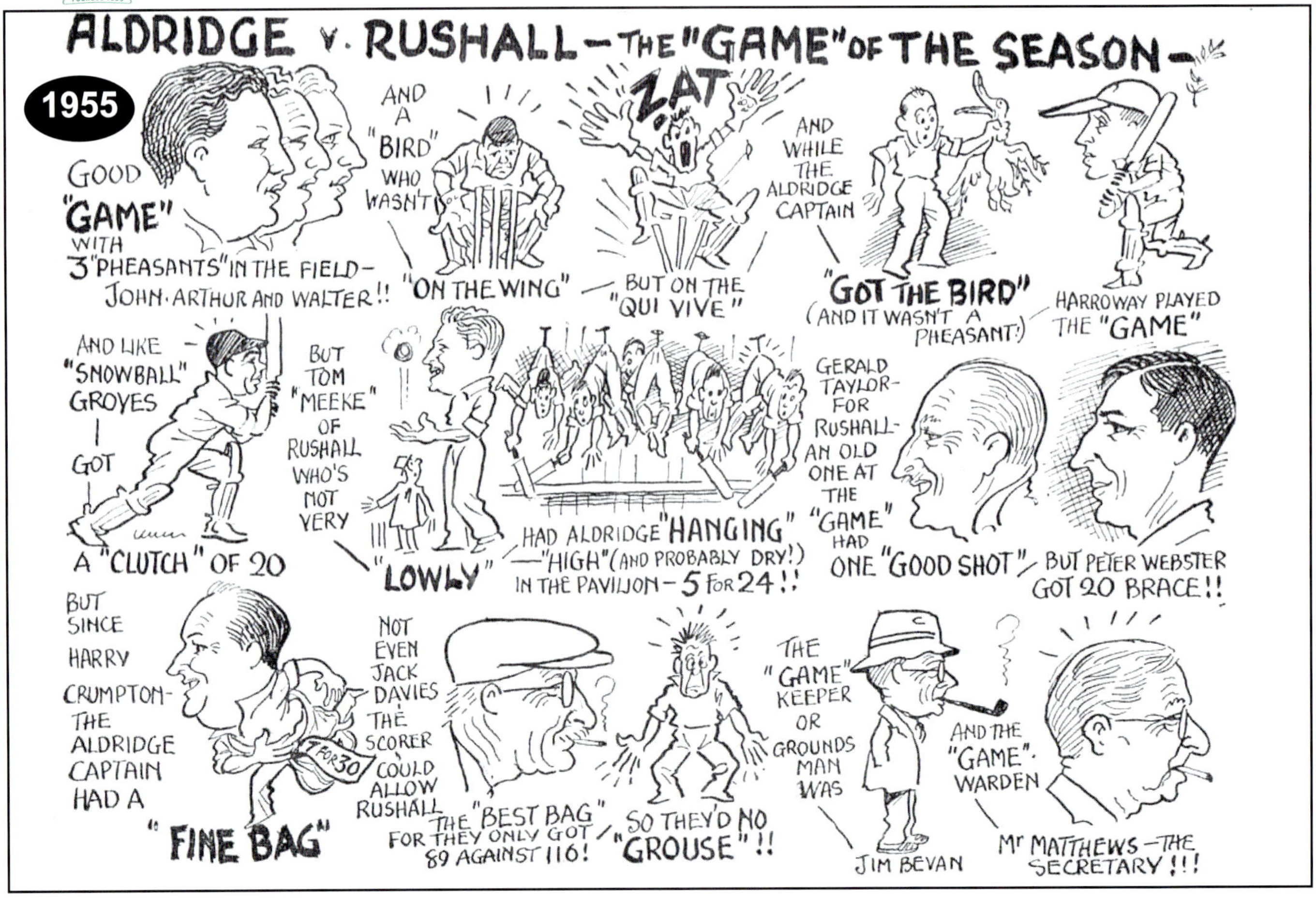

Aldridge Cricket Club 1853 - 2003

ALDRIDGE v. RUSHALL — THE "GAME" OF THE SEASON — 1955

awe, to the long service of the Aldridge officials. In centenary year, 1953, the aggregate service of these officials amounted to no less than 278 years. Jack Matthews with his forty years of service as Club Secretary was functioning, as Howard Walton put it: *'... as the most important official.'* He also stated: *'Others may go in first, and grumble, others may go in last and grumble; but a secretary is in all of the time.'* Jack Matthews wore a splendid blazer emblazoned on the pocket by a Staffordshire Knot. He was, along with countless other jobs, responsible for cricket sundries and sold Club blazer badges. Sam Harvey recalls going to a shop in Station St. in Walsall to buy a made to measure Blazer... total cost an economical £2.00. In fact, it needed four clothing coupons. When he got his badge from Jack he was told it would be a further £5.00, more than twice the cost of the blazer! Sam added: *'The badges were very good, bullion type, and you didn't argue with Jack ... he was doing you a favour'.*

Centenary year was, like 1950 and 1951, a winning year in the Knock-Out competition. For the third time Aldridge, led by captain Harry Crumpton, romped home with a sound defeat of neighbours Rushall. In fact, so superior had been the Club's route to the final that they had scored an average of 19.8 runs per wicket compared with Rushall's 6.4. So yet again the team were drinking from prize-winners pint tankards. The big game of the 1953 season should have been the one versus Walsall on the day of the opening of the new pavilion, but the weather intervened and the match was abandoned. For a while Cliff Myring and Sam Harvey were batting against the West Indian bowling duo of Ramadhin and Valentine but Sam was to be disappointed and not receive a single ball from Valentine, something he had been really looking forward to. The good form of the team continued through the 1954 season with the first team winning ten matches, drawing six and losing seven. Sam Harvey scored a century for the first team. Unfortunately, in the Mellor Cup final victory was snatched from Aldridge by Walsall Trinity in the last over of the match. In 1955 the Cup found its way back to Aldridge after a sound thrashing of Bloxwich in the final. Harry Crumpton taking five wickets in seven balls, including a hat-trick. In the 20 overs Bloxwich were all out for 66 with Aldridge 103 for 5. Batting stars for Aldridge were Arnold Ballinger 16, Sam Harvey 21, with an unbroken partnership from Arthur and John Pheasant of 24 and 20 respectively. Somehow, these Cup games were always just that bit more serious than the usual 'Friendlies'.

In the 1950s a number of cartoons appeared in the 'Walsall Observer' which captured the essential qualities and quirks displayed by the characters of the team as well as the inevitable play on words associated with the names. A real gift for such an artist was the clutch of 'bird' names at the time. Three 'Pheasants' - John, Arthur and Walter,

Aldridge Cricket Club 1853 - 2003

1st XI c.1957

Jack Matthews, Dr Mearns Milne, John Swann, Arthur Pheasant, Walter Pheasant, David Franks, John Morgan
Sam Harvey, Eddie Bird, Arnold Ballinger, (Capt) Derek Edge, Phil. Butler

Walsall Observer, Friday, May 31, 1957

ALDRIDGE v WOMBOURN

THE ALDRIDGE CHAIRMAN HOWARD WALTON WAS THERE — HE USED TO SCORE SO MANY — THOUSANDS OF RUNS — FOR ALDRIDGE — THAT OPPOSING FIELDSMEN THOUGHT THEY'D ENTERED FOR "THE MARATHON" — "I'VE RUN MORE THAN 26 MILES" — AND THE POOR BLOKES ON THE SCOREBOARD WERE OFTEN "OUT OF THE RUNNING"

AND SOON — SO WERE WOMBOURN! — ALL OUT FOR 96 — BECAUSE VETERAN HARRY CRUMPTON ("21 YEARS HARD LABOUR") WITH ALDRIDGE — ARTHUR PHEASANT — AND JOHN SWANN — "PUT 'EM OUT OF THEIR STRIDE"

AND SO — WITH ARNOLD BALLINGER — SAM HARVEY — MAURICE HARROWAY — PHIL BUTLER — DEREK EDGE — DAVID PARTRIDGE — "RUNNING INTO FORM" — ALDRIDGE TOTAL 1000 WICKETS 1 — THEIR NEW SCOREBOARD SHOULD LOOK INTERESTING SOME DAY!

The 1940s & 50s

Aldridge Cricket Club 1853 - 2003

John Swann, Eddie Bird, and David Partridge. This, combined with the idea of getting a 'Duck', the 'flight' of the ball etc. was just too good to miss. One year, Frank Hastilow wrote to Brian Johnston and the team at the BBC's 'Test Match Special' to let them know about the 'birds' in the team. Brian read-out the letter 'on air' and Fred Trueman made some of his usual witty, dry Yorkshire comments about it.

Dr Mearns Milne, son of Dr Victor Milne, was a regular batsman, contibuting many runs to both 1st and 2nd XIs. It could be assumed that to have a medical man on the field of play would be of great assistance in time of injury or illness. In fact, Mearns Milne, it seems, would frequently be the last person to arrive at the scene of any accident or suspected illness on the pitch!

John Swann's parents kept the Greengrocers in the High Street. The 'Team List' for the forthcoming match was always posted in the shop window, far more convenient than in the Pavilion. John was a rather erratic bowler. When he was on target he was lethal, but some balls were a touch wayward. At Rushall, for instance, the ball would fly past the crease and hit the tin pigsty on the adjacent farm making quite a racket. I expect the pigs didn't offer any grunt of approval either.

Changes in personnel happen regularly in all cricket clubs but during the latter part of the 1950s decade the faces at Aldridge were to alter remarkably, both on and off the pitch. With Aldridge village expanding rapidly in the mid to late 1950s it is not surprising to find a further influx of young players. David Franks, Jonathan Franks, Derek Edge, John Morgan, Jack Newsome, Ken Brown, Martin Tyas and others were all starting to make an impact in the scorebook. Other stalwarts such as Bill Groves, Stuart Joberns, Cyril Beasley, Cliff Myring, George Newall, John Pheasant, Harold Ray, and George Simmons, would stand down from 'active service' in Aldridge teams. In 1957 the death was announced of Mr T. H. Partridge, who was a Vice-President and Mr Jack Davies (Snr) who had been the Club's oldest member also passed away. Sir J. Cliff-Tibbits, the owner of Cedar Court, and always a big supporter of the Club, was elected as a Vice- President in 1959. Cliff-Tibbits' leather company had employed Alf Buckley and later also Frank Hastilow. In fact, Frank says that in the early days he would get two 'pay packets', one was for his work and the other, an extra payment, was the money for his cricket coaching. In June of that year the Club President Mr Alf Buckley died and his widow Mrs Jessie Buckley, always a tireless worker for the Club, was invited to succeed her late husband.

To finish this chapter we can go back to Jack Matthews and his book which chronicled the Club up to 1948, when it was truly a 'Village' Club. It was in the 1950s that Aldridge itself changed dramatically and the Club with it. He talks about games against Wombourne in the late 40s, games which still take place in 2003.

The Walsall Knock-out 'Mellor Cup'
Won by Aldridge three times in four years
in the early 1950s.
The Club has won the trophy so many times
it seems appropriate for Frank Hastilow s cap to sit proudly on top.

'In recent years the Club has greatly enjoyed the outings to Wombourn (sic) where they are assured of meeting a really good sporting side. The Wombourn ground has a perfect setting for a village club, being in the centre of the community and having the Church, with its lofty steeple, dominating the scene. Matches between the two clubs have generally been finely contested, and have resulted in very close finishes.

A little incident that took place in one game is well worth recording. While Aldridge were batting, a small lad ran on to the field, and accosted one of the Wombourn bowlers with "You'm wanted at 'ome, the bees are swarming!" The over was duly finished, a substitute was readily found, and off went the excited apiarist to attend to his bees. Returning after an interval of about an hour, he was pleased to announce that he had been successful in getting the swarm safely hived.

Such an incident could surely only happen in truly English village cricket.'

The 1960s & '70s
Aldridge Cricket Club 1853 - 2003

The death, in April 1960, of Jack Matthews, a man who had been 'Mr Aldridge Cricket' for longer than most could remember, could have set the Club back for many years.

However, such was the reputation of, and depth of skill and talent at the Club, much of it nurtured by Jack over some 58 years, that the cry was to continue to develop and carry on with what he had created. It was a case of - 'onward and upward'. The dawn of a new 'modern' dynamic era in the country as a whole, was reflected in the attitude of those associated with Aldridge Cricket. To paraphrase U.S. President J.F.K. ... it was not a matter of what Aldridge Cricket could do for you but rather, what you could do for Aldridge Cricket. Aldridge itself was expanding rapidly, becoming a small town in fact, and the Club set about reflecting that improved status both within the team itself and with the ground facilities which would be on offer.

In the late 1950s and into the 1960s there was a very strong Junior team which encouraged local cricketing talent. The juniors would even occasionally take on senior teams and beat them! The early 1960s IXs proved the worth of establishing such a youth programme as many fine players began to emerge. For instance, in 1962 Aldridge Juniors, in order to make up the number of teams in the cometition, were entered into the Aldridge C.C. Works Knockout which involved eight local teams from places such as BIP Streetly, BRD, McKechnie, and T.I.. The team displayed precocious talent by winning it! The Junior Team was: M. Moseley (Capt.), R. G. Evans, M. W. W. Baker, R. Baker, P. R. Burton, J. K. Mason, G. J. Nicholls, R. J. S. Moseley, R. Pickston, M. J. Tyas, and R. Warwood. The number of playing members had steadily grown since the war with an 'A' team, additional to the 1st & 2nd XI's operating from 1949 onwards. This 'A' team was very much a 'Social' side involving such folk as Rev. Martin Whitwell whose one 'strength' lay in always being able to catch the ball, no matter where he was fielding. The 'Saints and

1st XI 1964
(Taken at YMF Ground Walsall)

John Burton (Scorer) · Russell Pickston · Ken Brown · Mick Hall · Martin Baker · Bernard Hopley · Gary Nicholls · Harry Crumpton (Umpire)

Martin Tyas · Frank Hastilow · Arthur Pheasant (Capt) · F. Broome · Glynn Evans

Aldridge Cricket Club 1853 - 2003

Sinners' games continued for many years as did games against Walsall Rugby Club with the likes of Jan Webster and David Brown. Perhaps the standard of cricket was not high, but it did lead to a very good atmosphere within the Club. In the early 1960s the 'A' team played on Thursday evenings.

By the close of the 1960 season the Walsall Knock-out, 'Mellor' cup, was again in the hands of Aldridge, at least for six months since it rained on the final and the cup was shared with Walsall Trinity. The combination of youth and experience in the 1960s was a real winner for the Club and in 1966 the Cup returned to Aldridge hands, this time for the whole year. Gary Nicholls, Russ Pickston, Mick Hall, Martin Tyas, Mike Pemberton, Neil Castley, Mark Biddle, Mick Dufty, Glynn Evans and Keith Buller et al. linked up with other home-grown talent such as Bernard Hopley, Frank Hastilow, Sam Harvey, John Morgan, Ken Brown, Jonathan Franks, David Franks, and John Burton. Some players such as Arthur Pheasant, Geoff. Whitehouse, Maurice Harraway and David Partridge were entering their third decade with the Club.

In the match against YMF (See picture page 43) Mick Hall took six for 31 runs in 18 overs. Russell Pickston (32) and Gary Nicholls (18) got Aldridge off to a good start, followed by Bernard Hopley's fine 41. The winning run was taken from the last but one ball of the final over, with Frank Hastilow and Arthur Pheasant together at the wicket. Many teams fell victim to Aldridge in the 1960s; Rushall, Bridgnorth, Lichfield, Coleshill, Birmingham Co-op, Birmingham Gas Officials, Wombourn, Himley and of course old rivals Bloxwich. In 1966, Bloxwich were the victims in yet another Walsall Knock-out final victory. However, it should not be assumed that all was rosy insofar as winning was concerned. With so much talent and such a good reputation some of the statistics do not really measure up. For instance in 1965, a summer spoilt by the weather, as it had been in 1960, the record for the 1st XI was: Played: 23, Won 5, Drawn 8, Lost 9 and 1 Abandoned. Arthur Pheasant topped the batting averages and Glynn Evans took 28 wickets for an average of only 9.9 to top the bowling. Russell Pickston was second in the batting averages. Lionel Webb, second team skipper topped the averages in that team with 52.8 and John Burton although mainly a bowler was second with 12. Brian Latimer just pipped off-spinner David Franks for the bowling honours. By 1969 it had improved a little: 27 matches, Won 7, Lost 6, Drawn 7, Abandoned 1, Postponed 6. These somewhat mediocre results are typical of much of the 1960s and well into the 70s.

Perhaps it would be realistic to say that the Club with its improving facilities, was now expected to be 'big league' but the worthy mentality of simply having a good game, no matter what the result, seemed to prevail. For a club weaned on the rivalry of spirited village cricket and following what had been a true 'golden' era, it was not a familiar game plan. This state of affairs would dominate the committee agenda in the pavilion and with players on the field throughout the coming decades.

Howard Walton stepped down from his position as Chairman in April 1962 and in May 1964 he died. Six members of the Committee acted as bearers at his funeral. This was the end of an era for Aldridge. Within the space of five years the glorius triumvirate of Alf Buckley, Jack Matthews and now Howard Walton had passed away. Mr Stephens also resigned his position as umpire. The Club was now being transferred into new hands. Mrs Buckley had accepted the position of Club President and would prove to be no mere 'figurehead'. Bill Groves took on the position of Chairman and Mr J. Newsome who had been Treasurer since the death of Jack Matthews but had to leave the district with his job, was replaced by Ken Brown. Harry Crumpton, now finished with his illustrious playing career in two stints for Aldridge between which he was opening the bowling for Walsall in the Birmingham League, was established as Club Secretary. According to the minutes of the 1963 AGM the '*Spirit of the Club*' was '*very much alive.*' However, spirit was not enough on its own, for the Club to progress the playing standard had to improve. Some of the playing members became frustrated that committee discussions seemed to revolve around electricity supply, bar profits and advertising. At the meeting in July 1964, when the position of Club secretary became vacant with the resignation of Harry Crumpton, most discussion was not about who would replace him. Talk was of the request from Arthur Pheasant that the Club should pay much more attention to the 'playing' side. The question was asked; what came first, facilities for practice or the electricity supply? At the following meeting it was announced that Mr Geoff Walker had agreed to take on the job of 'Ground Secretary' only, leaving David Franks to be 'Fixture Secretary'. By 1966 Geoff was 'Hon. Secretary'. As Mike Pemberton states in his book 'The Wisdom of Aldridge Cricket Club': '*Geoff was not to know that his fouteeen years in office were to see the most rapid growth and expansion of the Club.*'

A new Walsall and District Mid-Week league was formed in 1964 which involved matches consisting of 15 eight ball overs. Frank Hastilow, Martin Tyas and Harry Crumpton had much to do with the inauguration of this new venture. Martin Tyas went on to do an immense amount of 'back office' work for the Club in the role of Assistant Secretary and member of numerous committees as well as being a regular 2nd XI and 1st XI batsman. He would, it seems, always write in green ink. In 1977, after obtaining his doctorate, he went to work in Australia as the 'Flying Dentist' and was added to the list of Club Vice-Presidents joining both Frank Hastilow and Harry Crumpton in this elite squad. In 1963 Martin Tyas, along with Martin Baker, who also became 'Dr' Martin Baker, were the first Club members to produce a record of each season's matches

Aldridge Cricket Club 1853 - 2003

1st XI 1966
Winners of the Walsall Knockout

| Geoff. Walker (Hon. Sec) | Gary Nicholls | Glynn Evans | Mick Hall | Bernard Hopley | Jonathan Franks | T. Fazey | Bill Groves (Chairman) |
| | Martin Tyas | Arthur Pheasant | Frank Hastilow (Capt) | Sam Harvey | Bob Shelton | | |

1st XI 1967
At 1st Ox-Roast August Bank Holiday

| S. Brown (Scorer) | John Morgan | Sam Harvey | Jonathan Franks | Arthur Pheasant | Mick Hall | Ken Bourne | Harry Crumpton (Umpire) | Bill Groves (Chairman) |
| | Bernard Hopley | Malcolm Moseley | Frank Hastilow (Capt) | Gary Nicholls | G. Rutherford | | | |

The 1960s & 70s

Page 45

Aldridge Cricket Club 1853 - 2003

1st XI 1969

S. Hough (Umpire) H. Pickering John Walton David Franks Sam Harvey Keith Buller John Burton M. Hobday (Scorer)

Brian Holsey Jonathan Franks Frank Hastilow (Capt) Arthur Pheasant Russell Pickston

going back to 1910. These details were very helpful to Mike Pemberton when, in 1978, he produced his book, 'The Wisdom of Aldridge Cricket Club'. Like Martin Tyas, Martin Baker left the area to work - in Batley, Yorkshire.

Jack Wright was a regular Aldridge Umpire. Frank Hastilow reckons that because Jack had to get the last Harper's bus at 7. 30… no matter what, sometimes he would be rather enthusiastic to give batsmen out in order to finish the game. Frank remembers one occasion when he was batting he had missed the ball, no one appealed but Frank happened to mention to Jack that he had missed the ball, Jack lifted his finger and gave him out … possibly the only occasion when a batsman has 'asked' the umpire himself. Frank admitted that it was getting quite late and the green Harper's bus wouldn't wait.

Junior cricket at Aldridge was continuing to provide a constant stream of new players and the senior players were always there to help them. In April 1966 it was announced that the 'Juniors' would henceforth be called 'Aldridge Colts'. A year later, it was also decided that the Colts should elect their own Captain. Swingin' 1960s 'youth culture' was really taking - off in Aldridge!

The Club President, Mrs Jessie Buckley, sadly, passed away in 1969. Provision had been made for the Club to have first option on the purchase of the ground from the estate. As a direct result of speedy negotiations and the Buckley family's generosity, the land was secured for a fraction of its market value. The way was now open for a brand new pavilion-clubhouse to be considered and the opportunity arose sooner than expected. The outcome, building of the 'Stick & Wicket', is detailed elsewhere. That year the 3rd XI was officially constituted with limited fixtures, although there had been an 'A' Team for many years as well as a 3rd Team usually assembled on an ad - hoc basis.

Aldridge went into the seventies with a number of exciting changes in addition to the building of a new clubhouse. Sunday Cricket for instance started in Aldridge on May 17th 1970. Bill Groves took over as President after many years as Club Chairman with Treasurer Ken Brown following him into the Chairman's seat. Jonathan Franks took charge of the 1st XI and John Burton the 2nds.

Spectators have always been welcome at cricket grounds and Aldridge is no exception. The days when cash collections were taken had long since passed, even in the 1970s,

3rd XI 1972

Geoff Walker (Hon. Sec)	Pete Burton	Pete Williams	Colin Warner	John Wilson	Kevin Phillips	Tony Warwood	Gordon Popple (Umpire)
	Austin Dancey	Frank Hastilow		Ken Bourne	Chris Murphy	Keith 'Ticker' Davies	

but occasionally certain characters would emerge on the other side of the boundary. Sometime in the 1970s and into the 1980s, although it remains unclear exactly when it started, there was a small procession of 'supporters' who would emerge from the side of the Rectory wall led by George Edwards and 'Grog' Crumpton, Harry Crumpton's father. George was the father of well known local councillor Mavis Foden. Not reliant entirely upon their loud voices, they would ring a large handbell to celebrate Aldridge boundaries and the fall of opposition wickets. A typical humourous quote from George was:

'They'm a funny team, this fost team of ow'en; when yow think they'm gonna win - they lose, and when yow think they'm gonna lose - they do!'

Notwithstanding the 'prophets of doom' such as George Edwards, the 1970 season was the most successful for several years. John Burton, Fixture Secretary extraordinary, managed to upgrade the standard of fixtures providing a distinct improvement for the 1971 season. 1970 had been a great Inaugural year for Sunday cricket with teams such as 'Hendon Buccaneers' turning up to play; the start of a number of fine home and away fixtures over the ensuing years. The 1st XI played 27 matches, won 11, lost 3 and drew 11 with 2 being abandoned. Honours went to the feisty, no nonsense Terry Pendry, (Batting) and Bob Shelton (Bowling) in the 1st XI, Keith Davies (Batting), and Geoff Whitehouse who had by this time taken nearly a thousand wickets (Bowling) in 2nd XI. Richard Hawkley took the batting and Steve Randall the bowling for the 3rd XI with Terry Pendry taking the batting supported by the pace of Mark Biddle bowling for the Sunday XI. In 1971 the irrepressible and voluble Russell Pickston headed the batting in the 1st XI with Bob. Shelton leading the bowling averages.

For the start of the 1971 season Aldridge had the enviable situation of having six umpires of its own: H. Crumpton, S. Hough, F. P. Stephens, R. Biddle, E. Orton and L. Webb. That same year the 'Sutton and District Panel of Umpires' was set - up with Ron Biddle as Secretary.

One of many changes in the 1971 season included the introduction of a Sunday 2nd XI. The 1972 season however would see Aldridge participate in real 'competitive cricket' for the first time. The newly formed 'Warwickshire and Staffordshire Club Cricket Championship' provided strong competition, a league which Aldridge helped to found through the auspices of Club Captain, Jonathan Franks. This one move would dramatically increase the number of games played in the

Aldridge Cricket Club 1853 - 2003

season. A total of 43 games were played by the 1st XI in 1972 with Aldridge finishing almost halfway up the table in the Warwickshire and Staffordshire Club Cricket Championship. Russ Pickston still topped the batting with the newly arrived Terry Clews, the classic opening bat, in second spot. Steve Dean was at the head of the bowling averages with Bob Shelton in second place with a very creditable 84 wickets.

Further strengthening of the fixture list in the 1973 season found the Club participating in the short-lived 'Staffordshire Cricket Alliance' as well as the Warks. & Staffs. games. Overall results didn't look quite so good against better opposition. Left hander Gary Nicholls, in his first season as Club Captain topped the batting averages with Bob Shelton yet again at the top of the bowlers. This was the year Gordon Popple joined the list of Club umpires, although he had started in 1972. Sam Harvey and Frank Hastilow now in the ranks of 'older players' topped the batting for the 2nd & 3rd XIs with Arthur Pheasant doing the same, bowling in the 2nds. The Club did well in the Sutton News Knock-out Cup and won the Walsall Knock-out Cup, after one of the most exciting finals witnessed at Gorway. It had been some thirty five years since Aldridge went on tour, but in 1973 the exotic Greek island of Corfu was the destination for what turned out to be an interesting weeks' cricket. (See page 88)

1974 will not be remembered as a cricketers' summer. The weather was most unkind with a high percentage of matches ending with no result. Terry Clews and Mike Reaney topped the 1st XI batting and bowling averages. Martin Pinfold joined the Club, strengthening the batting line-up. Aldridge reached the semi-final of the Sutton News' Knock-out Cup being beaten by Walsall. However, revenge was sweet when, just a week later, the tables were

Walsall President Mr Jack Hight hands over the Mellor Cup, the Walsall Knock Out Trophy, to Aldridge skipper Garry Nicholls for the third successive time after beating Walsall Phoenix. July 1975.

1st XI 1975-6

| Mrs Nicholls (Scorer) | Richard Lowe | Martin Pinfold | Mick Dufty | Terry Clews | Derek Egerton | Roger Green |
| | Jonathan Franks | Keith Buller | Gary Nicholls | Les Pullen | John Milner | |

Aldridge Cricket Club 1853 - 2003

Aldridge C.C. 3rd's are pictured at Cedar Court. From left to right, back: M. Richards, N. Taylor, K. Ford, J. Heming, I. Hastilow, S. Machin. Front: A. Brown, F. Fitzpatrick, M. Cooper (captain), M. Windsor, R. Dyer, Mrs. B. Popple (scorer).

More cricket on page 29

Pickston 105, then thrills galore as Aldridge draw

Walsall Observer — July 11th 1975

It was a really close thing at Aldridge on Sunday, when Highcroft Hospital were the visitors. Russell Pickston hit a great 105 not out, from Aldridge's total of 198-6, in a chanceless knock.

Highcroft scored quickly in reply, but also lost wickets at a fast rate and the tension mounted until, with an over remaining, they needed eight to win with one wicket in hand. But Peace and Brown could manage only two runs and the spoils were shared.

ALDRIDGE
Nicholls c Pearce b Brown	0
Clews c Woolfson b Revan	32
Pickston not out	105
Buller c Sissons b Woolfson	7
Pemberton run out	3
Pendry b Woolfson	22
Lowe c Brown b Revan	15
Reany not out	2
Extras	12
Total (for 6 wkts. dec.)	198

Bowling: Brown 1-60; Revan 2-53; Woolfson 2-43.

Aldridge 2nd's defeated Walmley 2nd's by 66 runs.

ALDRIDGE 2nd's
Pendry c Jones b Blake	7
Burke b Raines	25
Harvey b Mees	1
Kean b Mees	0
Warwood run out	30
Castley b Blake	36
Hirst c Bromley b Finlay (J.)	26
Lewis c Finlay (L) b Finlay (J.)	22
Green c Evans b Finlay (J.)	7
Dean b Mees	5
Franks (D.) not out	5
Extras	22
Total	186

Bowling: Blake 2-56; Raines 1-20; Mees 3-38; Finlay (J.) 3-33.

WALMLEY
Raines b Dean	24
Bromley c Harvey b Dean	9
Evans c and b Franks (D.)	5
Jordan c Lewis b Dean	2
Finlay (L.) c Warwood b Franks (D.)	41
Briggs b Franks (D.)	9
Jones b Franks (D.)	15
Brassington b Hirst	11
Finlay (J.) b Hirst	0
Blake c Pendry b Hirst	0
Mees not out	3
Extras	1
Total	120

Bowling: 4-46; Dean 3-24; Hirst 3-9.

Aldridge 2nd's won by four wickets against Highcroft 2nd's.

Aldridge 3rd's received Old Edwardians 3rd's on Sunday, but lost by seven wickets.

ALDRIDGE 3rd's
Holsey c Byrne b Bennett	32
Groves c Byrne b Glover	13
Ford b Hunt	6
Burton not out	15
Cooper c Bennett b Hunt	3
Machin b Bennett	0
Hastilow b Hunt	6
Bourne b Hunt	2
Dyer run out	6
Randall c Bennett b Hunt	4
Williams st Cashmore b Hunt	0
Extras	6
Total	89

Bowling: Hunt 6-36; Glover 1-20; Bennett 2-26.

OLD EDWARDIANS 3rd's
Otto b Bennett	0
Glover c Ford b Williams	1
Cashmore c Bourne b Randall	24
Lewis not out	26
Cull not out	27
Extras	13
Total (for 3 wkts.)	91

Bowling: Randall 2-22; Williams 1-14; Dyer 0-22; Cooper 0-8; Bourne 0-7.

...breaks ...ecord

...scored his maiden half-century for the club.

Wood quickly ripped through the Tipton batting but a fighting innings of 59 by Butler delayed victory until the closing overs.

WALSALL WOOD
Smith not out	75
Wagg c Pearce b Tranter (S.T.)	37

Terry Whitehouse Rushall's fine 135 ru... ton Regis, on Sunday...

Whitehouse took a ...half-century off the N...ton attack and with g... support coming fr... Evans, Pittaway and ...loway, they totalled 2... declared.

After their hard toi... the field, the Newton b... men were unable to ge... grips with the situat... and Whitehouse sp... headed the Rushall att... with fine figures of 7-53 the visitors were shot ...for 105.

RUSHALL
Williams c S. Tomkinson b Wood ...
Evans c S. Tomkinson b C. Hill ...
Heath b Wood ...
Pittaway c Norman b Barber ...
Whitehouse c Barber b D. Tomkinson
Holloway c D. Tomkinson b Wood ...
Wiggins run out ...
Cooke not out ...
Hartshorne not out ...
Extras ...

Total (for 7 wkts. dec.) ...

Bowling: Wood 3-67.

NEWTON REGIS
Hill c Wiggins b Whitehouse ...
Norman lbw b Whitehouse ...
Knight b Whitehouse ...
Tomkinson (S.) b Whitehouse ...
Barber st. G. Horner b Wiggins ...
Bryan b Whitehouse ...
Tomkinson (D.) b Whitehouse ...
Wood st. G. Horner b Wiggins ...
Roberts lbw b Whitehouse ...
Ireland c K. Cooke b Wiggins ...
Hill not out ...
Extras ...

Total ...

Bowling: Whitehouse 7-53; J. Wi... 3-23.

NO T... FOR P...

Pelsall had little trou... in winning a low scor... home match agai... Goodyear, on Saturday.

Batting first, Goody... were always in difficu... against the bowling Hooker, Farmer a... Stringer and only a l... unbeaten 23 from M... enabled them to reach...

BILL'S UNBE...

turned when Aldridge knocked Walsall out of their own Knock-out Competition in the final! In August a Warwickshire XI turned out at Aldridge to play an exciting game for John Jameson's Benefit year. The following year, unlike 1974, was very much a 'Cricketers' Summer'. Keith Buller bowled and batted extremely well and, as the Secretary's Annual Report stated: *'on the few occasions when he didn't, made up for it by his enthusiasm.'* The Mellor Cup for the Walsall Knock-out competition was won again for the third year running when Walsall Phoenix fell victim to two nights of Aldridge cricketing flair. Success in the other Knockout Competitions, Sutton Coldfield and Douglas Concrete, eluded the Club however. The first printed 'Colts' fixtures appeared in the Fixture list with games v Rugeley, Bloxwich and Wednesbury.

The hot and dry summer of '76 produced ideal weather but, as a result, many clubs were able to produce fine wickets which led to inconclusive results. The Club won the Staffs Alliance Championship and reached the final of the Douglas Concrete Invitation Knock-out Cup. Gary Nicholls scored over 1,000 runs leading to his winning the 1st XI Batting Trophy. The new practice wicket and nets came on line and would prove to be an invaluable resource in the right hands. For instance, a young man by the name of Bob Dyer (aka 'Dottie' because of his diminutive stature as a lad) who had grown up in the Aldridge Junior Side from the age of 13, took the bowling award for the 2nd XI in 1976. Under the expert guidance of Warwickshire coach R. W. O. (Don) White, himself a bowler of the left arm 'chinaman', Bob was developing an orthadox off-spin technique which would take him far over the next few years. Don White's regular Tuesday and Thursday nets for the Colts became very popular. The growth of League cricket was now unstoppable, any club which decided to abstain from this form of competition would be left behind, so Aldridge could not afford to sit and watch. Terry Clews took the 1st XI batting honours and Mike Reaney the top bowling spot. The ground certtainly looked parched and was in poor condition by the end of that summer.

Almost a repeat of the wet summer of 1974, the 1977 season was disappointing. Perhaps this was again due to the weather. The figures speak for themselves: Played: 49 Won: 9, Lost: 10, Drawn: 18, Tied: 1, Abandoned: 6, and Postponed: 5. Results for the 2nds and 3rds were no better. The 'Colts' matches were now officially being called 'Junior' fixtures. For the first time the 2nd XI took part in a Knockout competition - the Wolverhampton News Chronicle K. O. A midweek tour to south Devon was organised which proved to be a great social boost for the club. Special Bank Holiday home fixtures were arranged against Hendon Buccaneers and Aluminium Bronze which would be repeated for the next few years.

For the 1978 season the league became sponsored and was changed from 'Warks. and Staffs. Club Cricket Championship' to 'The Kendrick Construction Warks. and Staffs. Championship'. Now, worthwhile cash prizes were on offer to the total value of £2,000. Even with the participation in competitive league cricket for much of the 1970s, the ethos at Aldridge was still very much centered around 'friendlies'. Attitudes on the field were often somewhat 'laid-back' and declaration matches, to give the youngsters a game, were not uncommon. Needless to say this situation brought about tensions on and off the field with the most 'competitive' players often finding themselves frustrated. Bob Dyer, now aged 19 and restless for competition, moved to the Birmingham League Club Aston Unity, eventually sharing with them the honour of winning that famous old League. Fordhouses C. C. ran a Knockout, the second competition in which the 2nd XI took part. Following the success of the Devon Tour in 1977 the Club headed back to that county for another week long tour in June.

In July 1978 a nine - day Cricket festival was organised to celebrate 125 yrs of Aldridge Cricket. Unfortunately it didn't quite turn out as hoped. Visiting sides appeared from Moseley Rugby Club, Warwick & Staffs League, West Midlands Police, Coleshill, Kendrick Construction League, Streetly Colts and the like. Aldridge teams lost all of the matches except for the final game when they just managed to beat an Aldridge Hockey Club XI on the third ball of the last over!

At the end of 1978, Mike Pemberton produced a wonderful little book entitled 'The "Wisdom" of Aldridge Cricket Club'. This was a review of playing records and individual achievements to celebrate 125 years of Aldridge Cricket. In the course of his research Mike had spent the best part of three years carefully and painstakingly going through the score books. He produced the most detailed analysis of players and team performance from the period

Aldridge Cricket Club's members enjoyed their annual dinner at Druids Heath Golf Club, last week, when the main guest was Warwickshire and England opening batsman John Jameson. He is seen (third from right) handing the W. H. Bunn Award, for the club's best young player of 1975, to Bob Dyer. On the extreme left is chairman Ken Brown and next to him stands secretary Geoff Walker. Holding the tankard is the first team's top bowler of 1975, Tony Field and on the extreme right is skipper Keith Buller. Other awards for top performances, last season, went to: Russell Pickston (1st team batting); Ted Burke (2nd XI batting), Keith Davies (2nd XI bowling); Steve Machin (3rd XI batting); David Franks (3rd XI bowling); Russell Pickston, Terry Clews, Malcolm Keen (centurion ties).

1905 (The earliest records then available), to 1978. Mike was ably assisted by Arthur Pheasant, Gary Nicholls and Ken Brown. 'Wisdom' has provided the author with a great deal of information whilst writing this volume for which I am most grateful. Some of the outstanding records in the book were, naturally, those created in the 1970s, some remain in place even today. The First XI statistics make particularly interesting reading.

The two highest Aldridge totals to that date were scored in 1976, 256 for 3 v. Highcroft Hall and 241 for 5 v. Cannock & Rugeley, the latter producing the greatest winning margin with Cannock & Rugeley being all out for 50. Russ Pickston features second only to the great Howard Walton in the number of times he won the batting averages - six times between 1963 and 1975. In 1976 Gary Nicholls with 36 innings and 1,117 runs tops the list for the highest individual total in a season with Russ Pickston's 1,108 from only 27 innings in 1971 coming a close second. Russell was also number two to Howard Walton in the 'Top Twenty' batsmen having scored 7,635 runs (the majority on the leg side) compared with Howard's 9,862... but Russ was still playing!

Bob Shelton occupied the top three places for taking the highest number of wickets in a season, 89 in 1971, 84 in 1970 and 84 in 1972 a fine achievement even from a large number of overs. Although only at Aldridge for ten years, he entered the 'Top Twenty' bowlers list. In 1978, Bob, with 490 wickets, finished up in fifth place behind Arthur Pheasant 968 wickets, Harry Crumpton 753, Ray Clare 550 and W. Emery 534. David Franks, in June 1971, had the most successful weekend of his career when he took no less than 17 wickets for only 33 runs in two matches. On Saturday in the 2nd XI v M & B Springfield he took eight for 20 off 15 overs then v. Knowle & Dorridge on the Sunday, bowled 18 overs including 10 maidens for only 13 runs, taking nine wickets. This extraordinary feat put him in third place behind Dr. Victor Milne's 1926 10 wicket haul v. Moor End when he bowled 12 overs, 7 maidens for only 17 runs. Ray Clare's 1945 performance v. an RAF XI equalled Victor Milne's totals except for his conceding only 14 runs.

Some excellent fielding records were achieved in the 1970s. Only two names appear in the top four places for total number of catches in a season other than by the wicketkeeper. Russ Pickston in 1971 - 30 catches and 1970 - 27 catches and Keith Buller in 1973 - 21 catches and 1976 - 21 catches. Both players enjoyed fielding close in to the batsman and were highly competitive, going for everything with very safe hands. Russell usually stood at a suicidal foward short leg. Keith set high standards for others and himself, his cap frequently coming in for punishment as it hit the ground hard when those standards were not met, often accompanied by somewhat 'colourful' language. There were a number of excellent wicketkeepers during the 1960s and 70s, Brian Holsey, John Frankham, Terry Pendry, and Dave Lewis all figure in the table for most victims in a season. John Milner however took the top two slots with 34 catches and 6 stumpings in 1975 and a massive 51 catches and 9 stumpings in 1976. John's premature accidental death was a great shock and a real tragic loss even though he had left the area.

Some records of course, do not eaxactly 'grace' the scorebooks. During the 70s there operated a 'Duck Club' whereby there was a tarrif for each 'duck' achieved and dependant upon the number of balls faced, cash would have to be put into the 'Duck' A/C for conversion into drinks at the end of the season. There was, it seems, always enough in the kitty for a really good 'piss up' at the end of the year!

The Club has much to thank Mike Pemberton for, since his work remains unsurpassed. It must be added that whilst playing, Mike, who came up through the Junior sides, was a regular 1st and 2nd Team hard hitting batsman with a good eye. Another side of Mike's activities were his sartorial adventures. He once took to the field wearing white shorts and socks instead of flannels. Perhaps most famously, after a match at Hendon Mike, wearing his suit, was happily winding-up the Hendon players when they threw him in the bath. Poor 'Pem' had to travel home wearing his cricket gear and getting some very peculiar looks in the motorway services toilets! Hendon fixtures were always a very good social occasion and very often the 'drinking games' which included running around stumps, went on long after stumps had been officially drawn.

The 1979 season included more new fixtures. As well as the regular Holiday event v Hendon Buccaneers and Aluminium Bronze, there were home matches against the touring sides of Heathcoats Tiverton, rivals from the Devon Tours of the previous two years, and Prestatyn. On the other hand, it had been a small matter of 97 years since Aldridge 'toured' N. Wales, winning comfortably at Llandudno. So the Welsh reply had been somewhat delayed!

Aldridge Cricket Club 1853 - 2003

Into the eighties ...

1st XI 1981

| Ron Biddle (Umpire) | Steve Lydal | Terry Clews | John Frankham | Richard Lowe | Martin Pinfold | Ian Manwaring | Andy Roberts |
| | Andy Brown | Keith Buller | Russell Pickston | Jonathan Franks | Jo Franks (Scorer) | | |

A visit from the Singapore National Team, on Monday 21st May 1979, as part of the warm-up for the World Cup, provided the first of what would become almost regular International fixtures at Aldridge. The result was, as is often the case, dictated by the weather. Singapore made 212 for 5 before the heavens opened, including hail - which the visitors had never seen before. Singapore batsman Mukhtar Ahmed, who made 73 runs, took the man of the match award.

By the end of the seventies, clearly, much had been achieved. Aldridge C.C. as an institution was riding high on the benefits of much improved ground facilities. Bill Groves was still at the helm as President and Geoff Walker was able to hand over the Secretaryship to John Heming enabling Geoff to become Chairman. Ken Brown was quite happy to employ his safe hands as Treasurer. The 'Colts', now called the 'Junior Section' of the Club were able, for the first time in 1979 to take part in a competitive league system. Participation in the 'Alpine Junior Cricket League' would according to coach Don White, be a great introduction to what cricket would become for them and the rest of Aldridge C. C. in the 1980s and beyond.

A scene at Hendon.
The Aldridge ladies taking it easy in front of the pavilion.

The 1980s - 2003

Aldridge Cricket Club 1853 - 2003

1st XI 1982

| John Westwood | Ross Pearsall | Terry Pendry | Ian Manwaring | Martin Pinfold | Andy Roberts | Gordon Popple (Umpire) |
| Terry Clews | John Frankham | | Keith Buller | | Jonathan Franks | Andy Brown |

At the start of the 1980s there had been very little change in the playing members since the mid 1970s. The facilities on offer were now excellent and the Club had a high profile including the hosting of International matches. Compared with only three Club Captains in each of the 1950s and 1960s, there would now be six changes of Club Captain within ten years, setting the pattern for the 1990s. Sadly, the results of the 1st XI did not quite match the expectations of such lavish surroundings. Much of the 80s was spent trying to lift the playing standard of the team, and as we shall see, the decade was, as Ron Biddle put it, one of being 'So Nearly'.

There was considerable enthusiasm in the Club at the start of the 1980s, the pitch was in good shape and the facilities much improved. Hon. Sec. John Heming in his Annual Report made the rather gloomy comment however, that both the 1st & 2nd XIs had finished mid-table in the Kendrick Construction Warwicks & Staffs League. It was left to the Under 16 side to take the honours by winning their section of the Alpine Youth League only being beaten in the semi-final of the knockout. It wasn't all bad news in the senior sides either, with Terry Clews, Russ Pickston, Keith Buller and Terry Pendry all getting centuries. Other talent was emerging on the bowling front with young Andy Roberts, one of the successful under 16 side, actually finishing 2nd to David Franks in the bowling averages! David had taken 73 wickets that year. Figures for the year, however, confirmed the position; 1st XI Played: 49, Won: 7, Lost: 12, Drawn: 24 with 6 abandonments. 2nd XI Played: 46, Won: 16, Lost: 11, Drawn: 12 with 5 abandoned. 3rdXI Played: 40, Won: 7, Lost: 10, Drawn 15 and 8 abandoned.

When new Hon. Sec. Mike Cooper reported for 1981 he could say that so many wanted to play that a 4th XI had been started, which was christened 'The Cedars'. Actually, they were often not able to play at home on Cedar Court because the pitch was already being used! The standard of play however was not much better than the year before, although the 2nds did manage a worthy 2nd position in the Warks. & Staffs League. The results

Aldridge Cricket Club 1853 - 2003

were: 1st XI Played: 42, Won 7, Lost 7, Drawn 24, Abandoned: 3 and Tied: 1. 2nd XI Played: 37, Won: 18, Lost: 6, Drawn: 10, Abandoned: 3. 3rd XI Played 34, Won:12, Lost: 11, Drawn: 7, Abandoned: 4. 4thXI Played: 11, Won: 5, Lost: 5, Drawn: 1. In the Warks & Staffs League: 1st XI Played: 14, Won: 3, Lost: 3, Drawn: 5, Abandoned: 3. Points: 119, Merits: 11, position 6th. 2nd XI Played: 14, Won: 7, Lost: 3, Drawn: 2, Abandoned: 2. Points: 134, Merits: 6, Position: 2nd. There was much discussion and debate in 1981 that Aldridge was 'A Social Club playing sports'. A new playing member, who joined in July of that year, Stephen Peak, would be one of the players who would try to turn things around.

Reproduced on page 53, the 1982 team picture was taken in June on a day when they lost at home to Tamworth in a Warks & Staffs League Match. In fact the game was not much better than a humiliation with Aldridge managing only 150 and Tamworth cruising to an eight wicket victory. June, however, was a month of gripping International Action at Aldridge with the splendid club facilities being used to host three of the I. C. C. matches. On Sunday 13th, Aldridge took on the might of the Dutch National Side in an entertaining game but were beaten by 93 runs. Holland, one of the 'fancied' teams in the tournament, showed what their batsmen could do as they hit a wide range of strokes. Raskamp (16) and Lifmann (41) put on 55 for the first wicket before Bob Dyer (1-31) and Club Captain Keith Buller (2-38) put a temporary brake on proceedings. Elferink (52) and skipper Abed (40) added some pace to the scoring in the middle of the innings but this was reigned-in by the superb bowling of Keith Parnell (4-32 in 9 overs). The outcome was a quite reasonable total of 181 for 8. The Dutch bowlers were soon to display their talents however, with Van Heyningen bowling five successive maidens while at the other end it was Elferink again doing the damage, this time by bending the ball 'like a banana' to demolish the cream of Aldridge batting.

Andy Brown, Simon Bates, Mike Pemberton and Terry Pendry were all dismissed without score as Aldridge slumped to 11-5, Elferink taking 5-17. Only Terry Clews remained to display his superior technique and courage and restore some pride. Clews eventually ran out of partners being undefeated on 41 with the home side on 88 at the end of the game. On Tuesday 15th a Warks & Staffs League XI, including Aldridge players, played Fiji at Aldridge and on Friday 25th the U.S.A. played Hong Kong.

Warks. & Staffs. League v Fiji at Aldridge 1982

The 1982 season finished off without any major titles being taken, although there were a few highlights in the latter part of the season as one or two of the younger players started to get into the Aldridge 1st XI. In a game v. Dorridge on Saturday August 7th at Aldridge for instance, there was that most rare of occurences that year, an easy win. Dorridge were shot out for just 57 with Andy Roberts taking 5 - 28 from 19 overs including three wickets in four balls. Young stand-in wicket keeper Mark Rasmin took five catches that day. On the same day the 2nds also won away at Dorridge by 7 wickets to keep their place at the top of the 2nd Division.

1983 was the year Aldridge's prodigal, or should it be 'prodigy' spin bowler - Bob Dyer, returned to the fold, taking over from Keith Buller as Club Captain. Whilst

2nd XI Winners Fordhouses Knockout 1985

Dave Edge   Clive Lee   Mick Dufty   Keith Smith   Roger Wagg   Andy Roberts   Steve Peak

Howard Shippey   Martin Pinfold   Trevor Harvey   Russell Pickston

Aldridge Cricket Club 1853 - 2003

Walsall K.O. Winners 1985

Standing: Mike Cooper (Hon Sec.) Peter Hills, Ross Pearsall, Dave McKecknie, Dave Edge, Keith Smith, Andy Roberts.
Kneeling: Bob Eardley, Bob Dyer, Keith Buller, Simon Bates

being experienced in the game, after years of League Cricket at Aston Unity, Bob was still only 23 years old and remained as Captain for just one year. In the Secretary's Annual Report, 1984 was labelled as a 'good' season, but yet again the proviso was added that the 1st XI could have challenged for honours. Perhaps Bob Dyer's professional attitude needed to rub off on the other players? For instance that year Bob took 10 wickets for 53 runs in a League match at Hampton In Arden. Bob's attitude was to give 110% effort in his game. Before returning to Aldridge for Saturday games he had often played on Sundays at Aldridge. On one occasion, after breaking an arm playing for Aston Unity he went out to play for Aldridge on Sunday with his arm in plaster and took a fine catch in the outfield. The 2nd XI, captained by Trevor Harvey, performed with distinction, taking major honours in their Division with a record performance. Aston Unity feature in the Club Minute Books for April 1984 when they proposed a merger with Aldridge. The main stumbling block was the suggested name change, rejected outright by the Aldridge committee.

Ron Biddle in his first Annual Report as Hon. Secretary in 1986 looked back on the 1985 season with some pleasure since things seemed to be taking a turn for the better. Terry Clews won the Warwicks & Staffs League 1st XI Batting Award. During the season he had helped Aldridge to get very close to winning the honours in the Mallin League. The 2nd XI again took honours in Div 2. The 1sts won the Walsall Knockout and the 2nds won the Fordhouses Knockout. The 3rd XI finished in 8th place. Steve Peak was particularly outstanding with bat and ball - 3rd in batting averages and 7th in bowling. There were only a few 'Cedars' games due to availability of players.

The second half of the 80s and early 90s was to turn out to be a fruitful few years for winning the Walsall Knockout tournament, for what was now re-named the 'Walsall Observer Cup'. On 1st June 1985 it was Afro-Caribbean which suffered at the hands, or should it be bats of Peter Hills and Bob Eardley as they knocked a sparkling 77 runs between them in the summer sun, Eardley earning himself the Parry Cup as top batsman in the finals and semi finals. Peter Hills was voted 'Man of the Match' for taking four catches in the first innings and scoring an unbeaten 39. Caribbean were chasing hard for runs but accurate bowling and two tragic run-outs brought Aldridge out on top. Andy Roberts took 3 - 24 and Ross Pearsall 5 - 22. Bob Eardley was a good all round cricketer who perhaps should have played more 1st team cricket. Although diagnosed with Leukaemia he carried on playing showing great courage in the face of adversity, and exhibited a great sense of humour even in his final hours.

The Club reached the final in 1986, unfortunately without winning the game. However, the Mellor Cup/Walsall Observer Trophy did return to Aldridge again in 1987. In 1988 Aldridge were back in the two day final yet again, this time v. Pelsall. Batting first on the first night Aldridge reached 101 - 9 off their 15 eight-ball overs thanks mainly to 38 from Russell Pickston. Fielding was the forte of Aldridge that night however limiting Pelsall to 73 all out. Taking the lead of 28 into the second night it looked a foregone conclusion especially when Russell Pickston knocked 44 out of a total of 98-9. Pelsall needed 127 for victory in the gloomy conditions. After great application from the Pelsall side including a fine half century from Bob Hobster, they came within sight of the target. However, it was not to be - Aldridge, like true champions, held their nerve by taking more vital wickets in the closing overs to win by just seven runs. Russell Pickston, who was now more used to skippering the 3rd XI and had been drafted in at the last minute, proved that he couldn't be written off, by winning the 'Man of the Match' award for his two vital knocks. Martin Calkeld received the Parry Cup for the highest score in the semi-final or final, for his 89 not out against Wednesbury.

Walsall K.O. Winners 1988

Dave Edge, Gary Harris, Martin Calkeld, Russell Pickston (Man of Match), Geoff Middleton (Walsall Observer), Ian Manwaring, Keith Buller, Steve Peak (Capt), Keith Smith, Ross Pearsall, S. Jenkinson, Andy Roberts.

Aldridge Cricket Club 1853 - 2003

I.C.C. ASSOCIATE MEMBERS' WORLD CUP COMPETITION, 1986

Success in the Walsall K.O. for teams led by Keith Buller and Steve Peak kept Aldridge fairly competitive in the late 1980s, but only at local 'Walsall' level. It was clear that the Club should not be 'resting upon its laurels' in the truly competitive scene of the 1990s. In fact for the first couple of years of the 90s Aldridge struggled, but more on that later. By 1993, winning ways were back and the team won both the Walsall and Bloxwich K.O. competitions. 1995 saw them back again in the Walsall K.O. final. However, on the same evening as the first leg of the final the 1st XI were elsewhere! In fact they were playing in the Birmingham League Knockout. As an indication of just how far the team had progressed by then, it was left to a 2nd XI side to play the first leg. The 1sts need not have worried, with what turned out to be a sensational first leg being easily won. Phil Perchard, putting in a remarkable spell of bowling, took six wickets for one run in just four overs. In fact, when the 1sts returned for the second leg they only just managed to win, emphasising the in-depth strength of the 2nds. When it came to giving out the traditional engraved winner's tankards after the game, both the 1st XI and the 2nd XI were presented with them, and rightly so.

But what of the 'So nearly' 1980s, outside of the Walsall K.O. competition. Ron Biddle's comments about the late 1980s were really an appeal for the Club to adopt a higher level of commitment. In 1986 they were bridesmaids not brides as runners-up in the Warks. and Staffs. League, even though they managed to notch up a win against a full Walsall XI in the Birmingham League Knockout. To quote Ron: *'Oh! how easily they could have gone that vital stage further!'*

While the team were perhaps just missing out on League glory, the Club itself retained its high profile ...on the world stage, by hosting an ICC Trophy match between Associate members Bermuda and Israel. Aldridge played Kenya as part of the warm up for the competition. A month later and the exotic flavour of Aldridge C.C. continued with a visit from the 'Winelanders' a touring side from South Africa.

In 1988 an application was received from a Pakistani Test player to be the Aldridge 'Professional', little did he know that Aldridge were not yet really adopting the 'professional' approach. It was true that some 'professionals' would play in a few matches. Steve Farmer from Barbados, for instance. Unfortunately, Bob Dyer could see that his best chance to play at a higher level was to leave the Club. Joining Walsall in 1988, he went on to claim 50 Birmingham League wickets bowling his 'allsorts' spinners (he was known as 'Bertie Bassett'), and by 1992 was top of the Birmingham League averages and a regular Staffordshire player. In 1991 he proudly led Walsall out at Lords in the National Club Knockout and the next year was back at Lords with the Staffordshire side.

Unlike Bob Dyer, Aldridge's other Bowling sensation Andy Roberts, firing on all cylinders in the late 1980s, sadly shunned all offers tempting him away from the Club where he could perhaps, develop to a higher performance level. Some say that his batting potential was even better than his bowling and that it was something of a wasted talent, sadly, we will never know. A typical 'Robbo' incident was reported in the 'Walsall Observer' in September 1988: In a Barr Computers Warwicks & Staffs League match, Streetly batsman Micky Wooldridge sent a mighty six crashing through the windscreen of a car on the Aldridge car park failing to amuse bowler Andy Roberts for good reason. Not only had Andy sent down the ill fated delivery that had been hooked for six, but it was Robbo's car which had sustained the not inconsiderable damage! Spitting venom, Robbo, with poetic justice and just two balls later, sent Wooldridge's middle stump flying. Andy went on to take 4 - 39 as Streetly were restricted to 97 off their 48 overs. In reply Aldridge reached 98 - 5 with Pete Hills 42 not out, to win the match with ease.

Some of the 'Winelanders' from South Africa. July 1986

Aldridge Cricket Club 1853 - 2003

Steve Peak took over the captaincy in 1988 from Keith Buller and soon became a 'man on a mission' - to turn around the fortunes of the Club, on the field as well as off. Barry James writing in the 'Sunday Mercury' in May 1989, after making the usual visitor comments about the high plateau ground and 'cooling breeze' was quick to compliment the Club on its warm welcome and handsome facilities. He went on to say: '... *Aldridge are patently well organised and successful when it comes to staging numerous representative matches. The problem is that they can't quite match these attributes on the wicket. In short Aldridge are the Nearly Men. Barr Computers League runners' up for two seasons and fourth last year just about sums it up. Clearly, Aldridge have the potential to be among Midland club cricket's front runners.*' The reason for the comment was that since Aldridge had beaten League sides such as Stourbridge and Smethwick this indicated that if they could make it into the new Combined Counties League in 1990 they would probably cope with the standard. Vice-Captain Gary Harris when questioned by James looked forward to the coming 1990 season with relish stating that: '*The new pyramid set-up will give every club something very positive to aim at.*' Full of praise for skipper Steve Peak who he said had pulled the side around since his appointment in 1988, he added: '*...We're functioning as a unit these days, and Steve must take the credit for that.*'

The side was becoming much more balanced in the 1988 and '89 seasons. Steve Peak, himself a big hitter, once famously took on the 'Mad Monk', Astwood Bank's quick bowler whose surname was Monk. It was a hard track and by flicking the ball over point managed to score over 50. Gary Harris, Terry Clews and wicket keeper Martin Calkeld also being fine strikers of the ball and providing a sound batting base. The attack was starting to gel with Andy Roberts, who took 95 wickets in 1988, Ross Pearsall and Howard Shippey supported by change bowler Keith Smith.

As the 80s changed into 90s the 'professional' attitude, so much craved and encouraged by the nucleus of really competitive cricketers such as Steve Peak and Gary Harris, actually started to emerge. Initially, however, Steve was to be denied direct first hand contact with this change through personal illness, leaving Gary Harris to skipper the side halfway through the 1989 season. Dave Edge took over the captaincy for 1990 and for 1991, the latter being the year that Indian all-rounder B. K. Maruthi arrived. Maruthi was the nephew of a Gt. Barr doctor and had not originally intended to play for Aldridge. He was recommended to Aldridge by Jim Hartley who was then with Streetly C.C. but is now an Aldridge man. The team were very pleased that he did, for he was a very useful right-handed batsman and off-spin bowler which helped the Club win Division 2 for the second year. Returning home to India before the end of the 1991 season Aldridge were left to reflect upon the young man's performance. In 1991 John Burton, who had been something of a 'fixture' himself, stood down from his position as Fixture Secretary after 25 splendid years in the job.

Secretary Gordon Popple in his Report of the 1992 season, in which the Club was relegated to Division 3 of the Midland Combined Counties League, described it as a 'Disaster'. B. K. Maruthi, although willing, was unable to come to the UK. So after much hard work and being on the very verge of success in the previous few seasons it seemed as if all had been for nothing. The only good news was that the Sunday XI were fortunate to be boosted by West Indian legend Alvin Kallicharan who averaged over 100 for the season. Fortunately for Aldridge the next season saw the return of a Super Hero who took the form of 'Captain Courageous' - Steve Peak. Steve managed to get Bob Dyer to return home to Aldridge, to add a touch more professionalism to the team. B. K. Maruthi, re-called from India, had an exceptional season scoring 1,200 runs with an average of 38 and took 50 wickets with his spin bowling at 15 runs each and if midweek games were included his runs would have been over 2,000. Naturally, there was only one consequence of this uplift in quality, a return to Division 2 at the end of the season. For 1994 Steve Peak handed the captaincy to Bob Dyer who had all the experience of captaining Walsall to draw upon. With his first rate contacts Bob was soon drafting - in players; batsman Wayne Law from Walsall and seam bowler Bob Cattell from Aston Manor arrived and the Club's overseas favourite Maruthi returned. If the '93 season had been dynamic then '94 was really alive as Wayne Law, B. K. Maruthi, John Rowley, Gareth Cornick, and Howard Shippey performed as never before. During the season Aldridge amassed 3558 runs and took 143 wickets to produce Aldridge's first major title in its long history, the winning of Div 2 of the M.C.C. League and thus winning promotion to Div 1. This high flying promotion was not gained without cost however, maintaining good quality facilities at the club was expensive. A number of fund-raising initiatives were introduced such as the 'Aldridge Cricket Society' to help keep the Club in the black.

On November 6th 1994 Ron Biddle passed away, leaving the Club mourning the loss of a good friend and servant. The following year would bring the deaths of two other 'giants' of Aldridge C.C. Bill Groves and Geoff Walker. Geoff joined the Club in 1938 although he had time off to serve his country in RAF Coastal Command during the war. Retiring early from a playing career in the 1st & 2nd XIs, he embarked upon a long period of service to both the Cricket Club and the Stick & Wicket. He was Cricket Secretary and also, as one of the original Stick & Wicket steering committee, S & W Secretary until 1981. Becoming Chairman of the Club in 1979, he continued in the job until 1984. At the time of his death he was still a Trustee. As a printer by trade he was responsible for printing the Club's fixture cards etc. Geoff will always be remembered for his good humour and friendly banter and as a friend respected by all for his honesty and integrity.

Aldridge did well in the top division in 1995 even being the losing finalists in the League K.O. Competition. Dave

Edge held together the 2nd XI splendidly as they won the 2nd XI League. The Walsall K.O. was won, as already related. Without B. K. Maruthi after just an initial few weeks, the '95 season put all the pressure upon the likes of Wayne Law and Ian Manwaring. For instance in a game against Hampton-in-Arden the batsmen only managed to muster just 139 for the loss of six wickets in the allocated 50 overs. Wayne Law scored 45 and hard-hitting left hand bat, Ian Manwaring 35. Perhaps needless to say, the visitors fancied their chances of an away win. However, they had not accounted for Capt. Dyer whose mercurial talents bamboozled Hampton with what can only be described as a superb

1st XI 1997

Standing: Ian Manwaring Kester Sharpe Richard Bleakley Gareth Cornick
Richard Capewell Matt Higgins Barbara Popple (Scorer)
Seated: Andy Wylie Wayne Law Bob Dyer John Rowley Howard Shippey
Photo taken at Warwick

exhibition of bowling. He took 8 - 16 to rip the heart out of Hampton's batting line-up, only one of them managing double figures in a miserable 51 all out. Almost a repeat of his superb performance against Hampton in 1984. The youngsters at the Club were also doing very well with Gareth Cornick and John Hancox being chosen to represent Staffordshire & Midland Counties League under 18s.

Andy Bryan joined the Club in 1996 as 'Club Pro' which raised the standard of the bowling attack taking 39 wickets and averaging 23.8 with the bat. He was supported by Mark Gouldstone. Kester Sharpe had his first season in the 1st XI taking 22 wickets for an average of only 15.68 runs putting him in 6th position in the M.C.C. League. Batting was not so good in depth however. Wayne Law with 695 runs and an average of 34.75 and a top score of 136 was placed in 12th position and young Gareth Cornick with 439 averaged 25.82. Bob Dyer, remained as Captain through the 1997 season but unfortunately was starting to pick up injuries far too often for comfort. Talented Batsman - and right-arm medium pace bowler Andy Wylie from Boland C.C., South Africa, arrived at Aldridge in 1997 and was destined to feature large in the revival of the Club's fortunes over the next few years.

All through the 1990s the world of Aldridge cricket was changing. Young players continued to develop their potential before promptly leaving to go to university or moving from the district, a position the Club had reluctantly faced since the early 1960s. There were many other changes taking place in society however and Aldridge C.C. would continue to reflect those changes. The increased 'professionalism' had come initially with the

192 - **Andy Wylie** v Tamworth
16th August. 180 mins and 137 balls.

**Two top scorers for 1997
pose in front of the old scoreboard**

169 - **Gareth Cornick** v Blossomfield
13th July. 164 mins and 122 balls.

introduction of Leagues, better training and practice facilities and the massive improvement in social provision. Transport improvements meant that players were able to travel greater distances and the concept of 'village/community' cricket had diminished. The rise of 'other attractions' of course went against the nineteenth century idea that cricket provided something for the young men to do in their spare time, if anything there were far too many

Ian Manwaring Howard Shippey & Andy Wylie

Wayne Law took over the captaincy in 1998 with a view to raising the standard of the team still further. After 14 years at Walsall, playing in the Birmingham League, he was looking to gain promotion. Wayne had always set his sights high, ever since playing in an England schoolboy XI with Michael Atherton and Nasser Hussain. Newcomer Onkar Chagger from Aston Unity was starting to perform well with bat and ball as well as being a great motivator. Unfortunately, automatic promotion was not achieved, even with a win in the League Cup, but a third place in the Warwickshire League was enough to gain the coveted place in the Birmingham and District Premier League Div. 2. Wayne had led the side very well and in doing so had also gained for himself the accolade of M.C.C.C. 'Cricketer of the Year' one of only five players so named. Finishing fifth from bottom however was not good enough to stay in the League, so for 1999 it would be the Staffs Club Championship again.

Bob Dyer was captain again in 1999, which was to be his final year in the job. Andy Wylie, by now an established team member and top performer with both bat and ball, was elected Captain for 2000. With over 1500 runs per season Andy won the batting award in the Staffordshire Club Cricket Championship in 2002 & 2003 as well as finding time to return to his native Stellenbosch to get married in March 2002. An indication of his popularity can be gauged from the fact that no fewer than nine members of Aldridge C.C. attended the wedding.

other attractions. The 4th XI virtually died out in the 1990s even with an attempt to get a regular 'Veterans' (over 40s) team up and running.

Sunday games have, perhaps, suffered even more than most. It was, and to some extent still is, difficult to field even one Sunday XI on some weekends. Since 1999 the Cedar Court Meadow ground has been hired out to the Walsall Health Cricket Club for Sunday fixtures. The Sunday League itself has been sponsored by various groups since the late 1980s. Initially called 'Steak Out' League, then 'Bridgestone Tyre', 'Dave Berry' and more recently 'V - Sports International'. Aldridge won the 'Steak Out' League in 1998.

The old 'nearly, but not quite' mantra applied again to 2002. Throughout, the batting was anchored by the Andy's - Wylie supported by Cornick. There were, as usual, the consistent bowling performances from 'Howie' - Howard Shippey. Fourteen year old Nick James played and even represented Warwickshire under 15s. Andy Cornick and Ross Shelton represented Staffs under 18s. John 'Rowles' Rowley had the distinction of becoming the first Aldridge cricketer to score a double century with his 205 not out against Cannock & Rugeley 2nd XI in a Sunday League game. The story was to some extent repeated in 2003 which, although a special year for the Club as an organisation, was not extraordinary on the field. The under 10s did manage top spot however.

By way of a postscript, as this history is being assembled in 2004, it must be noted that the side improved greatly throughout the season having a really good chance of promotion right up to the final game. A few lapses in consistency over the summer, however, meant that even after winning the final game, promotion remains ever illusive. There is always next year and the years beyond as Aldridge Cricket Club continues to advance by drawing upon its heritage, providing excellent facilities for players and encouraging its youth.

Millennium Veterans 2000

Aldridge Cricket Club 1853 - 2003

The Ladies

It was always traditional to thank the Ladies for 'doing the Teas', at the Annual Dinner; not at the AGM of course, because ladies were not allowed to attend. The Ladies in Jack Matthew's day included the likes of Mrs Pheasant, and Edith Clare. There was usually an individual driving force behind this essential tea preparation, a role performed with singular aplomb for many years by the indefatigable Mrs Jessie Buckley.

In the early 1960s it was stalwarts such as Mary Baker, Sheila Hastilow and Helen Franks who set the very high standards of Aldridge teas. However, by the late 1960s the 'Tea Pavilion' was starting to show its age. A series of break-ins, problems with preparing the food in the rudimentary kitchen, lack of electricity, and the general state of the place caused some concern. Shiela Biddle, along with the ladies and some youngsters, on every Friday night before a game would clean out the place ready for the next days match, causing the mice to scurry in all directions! Attendees at the groundbreaking AGM of 30th March 1969 witnessed the presence of Ladies for the first time. Extra work, caused by the introduction of Sunday Cricket and more teams, meant Sheila Biddle then Rose Cooper were fronting an ever growing army of helpers. At the 1971 AGM the 'Ladies Section' was thanked for organising social events and helping to create a good spirit in the Club.

Tea preparation was an ever - present fatigue, and by the start of 1977 there was concern that there were insufficient volunteers for the 'Ladies Tea Rota' and a special meeting was held to resolve the situation. Ladies were performing various 'backroom' jobs at the Club, for example, Helen Franks was thanked for collecting-in £1860 of subscription money. In 1978 the Ladies requested that profits from teas be used to provide childrens' play equipment for use in the Stick & Wicket. It was the question of Teas, however, which dominated the early 1980s and evidently there were still too few Ladies willing to prepare them. At the start of the 1982 season a new notice was placed in the changing room: 'Selection Committee is empowered not to select a player who consistently refuses to provide a tea lady...'

In March 1984 it was decided to re-form the Ladies Committee to handle a whole range of functions including teas. For the first time there was to be a Ladies cricket team. Obe Edge and Ina Warwood spearheaded the attack with Jenny Franks being the mainstay of the batting. Debbie Edge struck a most imposing figure behind the stumps and had her own fan club of male admirers. On July 7th 1984 Aldridge Ladies played Brewood in a 20 x 6 ball over match, 11 a side. Aldridge were 123 for two wickets Jenny Franks 75 n.o. Obe Edge 27. Brewood were 58 all out. A. Quiney took 1-16, Obe Edge 4-16 off 7 overs, Jenny Franks 2-11, K. Franks 1-3. There is also a record of Aldridge Ladies v Aldridge U16s. which happened on the 11th August 1984. The under 16s batted first with messrs. Burton and Rowley dominating, by scoring 51 between them before retiring. Michael Pickston managed 8 and the whole side were out for 75. The Ladies were bowled in succession until A. Quiney took to the wicket and scored a massive 34. With M. Dando not out 17. Sally Buller reckons that success was short-lived due to a succession of pulled muscles and torn hamstrings - but there was never a shortage of men volunteering to administer rubbing oils! Ina recovered from injury to promise Tony that only he would ever see her googly again. Jenny Franks was the first girl to represent a senior Aldridge side although, unlike in the ladies games, she didn't have support on the field from her Auntie Christine. The Ladies camp was usually set up on the boundary at away games to support husbands and boyfriends whilst consuming copious quantities of Piesporter. (See photo page 52).

A re-vitalised Ladies section was in action in 1987 when Sally Buller organised a Ladies rounders K.O., but sadly, although successful this was a one-off event. Sally and Jo Clews sold raffle tickets after each match to raise funds.

Ladies Committee 2003 - 2004

| Sue Ward | Jean Cornick | Katie Lloyd |
| Dawn Chew | Margaret Jackson | Caroline Whittock |

The approach of the 150th season with many special events being planned was encouragement enough for the Ladies committee to excel themselves by turning their hand to fund-raising yet again - with great success.

Over the years the job of 'Scorer' has often been taken by ladies. Longest serving of these has been Barbara Popple who has also loyally supported her husband Gordon at the Club for more than thirty years.

In 2004 an official Aldridge Ladies Team entered the Warwickshire 8 - a - side League as well as keeping in form by playing friendlies. The all - round talent of Captain Mel Cuthbert held the team together throughout their first season. Mel scored plenty of crucial runs along with Jo Allsopp, Karen Ford, Kerry Taylor, Caroline While and Deb Leason. The side's bowling was in the capable hands of Bridget Ball, Laura Shortland, and Jenny Shipley with Mel also producing some excellent performances. Some very good wins were notched-up and much experience gained. A pointer to the future perhaps?

Groundsmen, Grounds & Pavilions

The present cricket field and the peculiar 'mound' known as 'Gossy Knob' have an interesting but somewhat mysterious past. The history of both field and feature has been seemingly inseparable for at least the last two hundred years.

Gossy Knob

'Gossy Knob'

After surveying work on Gossy Knob in 1997, the Black Country SMR, Historic Buildings, Sites and Monuments Record: 2608 - BL1716, was updated:

'Earthwork Mound. Back of Aldridge Church. Tumulus, 2.2 m. high. Certain identification as a barrow (Burial mound) not possible in present condition. Mound is c.25m diam. and 2-3m. high. Visible on aerial photos of 1948 & 1963. Prehistoric Barrows were often re-used as windmill mounds so identification of site does not preclude earlier use as burial mound.'

So there we have it … an official 'don't know'!

Drewed Field, The Butts, Play Piece & Windmill Field

The field itself seems to be better chronicled. The area to the back of the church was part of one of Aldridge's large open fields, the 'Drewed Field' with the area furthest north from the Church being 'Drewed Heath' the waste land. This simple division between useful and waste land continued until the time of enclosures at the start of the eighteenth century, certainly sometime prior to 1750.

One use for this area was as 'The Butts' for Archery practice. In the 14th Century, during the reign of King Edward III, parishes were required to provide an area for villagers to gain archery practice. Even after the Civil War shooting was still being encouraged. The minutes of the Court Leet at Aldridge for October 15th 1664 state:

"It was ordered that the Constable of Barr and Aldridge for the year ensuing shall, at the parish charge, set up a sufficient pair of long shooting butts in the ancient and accustomed place, where the old butts formerly stood, before the 25th March next upon pain to forfeit if he make a default, 39s. 0d."

Another use possibly made of the field as early as the 17th century was for dancing round the Maypole. The name 'Play Piece' or 'Play Green' crops up on maps.

The Aldridge historian, Mr J. Gould, alludes to a 17th cent. Windmill at Gossy Knob, but no mill is shown on Brownes map of 1682 nor on later maps, although there are many 17th century references to a 'Windmill Field' in Court rolls, deeds etc. In 1801 there are also references to land near the 'Old Windmill' (owned by Mr Homer). On a map of 1817 the field is called 'First Druid Heath' and is farmed by Joseph Fletcher as arable. Note the change of spelling from 'Drewed' to 'Druid'.

On the 1847 Tithe Map, the present field is labelled as 'Windmill' Flat (divided into Big Windmill Flat & Little Windmill Flat) suggesting that the hill in the field, Gossy Hill, could indeed be a mill mound. The field was farmed by John Woodhall and owned by Dorothy Croxall.

'Gossy Knob' as it is known today, was referred to as Gossy Hill in Jack Matthews' day, and had originally been called 'Gorsey Hill'. An adjacent field is called 'Gorsey Leasowe' on the 1847 Tithe Map, literally meaning pasture with gorse bushes. Even today, clumps of gorse can be found wherever there are exposed areas of the stony and sandy soil such as on nearby Barr Beacon.

NB: The term 'Flatt' sometimes spelt 'Flat' is an ancient term used mainly in the North of England but common around Aldridge, to distinguish a part of a pre-enclosure open field. It does not imply that the field is level.

Other Fields

We know, however, that the present field has not been used by the club since its foundation. For many years other fields around the village were pressed into service, suitable or not. In 1865, for instance, there is a record of a combined Aldridge and Little Aston team playing in the grounds of Little Aston Hall. No doubt the 'toffs' at the Hall could afford a properly laid out field! (The field is now the site of the BUPA Hospital, Little Aston.) It must have been a real pleasure for the batsmen to be able to knock up double figures for a change. Few match reports from this time exist, and those which do cannot throw much light upon the precise whereabouts of the field. For instance the earliest match details discovered were reported in the Walsall Free Press of Saturday Aug 24th 1861 of a match between Walsall Wood and Aldridge played on Monday August 19th.

'Elevens of the above Clubs played in a field belonging to Joseph Proffitt Esq., of Aldridge, which resulted in favour of Aldridge in one innings and thirty six runs to spare.'

Joseph Proffitt lived in Lea House, in Anchor Lane, now called Walsall Wood Road, not far from Cedar Court. Lea House still exists, although it has not been a farm for many years. The Proffitt family, well known in Aldridge, were farmers and maltsters. The pitch used that day could well have been on the area now known as Cedar Court Meadow, currently occupied by the 3rd Team pitch.

Fields near the Moot House and Hobshole Lane were used, perhaps from around 1868 after Joseph Proffitt started selling - off his land. Some, such as The Bithams, Druid Field and Cedar Court Meadow, ended up as part of Manor House Farm. According to Jack Matthews, a pitch at the top of Frank James' Hill (Little Aston Road), in a field behind the Moot House adjoining the School Playing Field, today the playground of the present Cooper & Jordan School, was used for some years. This field was part of the Moot House Farm which for a time, certainly between 1871 and 1874, was occupied by another member of the Proffitt family, William, who was a farmer and schoolmaster. William ran the Grammar School which ajoined the Moot House property. The school, significantly in 1874, according to the Aldridge historian Richard D. Woodall, advertised *'large cricket and recreation grounds'*. So this would seem to confirm the likelihood that the field was indeed used. Jack also states that a field in Hobshole Lane was used for a few years before the present field. This Hobshole Lane field may have been the field offered by Mr G. G. Potter at the special Cricket Club meeting as reported by The Walsall Observer of Sept 3rd 1881:

"On Monday last, the Committee of the Cricket Club resolved to accept Mr G. G. Potter's offer for the use of his field for the ensuing year, and to thank Captain Tongue for his kindness for the past season."

It is more likely, however, that Mr Potter's field was the same one formerly run by William Proffitt, since Potter had taken over the Moot House from Proffitt in 1875.

Manor Farm - the Tongues and Croxalls

In the 19th century, much of the land in and around the village was owned by either the Tongue or Croxall families. The Tongues were based at the Manor House near the church.

It is perhaps pertinent to summarise here the rather complicated background of the landowning Tongue and, Croxall families and the Aldridge Manor Farm which played host to the Club for much of the late 19th century and nearly half the 20th.

Manor House Farm was owned by Edward Tongue (sometimes ref. to as the 'Squire of Aldridge') whose family had owned land in Aldridge for many generations. Edward lived at the Manor House and had married Sidney the sister of Edward Croxall of Shustoke, who was officially Lord of the Manor of Aldridge and also owned land locally. To complicate matters, Edward Croxall who died in 1827 had himself married Edward Tongue's sister Dorothy! Edward Tongue basically 'assumed' the title Lord of the Manor until his death in 1879 although 'his' estates were actually divided between his two sons Vincent and Randolph/Randall/Randle?.

Randall, who had inherited the Croxall land in Aldridge which included Manor Farm (as distinct from Manor House Farm) added 'Croxall' to his name, when his aunt Dorothy died in 1862. He lived at Shustoke, leaving a trust to run his part of the estate in the capacity of 'Lord of the Manor'.

Capt. Vincent Tongue, an army officer, had allowed the club the use of one of his fields, but may have begun selling-off tenancies on his land in the early 1880s after his father died. The Cricket Club is recorded to have thanked him for the use of his field at the end of the 1881 season. The location of this field is uncertain, it was probably not the one by the Moot house since that was not part of Manor Farm or Manor House Farm, although it could not have been the present field since that was owned by the Croxalls! By 1881, Capt. Vincent was probably living in the Manor House with his wife Janet whom he had married in 1864. He wasn't a farmer and evidently he was not at all well, so understandably, he didn't want to run things directly. Having a cricket club in 'residence' on a particular field was probably not seen as being the easiest way to obtain a tenant. Capt. Vincent died in 1883, aged 57, having one son Edward Randolph Tongue. Vincent's wife Janet stayed-on at the Manor House until her death in 1914. Vincent's brother, Randolph (Randall or Randle) Francis Tongue-Croxall who had already inherited the Croxall estates, died four years later leaving Capt. Vincent's son Edward as male heir to both the Tongue and Croxall estates in Aldridge.

Edward Randolph Tongue, as had his uncle Randall before him, added Croxall to his name when he 'assumed' the title 'Lord of the Manor of Aldridge' in 1887. 'ERT Croxall' lived at Rocksall Sutton Coldfield and then at Shustoke but retained much influence in Aldridge, including of course, presidency of the Club. His mother, Janet, was still living in the Manor House and legally all the land and title would not be his until her death in 1914.

'...it affords the (Cooke) family great pleasure'

In 1884 the present field, part of the Manor Farm, came under the tenancy of Dr. W. H. Cooke MRCS who, besides being a doctor, was a J.P. and businessman. He owned and rented much land locally, including most of the Manor House Farm. He was not a 'hands-on' farmer however, and appointed a bailiff to look after his holdings. The good doctor was a keen Cricket supporter - his three sons being active club members. Dr. Cooke made the field available to the club, perhaps as early as 1885.

Evidently, the offer of the Windmill Flat for the Club's use, was an offer too good to refuse and Mr Potter's field, used since 1882, was abandoned, but there is no record of the date. In 1888, the Club was given permission by Dr. Cooke to adapt the field specifically for its use vindicating the decision to make it the new home. Eventually, even naturally we can say, Dr. Cooke like Mr G. G. Potter before him, took his place upon the list of those eminent personages appointed as Club President.

An interesting snippet of information regarding the field appears in the Walsall Observer of June 25th 1887:

'Jubilee Celebrations. (Queen Victoria's Golden Jubilee) Took place on Tuesday. Magnificent Weather. After a Service for parishoners they formed a procession led by Brass Band and proceeded round the village to the field called the Windmill Flatt which was kindly lent for the occasion by Dr Cooke. 900 were entertained in several tents for dinner. The Children, 600 - 700 in number took tea later in the day. Sports took place. At 10 p.m. a bonfire was lighted and fireworks set off. Mr G.G. Potter showed limelight views. During the afternoon a fountain of real water was playing. The whole thing was very successful...'

Jack Matthews alludes to Mr Jim Davies, the oldest member (in 1948) in his eighties, recalling that as a lad he witnessed the laying of the present pitch. This would put it at around 1887 - 1890 so he was very accurate. The following reference seems to confirm that, by 1888, Dr. Cooke's Windmill Flat was indeed the cricket field.

A report of the Annual Aldridge Cricket Club Dinner in The Walsall Observer of Sat. Dec. 1st 1888, and in particular the Chairman's remarks, is quite revealing:

'The balance in hand was scarcely so large as last year but he supposed that arose from the fact of the cricket field having had to be levelled. It was true the ground had been made wider, but he thought it would be much better if it could be made wider still, thus giving more space for the players.'

Later in the speech he added that he thought...

'...the club was deeply indebted to Dr. Cooke for allowing the use of the ground for the matches, as it was not every gentleman who would have allowed his ground to be interfered with for such purposes. The company fully endorsed the Chairman's remarks, and Mr J. Cooke said it afforded the family great pleasure for the ground to be put to such a purpose.'

Mr Joel Cooke & Mr A. Cooke both played for Aldridge C.C.

The First Pavilion

In 1890, a small pavilion was erected on a site to the east (Rectory Side) of the later 'Tea Pavilion' which now serves

Plan of the original cricket pavilion, built 1890.   - Drawn by Mr Edward Joberns -   Walsall Local History Centre

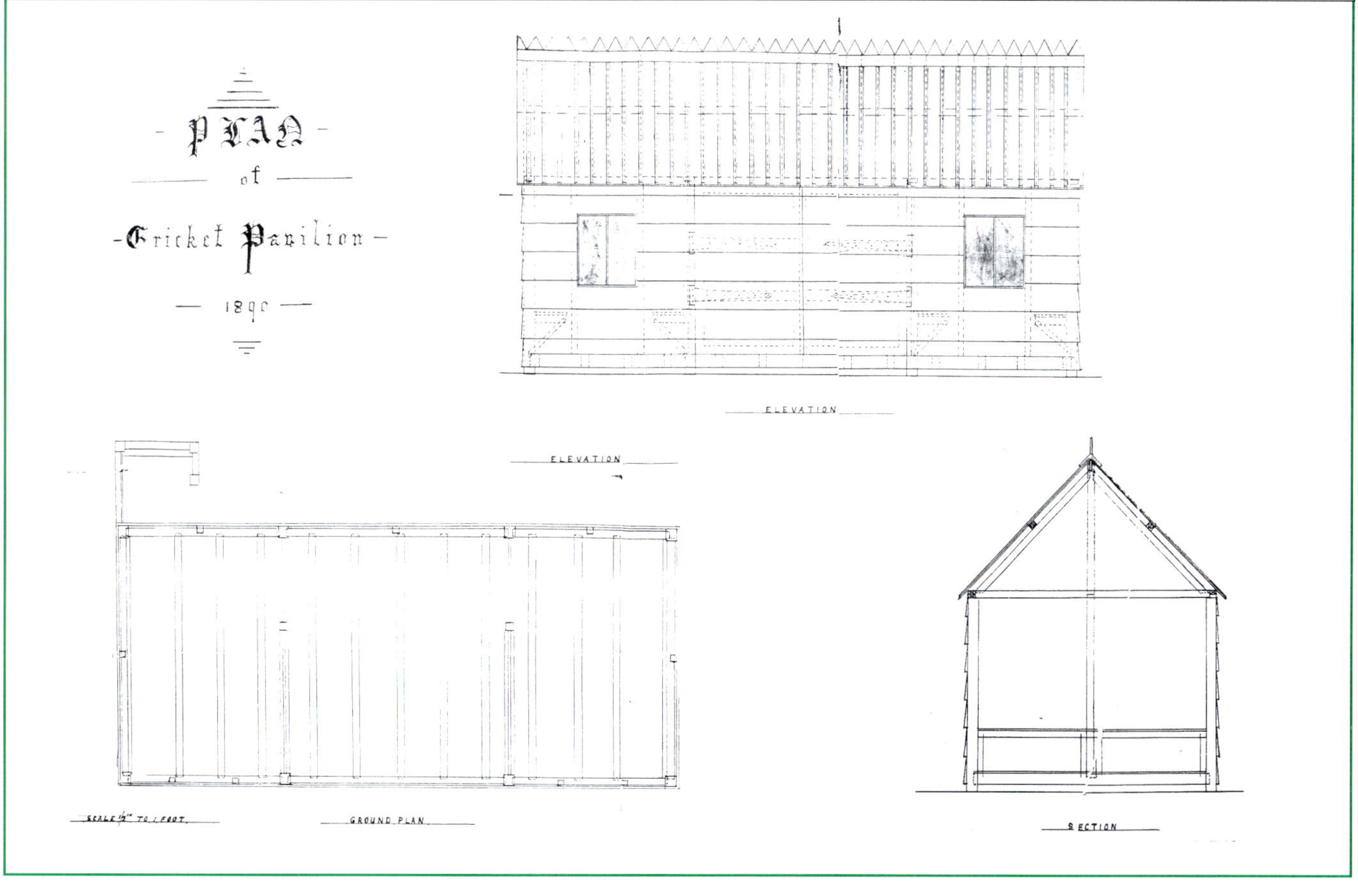

Aldridge Cricket Club 1853 - 2003

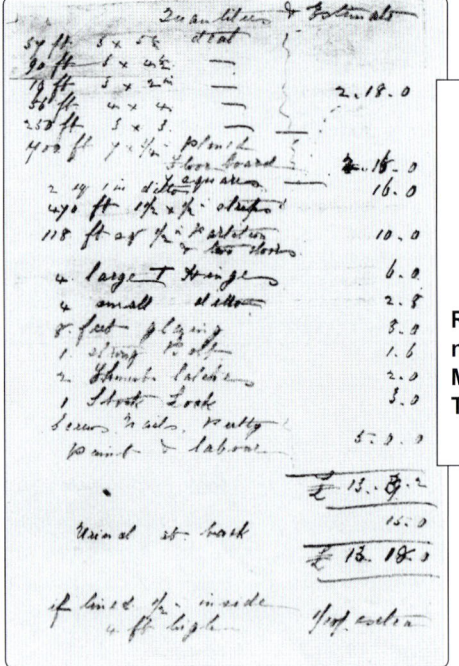

Left: The original quotation for building the 1890 pavilion.

Right: The 1949 note to Jack Matthews from Ted Joberns.

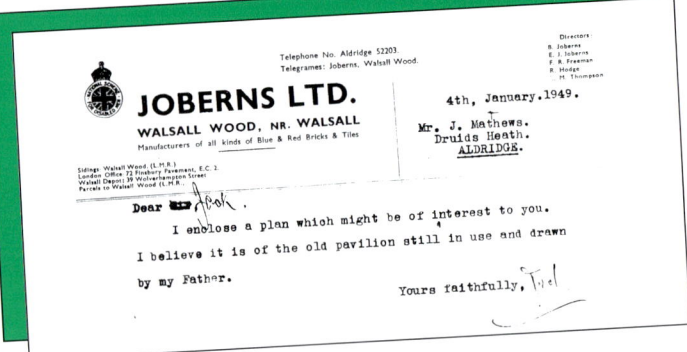

as the groundsman's hut and scoreboard. It was little more than a shed being only twenty feet by nine but had the distinction of being marked on the Ordnance Survey Map. The total cost was less than 14s! (See above) It served the club and often the Hockey Club too, until the Club centenary year of 1953 when changing facilities were added to the sides of the new tea pavilion. Its fate was then to become simply the groundsman's storage shed.

The plan, reproduced above, came to light in January 1949 when it was sent by Ted Joberns junior, to Jack Matthews, no doubt annoyingly, just after the publication of his book. The original quotation for the work has also survived along with the plan. Clearly, nothing had been forgotten; a lining inside to the height of 4ft was quoted at an extra £1. 10s, and there was also a quote for a 15s urinal at the back!

On Lady Day 1891, Dr. Cooke surrendered his lease on Manor Farm & Manor House farm. Mr Sam Bonner who had been Dr. Cooke's Bailiff took on the tenancy, and now began working directly for the 'Lord of the Manor' Mr E.R.T. Croxall. Dr. Cooke died in 1902.

The 'Cricket Field' is born

In the Walsall Observer of July 8th 1893 it was reported that there were rejoicings in Aldridge for the Royal Wedding. Shops closed, bells pealed and 600 children assembled; each child being presented with a medal. There was a parade to the Church and then through the village with all singing 'God Bless the Prince of Wales'. The article went on to say…

'... thence to the **cricket field** where tea was served on the grass. There were races in the evening, the winners being presented with toys of various kinds, also various kinds of entertainment.'

The tea was paid for by the results of a subscription list organised by Mr Frank James JP CC DL. The field was now being called the 'Cricket Field' and had, presumably, finally established its identity! Perhaps it now looked more the part, being levelled and having the relatively newly erected small wooden pavilion on its eastern edge.

On June 19th 1897, for the celebrations of Queen Victoria's Diamond Jubilee, the throng went to a field lent by Mr Marlow for 'Tea & Sports'. (Cricket field not now available ?) This field could even have been the one used for cricket in the early 1880s since Mr Potter & Mr Marlow had been partners. Mr Potter had since moved out of the area to reside in Lichfield. Mr Marlow lived at Cedar Court so it could even have been the Cedar Court Meadow used today as the 3rd team pitch!

It was reported in 1901, at the AGM, that the rent for the field had doubled. There does not seem to have been any reason given for this increase, but it is likely that as the club had rented the field for exactly ten years at the same rate, it was time for a review. The new figure was set at £5.0s.0d. per year.

Mr Samuel Bonner, the tenant farmer of Manor Farm from June 5th 1885 to 1920, was not simply a farmer but a deeply involved participant in the politics and social life of the local community. Already a Parish Councillor, in 1902 he stood for the District Council and was duly elected, replacing Mr Victor H. James and defeating other local worthies. Sam was a big supporter of the Club and there is a record, in the minutes of him being thanked for having the pavilion painted during 1904. His family was involved in founding many local activities such as the Hockey Club and a football team. Charles George Bonner, Sam's son, known as 'Gus', was not interested in farming, joining the navy and spending very little time at home. In 1917 Gus was awarded the Victoria Cross bringing much pride to his family and the village. Sam continued to work for the Manor Farm until it was sold to Thomas Hawkins in 1920.

Aldridge Cricket Club 1853 - 2003

In the early years of the 20th century the 'field' was gradually being transformed into something like the 'cricket ground' we know today. We don't know what it was like in terms of size, colour or location, but a scoreboard had been functioning well before 1907 when, according to the minutes, the figures were re-painted. Moveable seats were bought for the pavilion in 1908 along with a new rope for the Flag Pole.

In 1908, an athletic young man by the name of Howard Walton arrived in Aldridge to learn farming under the direction of Mr Bonner. Howard, who always saw himself as a 'Gentleman Farmer' was keen on playing cricket from the start, and needless to say had nothing but encouragement from Sam Bonner.

Thought was again being given to re painting the pavilion in 1909, but it was not done. The Rector was consulted however regarding the whitewashing of the rectory wall. Generally, the view was that the ground required a great deal of attention. In 1910 there was a recommendation made at the annual meeting that 'the ground be looked after properly'. Mr Sam Aston the groundsman was, however, complimented upon the splendid manner in which he undertook his tasks. The pitch was being 'railed-off' at this time with permission from Mr Bonner. In 1911 the paintwork on the pavilion was completed and the roof 'gas-tarred'. One of the major jobs was the removal of cow manure from the field prior to a match, cows were brought through the field at least twice daily to be milked. Perhaps because of the problems with the field Mr Sam Aston resigned as Groundsman and veteran player Mr Ted Milner took over. The pitch itself continued to cause concern however, evidenced by a Mr Brammer being brought in to inspect and give advice on same and a Mr Phillipson being consulted about new turf being laid.

By April 1914 the future for the ground looked bright. Cash was available for further painting of the pavilion and better enclosing of the pitch using metal standards and galvanised chain. A new Groundsman, Mr F. Dawson, was appointed at £6.0.0 per year. However, external events on the mainland of Europe would cast dark clouds over any sort of bright future during the next few years.

Neither the ground nor the pavilion were used for matches during the war years. Mr Bonner helped considerably by making the field available, rent free, for the general recreational use of the club. Much use was made of it however, by patients from the nearby Manor House which had now been converted into an 'Auxiliary Hospital' since becoming conveniently available for war use, due to the death of Mrs Tongue in 1914. The Pavilion was repaired in 1918 at a cost of £9. 6s 3d. In 1919, when the roof was examined and 'found wanting', it was covered with felt and tarred. A wash basin was fixed in the visitors side of the pavilion although as yet there was no water on tap.

In May 1919, Mr Godridge the newly appointed Groundsman had to seek the backing of the ground committee when, because of the dry weather, there had been complaints about the state of the pitch. The committee were supportive and: '...hoped that he would take no notice of remarks of ignorant people regarding last Saturday's wicket' No doubt, certain influential people were set thinking about the advantages that would be gained by getting water piped on to the ground.

The Minutes of Oct 3rd 1919 record: 'Re matter of attention to ground - owing to the unsettled state in regard to tenure of same it was thought advisable to let the matter rest till something definite is decided regarding the taking over by new Landlord.'

The annual rent for the ground in 1919 was re-established at the pre-war rate of £5.0.0 per year, given that it was now back in use. In 1920, it was doubled under the new Landlord, to £10.0.0 per year, but this still represented a good deal for the club. There was more than enough cash available from donations etc., in particular one of five guineas from the entertainment committee of the Auxiliary Hospital. The ground had been widely used by the hospital to aid recovery of the patients. (This figure of £10.0.0. remained the rental until it was bought by Mr & Mrs Buckley in 1947). The 'new Landlord' was Mr Thomas A. Hawkins, owner of Cannock Old Coppice Colliery, Cheslyn Hay. Mrs Tongue's demise in 1914 and the vagaries of war had no doubt increased the 'unsettled state' of the tenure of the farm and the condition of the fixtures and fittings of the institutionalised Manor House. In 1920, Mr Hawkins and his son Major O. C. Hawkins chose to live not at the Manor House but at Aldridge Court, formerly known as Portland House. Portland House, (See photo page 8) built by Mr Frank James in 1865 as his residence, and within a few minutes walking distance of the Cricket field, had always occupied an important place in the history of the club. Since 1898, when Frank James moved out, it had been the home of Walsall Tube manufacturer Mr John Gilbert Russell.

The 'Tea Pavilion'

Throughout 1920 there seems to have been almost continual concern about the long-term future of the ground. Representations were made to try to find out what Mr. Hawkins had in mind for the farm and in particular that part of it which constituted the cricket field. In September 1920 it was reported that the Committee were going to ' ...See Mr Loyns re use of ground.' Mr. Loyns was probably Bailiff to Mr Hawkins. A certain Mr. Jack Matthews, Club Secretary extraordinaire, was not concerning himself with such trifles however, he had his sights set upon no less a project than replacing the pavilion. In April 1920 Jack spoke to the meeting about the desirability of having an 'annex' to the pavilion; discussion on the matter was deferred. However in typical JM style a building was

Aldridge Cricket Club 1853 - 2003

The 'Tea Pavilion' c.1948   The old pavilion can be seen on the right

actively sought. By the end of May a hut had been purchased and removed from the nearby Streetly Works. An estimate of £57.10s from Mr Robson for adapting the building was considered and agreed. Mr Bert Myring was recruited to lay brick foundations and an offer of £100.0s.0d loan from Mr Joberns was accepted. The bill for constructing the pavilion turned out to be £85. 9s. 11fid the extra cost being due to additions requested by the committee.

The New Pavilion 'annex', actually much larger than the old pavilion, was erected in 1920. Described as *'The season's big undertaking'*. The cost of getting it finished was £240, 1s. 6d. However, it was not without some dissent, Mr Turner, one of the leading supporters of the project, resigned over the 'loan' which had been accepted, his own offer having been declined.

The 'Old' Pavilion, to the east of the new one, continued to be used for changing so the 'New' building acquired the name 'Tea' Pavilion because this was where the ladies would 'manage' the teas under the very capable direction of Mrs Buckley. The original pavilion continued to be kept in good repair, a new door being supplied in 1920 for £1. 8s 0d.

Having installed the new 'Tea Pavilion' the angst with regard to the tenancy of the ground remained, as noted in the minutes of Feb 24th 1921:

'The chairman remarked on the purchase of field by Mr Hawkins of Aldridge Court & Mr Mold moved & Mr Bonnett seconded that the chairman & Secty. Visit Mr Hawkins and if possible get his interest & support of the Club.'

In 1922, a letter from Mr Hawkins was received outlining his concerns re. the field. The groundsman, now Mr W. Herbert, was accused of taking manure from the ground and that was not all... there was damage and trespass which had to be stopped. Mr William, the Bailiff, was to be approached with a view to getting some lime on the pitch. Mr Hawkins, although not a cricket lover as was his predecessor, was not averse to the needs of the Club. Mr Partridge reported to the Club meeting that he had collected details about the cost of laying water to the pitch. Whereas in 1922 taking manure off the pitch was the talking point, 1923 saw a liberal dressing of Marl & Manure applied to the ground during the 'out' season. It was acknowledged that such dressing would need to be done regularly if the ground was to improve. In fact the ground still needed cash spending on it. Fortunately, Mr Hawkins assured the club that it should not be disturbed by him for at least five years. The lack of human interference was gratifying but during the next few years, particularly 1924 and 1925, the problems encountered were from pigs rooting around the ground and in 1925, gale damage to the old pavilion. Provision of sight screens was put to the meeting of 14th April 1924 but no action was taken. A ladies convenience was constructed in 1925 at the back of the pavilion. Perhaps the pigs were too much for groundsman Herbert, he resigned and was replaced by former player and serving umpire T. Pendry in July 1926. No one told the pigs however, they continued to create havoc. Mr Pendry had to re-lay the practice wicket in January 1927, which had been completely uprooted by the swine.

Privileges continued

A new motor mower, described as a 'Motor Machine' in the accounts, was purchased in 1926 for £40. 7s 6d. The usual method of payment was adopted; loans from members in the form of £5.0.0. 'shares' which soon paid for it. Mr Pendry resigned as Groundsman due to 'medical orders' in April 1927 and Mr J. Hastilow was asked to take on the job. His position being ratified at the 1928 AGM. Further ground improvement came in July 1928 when water was finally laid on to the field in the form of a standpipe, at a cost of £23. 3s 7d. Nine years of discussion had finally borne fruit. The Churchyards Committee and Mr Hawkins were thanked for allowing the pipes through their ground. Mr Hastilow announced in March 1929 that, due to taking on another position, he could no longer carry on as Groundsman. Mr J. Jukes occupied the position of 'Auxilliary Groundsman' by the end of the season.

In 1930, Mr Thomas Hawkins evidently auctioned off the tenancy of Manor Farm including the Cricket Field, but the visit of the Chairman and Secretary some nine years previously, had obviously brought Mr Hawkins 'on side'. When Jack Matthews, worried about the change of tenancy, wrote

Aldridge Cricket Club 1853 - 2003

The view from above ...

c.1891
The original pavilion is marked

1938
Both the old pavilion and tea pavilion are indicated

c.1999
The new 'Stick & Wicket' pavilion and the two pitches are clearly visible

Aldridge Cricket Club 1853 - 2003

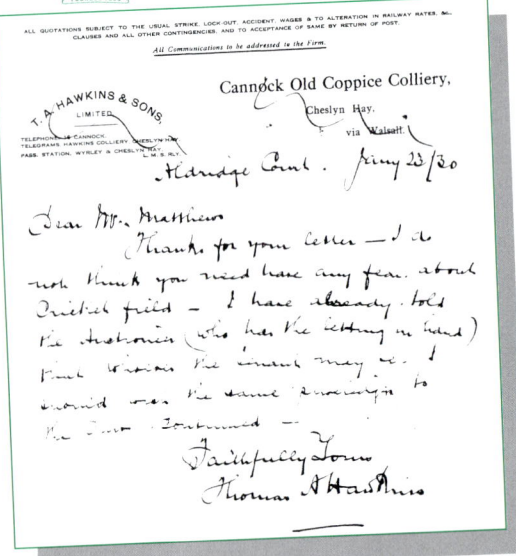

Thomas Hawkins' reassuring letter of January 1930

to him early in 1930, he was to express most positive feelings in his reply of January 23rd:

'Dear Mr Matthews.

Thanks for your letter. I do not think you need have any fear about Cricket field. I have already told the Auctioneer (Who has the letting in hand) that whoever the tenant may be I should wish the same privileges to the club continued.

Faithfully yours

Thomas A Hawkins.'

In 1930, the minutes record that Mr Hawkins & 'Mr Teece' were thanked for 'Privileges on Ground' so Mr Teece was, seemingly, the new Tenant. Clearly all was well with the new tenant farmer since there is a Vote of Thanks to him recorded at the 1933 Annual General Meeting. Club accounts in the early 1930s and 1940s mention paint and costs for cleaning both pavilions. A new mowing machine was purchased in 1932 for £31. 0s 0d. and the rails around the front of the Tea Pavilion were also repaired that year. Mr Jukes the Groundsman was provided, courtesy of teacher Jack Matthews, with the *'services of some boys to help rolling pitch'*. The pitch, however, was not in good condition. Mr Backhouse from Walsall was invited to give advice. So bad was the state of the playing area that in October 1933 a letter was received from Messrs Kynoch's refusing the fixture for the forthcoming season because of the state of the ground. A most unsatisfactory situation. Turf from Howard Walton's farm and a dressing of marl was suggested. 'Chemical manure' was seen as the answer in March 1935 and the Groundsman was invited to attend the Committee meeting to discuss the application of marl and the hire of a council roller through Mr Onions.

It was September 1935 before water was eventually piped directly into the pavilion at the cost of £6. 18s 4d. along with a 'heating chamber' constructed at the rear. That same year a concrete wicket was laid complete with practice matting. Evidently progress with the pavilion was not matched on the field and it was decided to 'sack' the Groundsman. Sutton's Groundsman, Mr W. Leonard was approached with a view to him advising on the restoration of the ground. An advert was placed in Mr Cope's window for a Groundsman and Mr H. Bounds duly appointed. Part of the pitch was re-turfed. Problems with the grass cutting machine led to the purchase of another and the erection of a shed and fence for its storage. Mr J. T. Davies was elected as Pavilion Manager in 1937. It was suggested that perhaps the farmer could be asked about the possibility of getting a lease on the ground.

In March 1938 the minutes record that Mr Hawkins should be considered as the new Landlord with rent paid direct to him. A new tenant for the Manor farm was due to take over later that month. Discussions were taking place at this time about the possibility of an extension to the Tea Pavilion in the form of a Verandah. Mr J. Ballinger prepared plans for the extension which were considred at the meeting in March 1939. Tenders for the work were opened and Mr Robson's estimate of £63 was accepted, including the painting of the pavilion.

World War Two

The 2nd World War had a similar effect on the club as had the 1914 - 18 conflict. Normal matches were not possible and the decision was made to launch an appeal to simply maintain the ground and its facilities for the duration. A letter was written to Mr Hawkins to ask him to allow the Club to retain hold on the ground by paying a small retaining fee. Major Hawkins, Mr Hawkins' son, in turn suggested that the farmer, Mr Gaul, be contacted with a view to concessions being made. In his usual style, Mr Gaul stated that he would rather the Major had made the concessions!

Alternative wartime uses for the ground were considered, for training the Home Guard and for the ARP wardens to play some matches. In 1941 the pavilion was thought to be in danger from Incendiary bombs and it was deemed advisable to have sandbags and buckets of water available with the keys left at the church rooms, although as an economy measure the water supply to the pavilion was dis-connected during the war. The back windows of the pavilion were boarded-up. The school, under the direction of Mr Tyas, made use of the field for boys PT in 1942 as it had the previous year. The Air Training Corps were given use of the pavilion and field in June 1942. Consternation was caused when Mr Gaul, the farmer, no doubt inspired by the government's 'Dig for Britain' campaign had intimated to Major Hawkins that he may plough up the field. Fortunately, the ground survived Gaul's arable aspirations.

Play resumed

Early in 1944, it was decided that a few limited games would be played during the season. Two of the games were arranged to raise funds for the Red Cross and it was reported that '...*the pitch and ground never looked finer, great credit being due to the voluntary work put in.*' At the end of the war, returning members realised that the Tea Pavilion was becoming rather small for the needs of the club and the old wooden pavilion was starting to show clear signs of its more than half a century of use. A new roof of corrugated sheets was approved for the old pavilion at an estimated cost of £7. The solution was in no doubt, a new pavilion was needed and consequently a fund was started. By the end of 1944 it had reached £156. 4s 8d. Day to day requirements were not forgotten, however, a roller and cutter was purchased for £9. 10s and a crease marker for £1.10s.

The matter of Ground tenure was back on the agenda in late 1944 due to expectations and requirements regarding the building of a new pavilion. Dr Milne and later Mr Partridge were asked to contact Major Hawkins to discuss the possibility of securing a lease. No reply was received from Mr Gaul or Major Hawkins until eventually, in December, a phonecall from Major Hawkins indicated that a lease would not be possible. Faced with growing uncertainty the Committee examined the possibility of transferring the Club to another field. However, it was stated that Mr Gaul, as tenant, was quite sympathetic- (clearly his 'ploughing' phase had been forgotten) and that may not be so with another farmer.

Mr J. Hastilow had been tending the ground during the war years on a voluntary basis and he was informed that after the hostilities he would be given the work on a 'paid' basis. So, in 1945, it was decided to employ a Groundsman at £2 per week between 1st April and 30th September and Mr J. Hastilow was, as promised, given first refusal. He was duly appointed, his position being ratified at the AGM in 1946. At the end of his first year Mr Hastilow informed the Committee that he would be unable to continue in the coming year. It was decided to write to Mr J. Bevan. At the October 1946 meeting Mr Jim Bevan was introduced. He would take up his position in April 1947. A gang-mower was purchased to make life a little easier for Mr Bevan who was used to having the proper equipment. Born in Aldridge in 1909, Jim had worked at Little Aston Golf Course, after leaving the village school where he had attended before the First World War. More recently he had been Green Keeper at the Sandwell Golf Club in West Bromwich. Jim Bevan did not wait until April to start work, however, because at the March meeting his excellent work was commented upon and an extra donation of £10 made to him.

Cows are always a problem on a cricket field. Should they actually stray on to the pitch itself then it can be little short of a disaster. In June 1947 Mr Gaul was rewarded for keeping his cattle off the pitch and given a present of £5 for his efforts. For many years the 'cowman' at Manor Farm was Mr Ivan Frost who lived in a small cottage near

the present Stick & Wicket site. (See photo on page 84) Ivan played for Aldridge C. C. and was noted for being something of a Swearer! Perhaps when he was out in the field he still thought he was talking to the beasts. Twice daily, cows would be led through the cricket field with the inevitable results. Youngsters who aspired to play for Aldridge were given buckets and asked to go and collect up the pats before the match started.

Ground secured

Due to Major Hawkins, Thomas Hawkins' son, leaving the area in 1947 The Manor Farm Estate, of which the pitch was part, was put up for sale. With the assistance of the buyer Mr Edgar Swain a local builder and supporter of the club, Mr & Mrs Alf Buckley managed to purchase the ground for the Club's use. Until this point the tenancy had been yearly. Mr & Mrs Buckley were consequently elected to Life membership of the Club. A machine shed was also purchased for £8.1s 6d. Actually, the Club continued to pay a yearly 'rent' of £10. 0s. 0d. which went straight into the new pavilion building fund. By 1948 this fund had risen to a splendid £524. 7s 2d.

Now the ground was secure, a number of improvements were scheduled to be undertaken. The Practice wicket would be enlarged, sight screens made a new pavilion constructed and the outfield improved. On a more immediate note, Jim Bevan would famously shave the wicket with a sythe to get it in really first class condition. He didn't have much in the way of 'Wages' but would often have tobacco and a certain amount of liquor. The liquor would invariably lead to much singing in the bar, in particular a special rendition of 'Who killed cock-Robin'.

Aldridge Cricket Club 1853 - 2003

In 1948, Calor Gas was installed in the pavilion for boiling water. Mr F. P. Stephens, speaking at the AGM that year praised the co-operation given by Mr Swain in giving the President the opportunity to purchase the ground. Mr Swain was present and briefly replied. 1949 brought the addition of the new 'Sight screens' constructed from tubular steel and canvas by Messrs W. H. Bunn and H. E. Swain, and a new fence and gates were purchased. 'Billy' Bunn was a well-known garage owner in the village and ideally placed to get welding and other construction jobs completed. It was during this year that the new 'Drive-In' from Hobs Hole Lane, specifically for car owners, was laid consisting of ashes tipped near the entrance to provide a better grip for cars although there were not many car owners in those days. It was also suggested that perhaps a calor gas light fitting could be installed in the pavilion.

Mr Ballinger reported that the Hockey Club were desirous of creating another pitch between the square and the pavilion which would mean removing the concrete wicket presently in that position and making another by 'Gossy Hill'. The new concrete wicket was approved.

The 'New' Pavilion

A building committee was formed in 1949 and Mr Onions was asked to survey the area and Mr Ballinger to prepare plans. An Excise Licence was registered from July 18th 1950 which meant that drinks could now be officially sold in the pavilion. A sub-committee was appointed to manage bar arrangements. Mr Ballinger's plans for a new pavilion were exhibited but there was still much discussion about the possibility of moving the existing Tea pavilion or using it in the plan.

Surveying the wind damage to the new pavilion.
Walsall Observer Photo: November 1952

The funds were available to start building work on the 'new' pavilion in 1951, but unfortunately the work did not commence on time due to labour problems. Mr Robson, the chosen contractor, whose quote was about half what the others had offered, felt that he should withdraw

The newly extended Tea Pavilion

because he could not get the workers. The plan was that the old Tea Pavilion was to be modified by having extensions to each side to accommodate home and away changing areas. By 1952, however, the extensions were reported as being 'practically complete' with a large proportion of the bricks and sanitary ware being donated by the Aldridge Brick & Tile Co and Messrs Joberns. Luck was against the project yet again when, on the night of 6th-7th November 1952, a violent storm struck the Aldridge ground and a severe gale stripped off much of the new roofing on the extension. The 'exposed' nature of the Aldridge ground is somewhat ledgendary, even during the playing season. Many a time players would insulate themselves with pyjamas under their whites.

After an uphill struggle the crowning glory actually arrived… appropriately with a formal opening of the 'new' pavilion on June 3rd 1953. Nationally, it was Coronation Week and the week that news of the conquest of Mt. Everest had reached the UK. The day was planned as an appropriate physical celebration of a hundred years of the Club. Mr Howard Walton officiated as chairman with a match versus an invited Walsall XI arranged. Mrs Buckley actually performed the official opening. However, the newspaper report (See opposite) adequately summed up the 'wretched' conditions prevailing at the opening, typical of Aldridge ground and of the year and of Coronation week in particular.

Cows were roaming the field once more during the summer of 1953 and by the autumn considerable damage had been done. The Old pavilion and the motor shed also suffered, from gale damage during the winter. With the imputus provided by a new pavilion and all the enthusiasm of the new Elizabethan age no sooner one project was finished others were initiated. Plans for the erection of a cattle fence on the farm side of the field and a new score box were put into place. It was 1956 before the cow problem was solved.

Aldridge Cricket Club 1853 - 2003

The Walsall Observer, Friday, June 5, 1953.

BIGGER PAVILION FOR VICTORIOUS ALDRIDGE

TRINITY CELEBRATE WITH A CORONATION "HAT-TRICK"

THE cold and rainy weather marred a notable day in the history of Aldridge Cricket Club on Wednesday. The official opening of the new extensions to the pavilion had to be curtailed, and the friendly match with Walsall Cricket Club was spoiled by the wretched conditions. Last week-end Aldridge won their sixth match of the season.

The Aldridge pavilion extensions were opened by Mrs. A. Buckley, wife of the club president, and afterwards Dr. V. E. Milne unveiled a plaque inside the pavilion, commemorating the work done by Mr. and Mrs. Buckley for the club. Mr. H. Walton, the club chairman, unveiled another plaque which records the service of Mr. J. Matthews, who has been secretary for over 40 years.

Aldridge Just In Time

With only a few minutes left to play, Aldridge snatched their sixth consecutive win of the season when Wombourn visited them on Saturday. Their victory by 48 runs was largely due to brilliant bowling by H. Crumpton, who had eight wickets for 36, backed up by fine wicket-keeping by H. Ray.

Aldridge declared after making 163 seven, to which S. Harvey contributed 44, F. Hastilow 43, and A. Pheasant 32. Wombourn started their innings disastrously by losing five wickets for only 18 runs. A good sixth-wicket partnership took the score to 81, but then Aldridge broke through again and finished off the innings for 105.

The second eleven match at Wombourn was one in which fortunes changed remarkably. After losing four wickets for five runs, Wombourn recovered to make 146, including 59 by W. Onions, a former Aldridge player, houses, and scored 163 for eight. Five bowlers shared in the dismissal of Fordhouses for 95, Appleby taking four wickets for 18 and Siverns two for 19.

A group taken at the opening of the extensions to Aldridge Cricket Club. On the right is Mr. H. Walton, the club chairman, and next to him are Mr. A. Buckley (president) and Mr. J. Matthews (secretary).

The Hockey club had complained about the cows during what was the cricket closed season, so as with all good committees the possible solutions were put to the vote. 'Controlled grazers' v 'Exclusionists'. The total exclusionists won by one vote.

Mr Robson's plans for a score-box complete with 'Eagle' scoreboard fittings were the topic for much discussion in January 1957. The score-box duly blossomed in the spring from Utopia bricks provided by Aldridge Brick & Tile and Blue bricks cement and sand care of Messrs Joberns. The whole splendid edifice was finished, at a cost of £147. 14s 0d, by the end of April, ready for the new season. In July, it was recorded as giving 'Great Satisfaction'.

Jim Bevan took on the job as Caretaker of the school in the spring of 1958 which meant that he could no longer be on the ground for 6. o'clock as was required. Born and bred in Aldridge Jim was returning to the same school in Aldridge he had attended as a child. He was also Verger at the Church and Grave-digger. Mr R. Davies was appointed as Assistant Groundsman to help him.

Under Threat

The Spring of 1958 also brought with it a looming threat to the field with proposals being published by the Staffordshire Education Committee to build a Further Education college for 2,000 students on Cedar Court Meadow. The meadow, owned by Alderman Sir J. Cliff Tibbits and used by the cricket club, was the home of the Hockey Club. Much of the surrounding land, some 20 acres, would be taken up by car parks and sports fields for the college if the proposals went ahead. Naturally, there was complete outrage at the very idea of taking away such a splendid facility from the people of Aldridge. Strong letters were penned to the Walsall Observer from the Cricket Club and the Hockey Club. Howard Walton stated:

'We are convinced that it would be a tragedy, contrary to good planning, and to the wishes of the vast majority of Aldridge people, if anything should be done to alter or curtail the freedom and enjoyment they have for so many years experienced on the Aldridge cricket field.'

Fortunately, support from Aldridge residents was overwhelming and the Urban District Council was also opposed to the plans. Its Chairman, Councillor H. E. Swain, the same Edgar Swain who had sold the ground to the Club some ten years before, stated that the County council would be urged to choose an alternative site. At the Annual Dinner in March it was announced by Secretary Jack Matthews that, due to popular opinion being taken into account the danger of losing the ground had passed. He added that the Club would need to remain vigilant in the future.

A piece of ancient history in respect of the field was brought to an end when, in February 1959, the Secretary reported that he had paid the Tithe Redemption Commission the sum of £36. 4s 5d and that as a consequence the land was now free from any further tithe for all time.

Aldridge Cricket Club 1853 - 2003

The Groundsman and the Club facilities in the late 1950s and early 1960s

Mr Billy Bunn's house was the venue, in 1959, for meetings of the 'Ground Committee'. Billy Bunn was the popular proprietor of the most well known Garage in the village. It was appropriate that recommendations for a new motor mower were made and accepted at the committee's February meeting and a machine ordered. When the mower arrived in April it was discovered that Billy Bunn had managed to obtain it at a good discount for the Club.

Jim Bevan resigned his position as Groundsman in October 1960 but stated that he would assist his successor if required. He was presented with two chairs and a hearth rug to make his retirement more comfortable! Mr Reynolds, Jim's replacement was unable to give the job as much time as it required and so by the start of the 1962 season it was Mr Bevan who was being re-called to prepare the square. By the AGM of 1964 Jim had been made Groundsman yet again for that season although he was often heard to say that it was physically getting too much for him. Mr P. R. Barton was appointed as Assistant Groundsman to Jim Bevan at the end of the 1965 season.

Electric heating and lighting for the pavilion was on the agenda in the summer of 1962, the cost would be in the region of £600. Mr Bunn had been offered a piano for use in the pavilion so perhaps it could have been used for singing and dancing to keep warm. The summer of 1964 finally brought an official estimate for bringing mains power to the pavilion. Agreement from the Rector was given, in principle, to bring the cable accross Ecclesiastical ground. Much discussion took place as to the emphasis which was seemingly being placed on the non-playing side of club activities. Nets and a roller were required. However, profits on the bar were hitting an all time record and new nets were donated anonymously so there was cash to spend. Mrs Buckley, the legal owner of the ground and now Club President, was not keen on the idea of a power line being put accross the field. Her permission was also required for work on the pavilion railings to go ahead on Sundays. Vandals hit the pavilion in April 1965 and again in July. Another break-in occurred in March 1966 and there was yet more in March and April 1967. It

Mr W. H. Billy Bunn outside his garage in Paddock Lane in the 1920s. A well - known local character and one of the first three car-owners in the village. He later moved to larger premises in Walsall Road. Billy was a very useful member of the Club Committee for many years.
His name lives on in the 'W. H. Bunn Cup' awarded to the most promising youngster.

was stated that it was rather difficult to install a burglar alarm without power. The pavilion kitchen was finally modernised in August 1967 and the triumph was minuted as: *'Ladies most pleased'*.

In March 1967, Jim Bevan announced his intention of retiring for good - since he would soon be leaving his job as school caretaker with the demolition of the old school and re-building commencing. His cottage was 'tied' to the job so he would now no longer be living quite as close to the cricket ground. However the new Assistant Groundsman, Mr D. Ball often failed to report for duty signalling the start of what would be a few unsettled years for pitch maintenance.

Aldridge Cricket Club 1853 - 2003

Jim Bevan Groundsman 1947 - c1968

Work continued on the ground facilities however, a decision to remove the railings from outside the pavilion being taken in April 1968 and a new Practice Wicket laid a month later. In July 1968 the old 'Implement Shed' was scheduled for demolition but reprieved until after the Ox-Roast. It would still be a further six years before a full-time Groundsman was appointed. Brian Davies acted as Groundsman between 1969 and 1971 with Mark Biddle taking responsibility during 1972.

Due to most successful fund-raising events co-ordinated by David and Helen Franks, particularly the annual Ox-Roast, the Annual Report by Sec. Geoff Walker was able to talk of the *'affluent state of the club'*. Great improvements were made to the interior of the Tea Pavilion, already being described as the 'clubhouse'. New seating, wood panelling, curtains etc., and in 1968, electricity. All the wiring and inside installation was done voluntarily by Mark Biddle. For the first time ever the Club was open socially all the winter of 1968-69 with permission granted to the Hockey Club to share the facilities of the pavilion. Tommy Hood stood down from the Bar Committee after good work in the previous seasons. The 'A' Team, which had become the embryo '3rd XI', were given permission to use McKechnie's Sports Ground for home team matches from 1969.

It is said that you should not have power without responsibility, and so it was with the Pavilion. The pavilion could now be used for the first time, during the close season, but it brought with it some new problems. For the early years after electricity installation, it was not uncommon to find that, in the middle of a particularly dark evening, the Pavilion had been 'blacked-out' by local youngsters who had found the outside main power switch. On one such occasion a 'Pyjama Party' was in progress and the sight of people running around in the outside gloom, clad ostensibly only in 'jim-jams', looking for the young offenders can easily be imagined. Today, such switches would be illegal and I expect that would apply to the party too! In the winter time particularly, It was very dark and a little treacherous to approach the Pavilion coming up the track from Hobshole Lane. At night many a couple would venture off the lane to a place where they thought it was totally secluded and isolated, only to be shocked and disturbed as the headlights of cars coming down to the lane put them fully in the limelight.

For the first year in the Club's history a full season of 3rd XI Cricket operated from 1969 and, along with the introduction of Sunday cricket that year, helped to put more pressure on the facilities at the ground. The 'Home' ground for all 3rd XI matches was either McKechnie's Sports Ground or the T.I. Ground, Walsall Airport. Sometimes, in the local paper the 3rd's were dubbed 'McKechnie's Marauders'. However, 'The Stick & Wicket', the all-new clubhouse, a joint venture with the Hockey Club, opened in 1971, improved matters considerably. This was further boosted by the creation of a second cricket pitch.

The 'Stick & Wicket'

In the late 1960s the Hockey Club was making plans to build a pavilion on Cedar Court Meadow, adjoining the cricket ground. Many members of the Hockey Club were also members of the Cricket Club, a situation which had existed since the former was founded in 1904. With the death of Mrs Buckley the Cricket Club received a letter from the Hockey Club stating that they were willing to postpone their own development if it was thought the two clubs could become more closely associated. Within two months of Mrs Buckley's passing her wishes that the ground be offered for sale to the Club had resulted in the Trustees purchasing it for the very favourable sum of £4,500. The idea was thus mooted whereby both clubs would

The vision... the Architect's drawing

The 'Stick & Wicket'

The reality... a photo taken in 2002

Aldridge Cricket Club 1853 · 2003

**Walsall Observer
Friday May 14th 1971**

Only the chairman of the committee, Mr. Arnold Ballinger is missing form this group seen in the new Stick and Wicket Club at Aldridge during the week. Seated at the table from left to right are Frank Hastilow, Bill Baker (club chairman), Brian Crabtree (treasurer) and Geoff Walker, (secretary of both the Stick and Wicket Club and Aldridge Cricket Club).

chaired by Mr Arnold Ballinger, was formed. David Franks, who had come up with the name, was the real driving force behind the venture, the culmination of years of effort by the two clubs. David had motivated the Cricket Club from the time it had been given the opportunity to purchase the ground in 1969, following the death of Mrs Buckley. Plans for the building of a new clubhouse, on land leased from the Cricket Club, to be sited directly opposite the old Tea Pavilion were drawn up. Those produced by John Meeson, an architect who played for the Hockey Club, were accepted. Rules for operating the new facility were also first formulated in 1970. In May of that year builders Messrs. Tomlinson & Son construction began work and twelve months later, on Friday May 14th 1971, the official opening of the new premises was carried out by Mr Billy Groves representing the Cricket Club and Sir Cliff Tibbits the Hockey Club. Facilities were spacious and luxurious, particularly after the vagaries of the old pavilion! Changing rooms and showers, a fully fitted kitchen, bar and stockroom, lounge and committee room all equipped with 'state of the art' fixtures and fittings. Needless to say, with such high quality facilities the membership of social and playing members of each club increased dramatically. The project included the cost of purchasing the ground and that of levelling of the centre of Cedar Court Meadow and the laying of a cricket square, thanks to the generosity of the late Sir Cliff Tibbits. The total cost of the project was some

Opening of Stick and Wicket club

Tonight (Friday) will see the opening of the new combined club of Aldridge Hockey and Cricket Clubs under the banner of the Stick and Wicket Club to forge the strongest sporting link in the ever growing village of Aldridge.

In the words of press officer David Franks the Stick and Wicket Club is a social club formed to administer a having the use of two home cricket grounds and four excellent hockey pitches, all served by a central pavilion and clubhouse. which

pool their resources and build a new, jointly-owned, clubhouse. Several exploratory meetings were held between officials of the two clubs and a steering committee formed. After a few meetings the planned Hockey Club pavilion was deferred in favour of the joint venture. Within a few months the decision was taken to form a new club to administer the 'amalgamation' of resources. So the House Committee of the 'Stick & Wicket Club',

David Franks & John Morgan

£21,500. The Hockey club ended up with four first class pitches. Celebrations of the opening continued into the Whit holiday when a cricket festival was held involving Streetly, Hendon Buccaneers, Shirley and Sutton Coldfield Cricket Clubs. The first Trustees of the Stick & Wicket were: Leslie Davis, Jonathan Franks, John Morgan and Dr Mearns Milne.

The old car entrance to the ground in Hobs Hole Lane was abandoned with the opening of the 'Stick & Wicket' with the club, in effect turning its back on what had been regarded as its 'address'. The new address was, for all of the 1970s and 1980s, stated as being 'Off High Street' but was later changed to the present title of 'The Green'. To celebrate his 50 years with the Club Billy Groves donated £50 for the planting of trees - estimated at £3 per tree. By April 1971 the trees had all been planted by Walsall Parks Dept., and Cedar Court had been levelled, seeded and limed. A 'members enclosure' in front of the pavilion was requested and Architect J. Meeson was given the go-ahead to establish this.

Membership of the 'Stick and Wicket', it was decided, would be automatic for all Cricket Club and Hockey Club members. A proportion of the membership fee being allocated to Stick & Wicket Membership. This did not, of course, apply to the under 16s!

New squash courts at Aldridge

Mr. Robin Manners put the bounce into The Stick and Wicket Club's new squash section when he poured a champagne toast for section chairman Mr. Brian Crabtree.

New nets which had been purchased were described as 'not altogether satisfactory'. The saga of 'nets' was to run for many years along with that of the score-box which seemed to be needing constant attention and maintenance. Following a donation of £30 in 1972, in memory of the late Dr. V. Milne, it was decided that a clock be purchased for the front of the Stick & Wicket. It was eventually installed in 1976 ... and they say that time waits for no man!

It was 1972 before the 3rd's were finally able to relinquish use of local factory grounds to play at home on Cedar Court for the first time. In 1973 a small changing pavilion, the former Aldridge Ex-Servicemen's Bowling Pavilion, bought at the great cost of £100, was erected just behind the clubhouse to serve the Cedar Court ground. Much work was done to make the building useable, including the provision of shutters on the windows following it suffering from serious vandalism in March 1975. In recent years this rustic edifice has been christened 'Chateau Cornick' in honour of the repair and renovation working party led by Club stalwart Brian Cornick. Following the death, in 1974 of Sir Cliff Tibbits, arrangements for the use of Cedar Court Meadow were formalised in conjunction with the Hockey Club which had been granted a long-term License for its use. The position of Groundsman, now essential, was not really stabilised until the aptly named Tony Field was appointed by the Stick & Wicket Committee in 1973. According to the committee minutes a 'considerable amount of new machinery' was purchased for his use. In addition, sight-screens were bought from the old Hilton Main Colliery ground to further upgrade the Aldridge facilities. Tony was a very able fast-medium bowler, taking the award for top figures in the 1st XI in 1975. (See picture page 50) He held the distinction... if that's what it was, of being the only cricketer playing for Aldridge who had taken more wickets than he had scored runs! Perhaps he never considered his own batting when he was preparing those excellent strips. In 1976 'home-made' frames for new outdoor nets were erected.

By 1975 the membership of the Stick & Wicket had grown to 343. The Clubhouse was being used regularly for discos, jazz nights, film shows etc. The fruit machine in particular, was making handsome profits for the Clubs. Two Squash courts were completed and in use by in May 1976 at a cost of £23,000. They were officially opened in September of that year, further adding to the facilities available, and ideal for keeping fit during the winter months. Further extensions were opened in 1977 which included an enlarged bar stockroom and an additional bar and lounge. In 1978 membership topped 500. All through the 1970s the Cricket 'Gang of four' - Ken Brown, Geoff Walker, Bill Groves and David Franks were working tirelessly for the Club.

Alan Parton took over the job as Groundsman in 1979 a position he was to hold with distinction for some 23 years until Andy Roberts took over in 2002. It was common for

Aldridge Cricket Club 1853 - 2003

Alan Parton Groundsman 1979 - 2002

Alan to work closely with nationally renowned groundsmen such as Warwickshire's Bernard Flack. Alan also spent much time assisting in the bar of the Stick and Wicket, occupying the position of Hon. Secretary during the 1990s.

On July 17th 1983, whilst a game versus Walmley was in progress, an unusual incident happened at the side of the main ground at Aldridge. In order to describe what it was, all I can say is that the newspapers reported the occurence without the expected puns such as 'Spinner takes Aldridge apart' or 'Spinner rips through the covers', 'more turn on the outfield' or other equally inventive 'cricket' headlines. Instead the headline was: 'Whirlwind stops play?'. The infamous weather conditions at the ground manifested themselves yet again with a freak mini - tornado which, in full view of players and some spectators who had only minutes before been sitting in 'harms way', picked up the wicket covers, spun them some ten feet into the air and brought them crashing down in pieces, all of this happening just short of the Rectory Wall.

The covers lie smashed after having been hurled into the air by a freak whirlwind in July 1983

The nearby sight-screen was completely unaffected by any wind at all.

The old changing room, the pavilion of the 1890s and early 1900s, ajacent to the former 'Tea Pavilion' was converted into a tractor shed in 1980. Major re-furbishment work on the scorebox also took place in 1982, including a new front and workings.

During the early 1980s it became clear that the Stick and Wicket was experiencing severe financial problems. Perhaps members of the two Clubs were taking the facilities for granted, or was it that the facilities were no longer meeting their requirements? In 1985 the decision was made to embark upon major re-furbishment at a cost of some £30,000. The roof was repaired, windows replaced with double glazing and central heating installed. A grand 'Re-opening week' took place in March 1986 which included special meetings of the Cricket Club, Hockey Club and Squash section. The new-look Stick and Wicket was a great success and much increased attendance was reported following the work.

In 1985 a new longer term lease was negotiated for Cedar Court Meadow. Although subject to a seven year rent review, it was good news for the 3rd XI to retain their 'own' lower field. Cedar Court, the home of Aldridge Hockey Club, was going to see many changes in the next decade, and by the end of the 1980s it was becoming clear that in future only an artificial 'Astro Turf' pitch would be allowed for use in all hockey matches. Both Cedar Court and the Cricket Club field had been used for Hockey over a period of nearly ninety years, so a re-evaluation of playing areas was required. Naturally, the Hockey Club was keen to get an Astro Turf Pitch laid somewhere on Cedar Court or on the 'Top Ground'. However, after proposals were put forward, starting in 1990, costs were escalating and eventually planning permission was refused. During the close season for cricket it would now be even more important to concentrate upon hiring out the grounds to local football teams.

Work on the Cricket pitches continued whilst the grounds were the subject of much discussion. The Ground committee reported in 1991 that Tony Orton had been brought in to advise Alan Parton on how to further improve the quality of the wickets. With more games being played throughout the 1980s it was clear that pitches were starting to wear out. This situation could simply not be allowed to continue since the standard of games played, now including International Matches, was improving. The advice was to extend the width of the wicket on the top ground and restrict the use. More matches would be diverted to Cedar Court. The vexed question of new nets was also raised frequently at Ground Committee meetings throughout the 1990s.

In 1994 the Groundsman was put on short time due to the

Aldridge Cricket Club 1853 - 2003

The new nets area

Andy Roberts

The old Pavilion, now the groundsman's hut, and electronic scoreboard

Hockey Club no longer using any of the fields. Over the last ten years, however, the use of the fields for football matches as well as regular cricket has provided plenty of work. The standard of grounds on offer and the quality of the cricket square has continued to rise. All over the ground, trees have been planted, hedges clipped and opened up where required in order to create a better environment. Memorial benches have been sited around the boundary and are much appreciated by spectators.

Before the bricking-up of the windows in the old pavilion, in the summer of 1973, the building had initially been used as a venue for Table-Tennis and a Friday Club for Juniors as well as a makeshift changing area for football teams. By the end of 1973 it had been turned over for exclusive use as the Groundsman's machine - shed. Somewhat optimistically, it had even been considered for conversion into a dwelling in 1976 but the idea was dropped. Incidentally, the 'famous' pavilion railings, pictured on page 32, were taken down and dumped behind the building before being officially taken away by 'Mr Dufty' in September 1973. The shed/hut became the 'plant house' after an expensive conversion in 1981 and has been the domain of new Groundsman Andy Roberts since 2002. That same year the matter of a replacement score board was finally brought to a spectacular conclusion with the installation of a state-of-the-art, electronic, remotely controlled board located in the shed's facade. The whole unit is able to be operated from on the field or from the scorer's room in the pavilion on the opposite side of the pitch. A roller shutter covers the unit when not in use. The old scorebox was demolished.

Also introduced in 2002 was a new nets area including three full-length Astroturf practice pitches with nets that retract into vandal-proof housing. 'Nets' and Scoreboard were things which for the best part of thirty years, had been deficient and inadequate but seemingly always left to another meeting. But now they were reality, thanks to much hard work, from C. C. Club, Treasurer and Stick & Wicket Chairman Jim Hartley. Finance came from Sport England and the Landfill Tax. These projects, which greatly improve the ground facilities, were brought to fruition for the Club's 150th year celebrations.

The new electronic scoreboard

Aldridge Cricket Club 1853 - 2003
Club Officials

PRESIDENT

Before 1883 details are not known but it could be presumed that Edward Tongue, as 'Lord of the Manor' occupied the position, if not actually in name.

G. G. Potter	c.1882 - c. 1885
Dr. W. H. Cooke	c.1886 - 1903
E. R. T. Croxall	1903 - 1911
F. James	1912 - 1923
E. Joberns	1924 - 1930
A. Buckley	1931 - 1959
Mrs J. Buckley	1960 - 1969
W. Groves	1970 - 1995
A. J. Franks	1996 -

HON. SECRETARY

A. C. Cooke	c1891 -
A. Buckley	c1900 - 1908
G. Hall	1909
J. Aston	1910
E. Smith	1911
G. Hall	1912
J. Matthews	1913 - 1959
J. H. Crumpton	1960 - 1962
G. Whitehouse	1963
G. T. Walker	1964 - 1977
J. C. Heming	1978 - 1980
M. D. Cooper	1981 - 1984
R. B. Biddle	1985 - 1989
A. G. Popple	1990 - 1998
K. Sharpe	1999 - 2001
R. Pickston	2002 -

CLUB CAPTAIN

A. C. Cooke	1890 - 1892
J. Dilks	1898 - 1900
E. Milner	1901
F. W. Stephens	1902 - 1906
A. Buckley	1907 - 1908
E. Smith	1909
F. W. Stephens	1910
A. Buckley	1911 - 1918
W. Stone (acting)	1919
A. Buckley	1920
H. Walton	1921 - 1922
A. Buckley	1923
H. Walton	1924 - 1939
W. Groves	1940 - 1953
J. H. Crumpton	1954 - 1955
A. D. Ballinger	1956 - 1958
M. Harraway	1959 - 1960
J. Newsome	1961 - 1962
A. Pheasant	1963 - 1964
F. C. Hastilow	1965 - 1969
A. J. Franks	1970 - 1972
G. J. Nicholls	1973 - 1975
K. D. Buller	1976
T. Pendry	1977
A. J. Franks	1978
T. Pendry	1979
A. J. Franks	1980
K. D. Buller	1981 - 1982
R. Dyer	1983
K. D. Buller	1984 - 1987
S. Peak	1988 - 1989
G. Harris	1989
D. Edge	1990 - 1991
A. Roberts	1992
S. Peak	1993
R. Dyer	1994 - 1997
W. Law	1998
R. Dyer	1999
A. Wylie	2000
M. Higgins	2001
A. Roberts	2002 - 2003
A. Wylie	2004 -

Geoff Walker

Ron Biddle

CHAIRMAN

Rev. J. S. ff. Chamberlain	c.1886 - 1893
V. H. James	1901
Rev. W. T. Newbold	1905
J. Myring	1906 - 1910
Rev. J. F. Tarleton	1911
F. Myring	1912
R. Bachelor	1913 - 1914
F. W. Stephens	1914 - 1923
T. H. Mold	1924 - 1928
T. H. Partridge	1932 - 1933
F. Myring	1934
T. H. Partridge	1935
A. Buckley	1936
T. H. Partridge	1937 - 1938
A. Buckley	1939
T. H. Partridge	1940
A. Buckley	1944 - 1945
H. Walton	1946 - 1961
W. R. E. Groves	1962 - 1969
K. Brown	1970 - 1978
G. T. Walker	1979 - 1984
A. J. Franks	1985 - 1991
R. Pickston	1992 - 1998
A. G. Popple	1999 -

HON. TREASURER

Harrison	c.1890 -1892
E. Joberns	1893 -
F. W. Stephens	1905 - 1911
J. Elkin	1912 - 1920
T. H. Mold	1921 - 1932
J. Matthews	1933 - 1959
J. Newsome	1960 - 1962
K. Brown	1963 - 1979
P. Williams	1980 - 1983
M. Clark	1984 - 1990
A. J. Walters	1991 - 1998
J. Hartley	1999 - 2002
Ms K. Lloyd	2003 -

Ken Brown

Gordon Popple

Club Presidents

Aldridge Cricket Club 1853 - 2003

1853 - c.1883 EDWARD TONGUE/CAPT. V. TONGUE-CROXALL ?

There is no definite information as to whether there was a Club President prior to 1888, and certainly there is no suggestion of who it may have been, if there was. It is likely that there was a President, and if that were the case Edward Tongue would probably have been the first choice. He owned the farmland upon which the various fields used by the club, from its earliest days c.1853, were situated. Edward married Sidney Croxall of Shustoke Warks. in 1814 changing his name to Tongue - Croxall and becoming 'Lord of the Manor of Aldridge'. He resided at the Manor House in the centre of the village, which still remains but is now occupied by the Youth Club. Edward, unlike some landowners, was certainly no stranger to the village, his grandfather Rev. Edward Tongue had been

Aldridge Manor House today

Curate of Aldridge from 1727 - 1777. He and Sidney had two children, Randall F. and Vincent R.. In 1881, Vincent Randolph Tongue - Croxall, Capt. 60th KRRC, and his brother donated gas lighting to the Church to replace the old fashioned 'dips'. The donation was a memorial to their father who died in 1879 after living all of his ninety years in the village. The younger of the two sons, Capt. Vincent Tongue - Croxall may have inherited the presidency from his father since, unlike his brother, he remained in the village following his army service. However, Capt. Tongue was to die prematurely in 1883. Capt. Tongue's brother, Randall Francis Tongue Croxall of Shustoke was Lord of the Manor in 1884 but he too was dead by 1892 leaving trustees to run the estate until Capt. Tongue's son Edward could take over.

1880s GEORGE GYBBON POTTER

It can be assumed that Mr G. G. Potter was appointed Club President sometime around 1883. The first known recorded details of him being President are in 1888. Mr Potter lived in the Moot House, then known as 'Moss House', near the church. In 1881 it was reported that, Capt Tongue 's field had been used, as it had been for years, but for the 1882 season Mr G. G. Potter's offer of a field was accepted. In 1894 it was reported that Mr G. G. Potter was a member of the firm 'Marlow, Potter & Marten.' He had for many years been in partnership with Mr Thomas Marlow who lived at Cedar Court, ajoining the cricket ground.

George Potter was born in Bridgeman Place Walsall and became a Solicitor in 1866. He was steward of the Manor of Walsall and on the death of his father, Mr Peter Potter he and his brother Frederick bacame the Walsall estate agents of the Earl of Bradford, an offfice which he subsequently held alone until the time of his death. He was also agent for the Preston-In-the Wildmoors Hospital Trustees, and for the estates of Morton Ellis Esqr. at Whitchurch. Some of the land for which he was responsible adjoined the Manor Farm. A staunch Conservative, he took very little part in public life in Walsall although he was a member of the School Board and of the Board of Guardians. He loved children and animals and was prominently connected with the Societies for the Prevention of Cruelty to Children and Animals. As an active member of the Church of England he was a frequent speaker at the church conferences in connection with the diocese of Lichfield. A great hater of shams, although not a popular man, he was much esteemed and resepected by all who knew him.

The Assembly Rooms Rookery Lane

Originally a farm building, converted in 1883 by Mr. G .G. Potter as the Anti-Botch Association meeting place. Purchased in 1922 by Messrs B. Joberns and E. Yardley for the Aldridge Women s Unionist Association, and renovated by W. Clare in 1926. Known thereafter as the AWU Assembly Rooms. Demolished in 1969.

In 1880s Aldridge, George Gybbon Potter Esq. was regarded as a minor celebrity and was very much the local philanthropist. He was founder of the 'Aldridge Anti-Botch Association' - a kind of 'do it yourself, carpentry club' which held exhibitions of members' work. A large facility in Rookery Lane was created by him in 1883, by converting the old granary, primarily for the meetings of the A.A.A., but available for the use of the Village. Many fund-raising concerts were held there for the Cricket Club the earliest being in April 1884 shortly after the building opened. Potter was involved with the Cottage Garden Society and many other local organisations. As a supporter of the Club, Potter was a good deal more effective than he was as a player. There are records of occasional games in the early 1880s in which he participated, without exactly distinguishing himself.

Aldridge Cricket Club 1853 - 2003

Surprisingly, he seems to have been a repressed 'showman'. Below the stern and serious exterior of solicitor and dour churchman of his adult connections, was a light fun-loving personality, particularly when in front of children. His entertainment speciality was providing 'Limelight Views' and performing illusions. The facility, known colloquially as the 'Anti-Botch' provided a superb location for all of his leisure interests. Mr Stan Brookhouse, the Aldridge octogenarian historian, once related to the author, that his mother, even in the 1920s, would often arrange to meet people outside the 'Anti-Botch'. Stan knew where it was, but he never knew what it meant. Eventually, the premises became known as the 'Assembly Rooms', and were widely used by the Club for Dinners, Whist Drives etc. They were demolished in 1969 to make way for the shopping centre. Mr Potter, vacated the Moot House in 1892 and died on the 4th October 1900 at his home in Netherstowe, Lichfield, aged only 58.

1890s   DR. WILLIAM HARRY COOKE MD J.P.

According to a report in the Walsall Observer, at the Annual meeting of 1893 Dr. Cooke was re-elected President, the club being grateful to him for the ground which he kindly lent, free of charge. Dr Cooke had come to Aldridge over 40 years before, from Wordsley. In 1857, he was appointed Medical Officer to the Union in the Aldridge District. He was Chairman of Directors of the Walsall Wood Colliery Co. and a large shareholder in other companies. One of the senior magistrates sitting at Rushall Police Court, he was also a staunch Conservative and Churchman, and for many years Churchwarden of Aldridge Church.

Before moving briefly to The Manor House and thence to Druids Heath, the present 'Richard House' in Stonnall Rd., Dr. Cooke resided in 'Walmer House' a large Victorian villa in Leighswood Road, now demolished. He was tenant of 'Windmill Flat' from c.1885, and by 1888 he had given his permission for it to be levelled for use as the cricket field. The Club moved-in sometime after 1882 and before 1888. Possibly as early as 1885. He employed farmer Mr Sam Bonner as his Bailiff from 1885. Mrs Cooke ran a Public Hall and Institute at Beech Tree House which was made available to the village. His sons, Joel G. Cooke & Arthur C. Cooke, both played for Aldridge C.C.

Surprisingly, Dr Cooke himself took very little active part in public life, particularly in later years when he was not well. He backed out of what few commitments he had taken on, such as dissolving his partnership with Dr Silver, and giving up various tenancies. In his last sitting on the Rushall Bench on Monday 17th February he had, in conjunction with fellow magistrates E. T. Holden & W. H. Brookes, granted an occasional licence to Thomas Wincer landlord of The Elms Inn for an extension of hours to 1.00 a.m. for a fund-raising dance in connection with the Cricket Club. He could not be accused of showing any favouritism however, the original request had been to extend the opening until 3.00 a.m.! On Feb 22nd 1902, he died in his 68th year.

c.1902 - 1911   EDWARD R. TONGUE-CROXALL

Capt. Vincent Tongue - Croxall died in 1883. By 1898, his son Edward R. Tongue - Croxall, had inherited all the Tongue and Croxall land in Aldridge and fortunately for the Club he continued in his father's generous ways. He lived for some years in the Manor House with his mother Mrs Tongue and his two sisters, but by the time Mrs Tongue died in 1914 he had moved away, first to live in Sutton Coldfield and then Shustoke. Whilst at home Edward must have spent much time watching the cricket matches but there is a record of him playing only once in 1881 as part of a 'scratch' team. The scratch team played Queen Mary's School Walsall, at Aldridge, and Edward batted number nine and was not out '0'. His main contribution to the game, which Aldridge lost, was taking a catch to dismiss one of the QM lower order batsmen. Although living away from the village 'E.R.T.C.' was keen to retain his influence in local affairs. One of his major avenues of influence was through the auspices of the Royal Antidiluvian Order of Buffaloes which included a number of Club members in its ranks. For instance, in 1898 he bought and donated, the land in Walsall Wood Road upon which the R.A.O.B. Orphanage would, eventually, be built in 1903. Mr J. Myring, RAOB Brother, the chosen builder of the Orphanage and member of the Cricket Club was with E.R.T.C. at the foundation stone-laying ceremony. The Aldridge RAOB Lodge which, like the Cricket Club, met at the Swan Inn, was officially designated the 'E. R. T. Croxall' Lodge. E.R.T.C. was President of the Orphanage by 1912, a job which may well have diverted his energies away from the Cricket Club.

1912 - 1924   FRANK JAMES DL JP

Mr Frank James was a wealthy Walsall industrialist who came to live in Aldridge in 1865. Born in November 1821, in 1845 he established a foundry in Walsall making Buckles and Saddlers Hardware, a booming business at the time. In his twenties he played cricket for Walsall and was elected Walsall Club President in 1847. He married Anne Wells Ingram and they had five children, Harry, Emily, Frederick, Arthur and George. Unfortunately, Anne died in 1858 but Frank was to marry again, at Fulham, in 1859. His second wife, Mary Emma Holland gave him another four sons who all had 'Holland' in their name; Frank Holland James, Charles Holland James, Herbert Holland James and Victor Holland James.

Frank James' career, outside of his business interests, was quite extensive. He became a prominent Conservative politician in Walsall, president in 1873. Elected as a Member of Parliament in 1892, for what became a very short career, truncated due to an embarrassing error made by one of his sons whilst campaigning on his behalf. A prominent Freemason and J.P. he had much influence in the Borough of Walsall. He was Chairman of the South

Aldridge Cricket Club 1853 - 2003

Frank James Esq.

After Frank James left the village in 1898, to live at Penkridge near Stafford, he remained in touch with the local community of which he had been such an important part. The Aldridge Cricket Club crest as worn on sweaters, caps, ties, notepaper and even the Club internet website, is a replica of his family crest. He died in 1924, 102 yrs of age.

1924 - 1931 EDWARD JOBERNS

As with all of the previous occupants of the position of Club President, Edward Joberns was involved with very much more than the Cricket Club. He was a churchwarden and local businessman. Joberns was a well known name in local brick and tile making, today still an important industry in the Aldridge area. His business, the 'Vigo Brickworks' in Walsall Wood, was very successful making tiles and pipes for local use and for worldwide export. It seems that he took pride in being one of the 'old brigade' and would always have a story to tell, some dating back to his first playing days with the Club in 1887. His business acumen made him the ideal choice for Treasurer, a position to which he was elected in 1893 and probably occupied for about ten years. Ted Joberns was the first of the line of 'former players' to occupy the highest position in the Club. Other Presidents had only ever played in a few games to make up numbers. As an ex-player Ted Joberns watched the games regularly and was not slow to

Joberns Brickworks is seen in the background, on the left, in this photograph taken in the 1920s. The Colliery on the right is Aldridge No 1 (Drybread)

Staffs Waterworks Co. from 1890 onwards and was given the Freedom of the Borough of Walsall in July 1913.

Portland House, just off Little Aston Road and just walking distance from the cricket ground, was built for him in 1865. It was substantial, brick-built and, contrary to popular myth, not constructed from Portland Stone, although some stone was quite evidently used as decoration. Frank lived in the house for 33 years during which time the house and family became very much a focus of village social life. Meetings and garden parties for local institutions were held in the grounds and because his sons were regular playing members of the Club, many post cricket soiree's took place at the house. Famously the part of Little Aston Road which runs past the house has always been known as 'Frank James' Hill.

criticise when he thought it justified to do so. He particularly disliked slack fielding, the result, he would say, of too much net practice.

Shortage of funds is a problem that seldom goes away from cricket clubs. Mr Joberns was always ready to help financially. One of the main movers in getting the original pavilion constructed in 1890, from plans he drew up himself, Ted Joberns was continuing his enthusiasm for seeing facilities improve when, in 1920, he lent the Club £100, free of interest, to assist in building the new tea pavilion. The family involvement with the Club continued with son

Aldridge Cricket Club 1853 · 2003

and grandson both becoming regular playing members. Illness and advancing years made Mr Joberns relinquish office in 1931.

1931 - 1959   ALF BUCKLEY

Alf was nurtured in Aldridge Cricket Club, it was a very important part of his life and he loved it. He was born in 1881 a few years before Aldridge were at the present ground and just as the team were starting to encourage youngsters to participate in the game. In 1893, when just 12 yrs old, this policy was to pay off. On July 1st that year the Junior Side played the team from Vicarage Walk (Walsall), and last but one man to take to the crease was a certain 'Buckley' playing what was probably his first game for Aldridge. He stated himself, at the Annual Dinner in 1933, that he had been a member for '40 yrs' so the year was certainly correct even if this wasn't his debut game. In 1896, Alf played again, this time for the 2nd Team, in games v Edward Butler & Sons, & YMCA (Home and away matches). Entering the 1st XI, on May 1st 1897 v. Pelsall Albion he made a wholly inauspicious start; he went in last and was out for a duck!

It is said, by those who played against him, that Alf was not an attractive player but he was very difficult to get out. He would stay at the wicket for what seemed an interminable time sctatching and poking the ball through gaps created by a fielding side becoming ever more weary. Alf's game frequently turned into a situation where dogged experience really triumphed. As a Factor in the Leather business in Walsall he worked for Sir Cliff Tibbits who had contact with a number of Aldridge families and was a great supporter of the Club. In the First World War he experienced the rigours of the Arctic Winters in Northern Russia, some would say a good grounding for standing for such a time in the middle of a windswept Aldridge pitch!

Alf married into a well known Aldridge family when he took Jessie Myring as his bride. The Myrings had been connected with Aldridge C.C. for many years. For several years he was President of the Conservative Club, again his involvement with that Club following on from many eminent Aldridge Cricketing men. As with countless Cricket Club members over the years Alf was also an active member of the Hockey Club and one elected to be Vice - President for a number of years. During the Second World War he served in the Special Constabulary.

The Buckley's house at Druids Heath must have been a real cauldron of ideas for Aldridge Cricket Club. Jack Matthews lodged with the Buckleys for all of his time at Aldridge, a period in excess of fifty years! In 1947, along with his wife, Alf purchased the Cricket Ground for the Club. Unfortunately, he suffered with poor health for nearly all of the final ten years of his life and this long-serving legend of Aldridge Cricket Club passed away on June 24th 1959.

1960 - 1969   MRS JESSIE BUCKLEY

The Cricket Club was where the young Jessie Myring met her husband and the Club was to be an important part of her life thereafter. She was however, a 'career' woman being involved in local politics for much of her life. She was adept at 'managing' the Teas in the pavilion a descriptive term employed knowingly by Jack Matthews. When not managing teas she was managing the affairs of Aldridge Urban District Council along with fellow councillor Howard Walton. It was actually a few months into 1960 before she formally accepted the position as the first woman President of the Club, but once in place there was no doubt as to who was in charge. For instance she refused to let the Club play games on Sundays. Needless to say this didn't stop the keen Aldridge cricketers who often did play on the Lord's day, but under another name, changed periodically just in case Mrs B. found out! In fact she was not only the President but the sole owner of the Ground with very strict views as to how it should, or should not be developed. There was no doubt however, that Mrs Buckley had the well being of the Club uppermost in her thinking about all aspects of the ground and served it well during her Presidency. She died, almost exactly ten years after her husband, on June 15th 1969.

1970 - 1995   WILLIAM GROVES

Like Alf Buckley, Bill Groves grew up inside Aldridge C.C. starting in 1919 as scorer, whilst still at school. In his working life he was employed by Walsall Electrical, becoming Foreman, a position he occupied until his 'retirement'. He became the Licensee of the Railway Inn at Pelsall for a further ten years, until 1972.

During the 1920s and 30s Bill was a successful local footballer in the Sutton & District League, having at least one trial for a Football League Club. But, second only to his family Bill had a love affair with cricket. Mainly playing in the 1st XI, he was Club Captain from 1940 - 1953 taking over from the legendary Howard Walton. He scored over 8000 runs for the Club including three centuries, quite an achievement considering this was from one game per weekend. In 1939 he achieved his best average of 52.7 also taking 61 wickets.

Between 1962 - 69 he was elected Club Chairman, becoming Club President in 1970 following the death of Mrs Buckley. His twenty-five year term of Presidency was second only to the remarkable Alf Buckley in its length. Bill was committed to Cricket and to Aldridge C.C. applying his sense of fair play, honesty and integrity to everything he did. As one of the Club Trustees, after the death of Mrs Buckley in 1970, Bill was able to negotiate the favourable purchase of the cricket ground, securing the future of the Club with its superb facilities. Bill was a proud but humble man, modest and unassuming, who will rank amongst the very greatest men of Aldridge Cricket.

1996 - A. JONATHAN FRANKS

Jonathan Franks, known affectionately as 'A. J.' is a former Club Captain, occupying that position five times between 1970 and 1980, and the post of Chairman 1985 - 1991. An elegant left-handed batsman of no mean ability and an agile fielder who was given the nickname of 'the cat'. He would sometimes come on and deliver his looping left arm spinners to display what was an all-round talent. Jonathan is most famous for being the real 'Gentleman' of the side, and that does not just mean the Public School accent! His family has been connected with the Club since the 1950s, his brother David was one of the Club's greatest wicket-taking off-spinning bowlers as well as being, along with Jonathan, a prime mover in the development of the 'Stick & Wicket'. Jonathan has always had close relations with the Hockey Club, in which his father 'Tas' played a significant role over the years. Jonathan is currently Managing Director of 'Strand Hardware' in Walsall.

Aldridge Cricket Club 1853 - 2003
Playing Statistics & Records

1905 - 1948

Highest Aldridge total
1st XI
240 for 7 v Wimblebury 1925 Home
2nd XI
No record

Lowest Aldridge total
1st XI
22 v Dunstall Park 2nd XI 1911
2nd XI
18 v Walsall Phoenix 1922

All - round performance
(300 runs plus 30 wickets in a season)
First: Cecil Lowe 1921 - 303 runs and 33 wickets
Ray Clare achieved this five times:
1932, 1934, 1935, 1945 & 1947.

Batting
First recorded century for Club
Ivor Wincer. 115 not out v Burntwood, 1911 - Away
Highest Total
Frank Myring Jnr. 148 not out v Birmingham Battery.
(Century in 62 mins.)
Highest aggregate for season
Howard Walton 1927 - 1270 (1st s & 2nd s)
Record average for season
Howard Walton 1929 - 66.2
(17 innings, 7 not out, Highest Score 110, 662 runs)
Principal Centurians
Howard Walton 6 centuries (1stXI) 1 century (2ndXI)
Cliff Myring 4 centuries (1st XI) 2 centuries (2nd XI)
Billy Groves 3 centuries (1st XI)

Wicket Keeping
Harold Ray 1st XI 5 stumpings in one innings 1944

Bowling
First to 50 wickets in a season
Arnie Bell 1919 (74)
50 wickets or more in a season
Bill Emery (3 times)
Arthur Beardmore (3 times)
Jim Holgate (3 times)
First to 75 wickets in a season
Ray Clare 1945 (82)
Most wickets in a season
Ray Clare 82 1945 1st XI
Percy Stephens 58 1925 2nd XI
Hat - Tricks
F. Baker (2) 1st XI 1926 - 1928
Percy Stephens (2) 2nd XI 1928 - 1935
4 wickets off consecutive balls
C. Taylor 1st XI 1910 v Hammerwich
Percy Stephens 2nd XI 1928 v Bournville
5 wickets off consecutive balls
J. Brown 2nd XI 1914 v Birchills 2ndXI
All 10 wickets in an innings
Dr. Victor Milne 10 for 17 1926
Ray Clare 10 for 14 1945

1949 - 1978

Highest Aldridge total
1st XI 256 for 3 v Highcroft Hall 1976 Away
2nd XI 258 for 7 v Aston Manor 1949 Home
3rd XI 231 for 3 v Studley 1976 Home

Lowest Aldridge total
1st XI 20 v Brewood 1960 Away
2nd XI 20 v Tamworth 1959 Away
3rd XI 20 v Lichfield 1971 Home

Highest Winning margin
191 (241 v 50)
v Cannock & Rugeley
1976 Home

Highest Losing margin*
167 (49 v 216)
v Y. M. F.
1911 Home
*Since 1905

All - round performance

(500 runs plus 50 wickets in a season)
Keith Buller 1975 - 537 and 72 wickets

(300 runs plus 30 wickets in a season)
Arthur Pheasant 1949 - 362 runs and 55 wickets
1953 - 332 runs and 42 wickets
1965 - 326 runs and 38 wickets

Wicket Keeping
3 Stumpings in an innings
Eddie Bird 1958 Dave Lewis 1970 Steve Key 1977
Most victims
John Milner 1st XI - 60
(51 catches and 9 stumpings)

Fielding
20 plus Catches in a season
Keith Buller 4 times -
1971 - 1972 - 1973 - 1976
Russell Pickston 3 times -
1964 - 1970 - 1971

Batting
Highest Total
Mike Pemberton 132 v Edgbaston Unity 1976
Highest aggregate for season
1st XI. Garry Nicholls 1976 - 1117
2nd XI Mike Kilgallon 1976 - 1006
3rdXI Norman Taylor 1976 - 479
Record average for season
1st XI Russell Pickston 1971 - 46.00 (1108)
2nd XI Sam Harvey 1971 - 42.9 (429)
3rd XI Norman Taylor 1976 - 47.9 (479)
Principal Centurians
Russ Pickston 4 centuries
Cliff Myring 3 centuries
Terry Clews 3 centuries

— Continued →

Aldridge Cricket Ground Facing SW c.1948

Playing Statistics & Records

Aldridge Cricket Club 1853 - 2003

1949 - 1978 Continued

Bowling
75 wickets or more in a season
Bob Shelton (3 times)
Mike Reaney (once)
Harry Crumpton (once)
Most wickets in a season
Bob Shelton 89 1971 1st XI
David Franks 90 1978 2nd XI
Mike Cooper 66 1976 3rdXI

Hat - Tricks
Arthur Pheasant (3) 1st XI 1950 - 1966 - 1973
John Fielding (2) 1974 - 1977
4 wickets off consecutive balls
George Simmons 2nd XI 1951 v Rushall 2nd XI
Best weekend performance by an Aldridge bowler
David Franks 1971 17 wickets for 33 runs

1979 - 2004

Highest Team Total
1st XI: 368 - 4 v Blossomfield 1997
2nd XI: 321 - 4 v Cannock & Rugeley 2002
3rd XI: 268 - 5 v Kidderminster 1987

Highest Opposition Total
1st XI: 354 v Highway 1990
2nd XI: 311 v Bridgnorth 2002
3rd XI: 319 v Gt Barr Unity 1989
U15: 333 v Weston Super Mare 1998

Highest Combined Total
1st XI: 554 Aldridge 306 Alvechurch 248 1991
2nd XI: 546 Aldridge 318 Alvechurch 228 1994
3rd XI: 525 Aldridge 206 Gt. Barr Unity 319 1989
U15: 558 Aldridge 225 Weston Super Mare 333 1998

Highest Score - Tied Game
1st XI: 225 Aldridge v Bronze 1993

Highest Partnership - All Teams
2nd XI 264 - 0 v Kenilworth
Andy Clews 139 n.o. Clive Lee 114 n.o.

Batting
Highest Total
John Rowley 208 n.o. v Cannock & Rugeley 2nd XI 2002
Totals over 150
1st XI Andrew Wylie 1997 - 192 n.o. v Tamworth
2nd XI Matt Higgins 1994 - 181 v Alvechurch
2nd XI Clive Lee 1988 - 180 v Five Ways
1st XI Gareth Cornick 1997 - 169 v Blossomfield
Clive Lee 1988 - 166 v Marston Green
1st XI Andrew Wylie 2002 -159 n.o. v Barlaston
2nd XI Stuart Wood 2003 - 155 v Coseley
1st XI Andrew Wylie 2003 -154 v Rugeley
1st XI Wayne Hughes 1991 - 152 v Alvechurch
1st XITerry Clews 1985 - 150 v Bridgnorth
Highest aggregate for season
Andrew Wylie 2001 - 2029
B. K. Maruthi 1993 - 2005
Record average for season
Andrew Wylie - 81.86 (1719)
Principal Centurians
Andrew Wylie 23 centuries
Wayne Law 10 centuries
Terry Clews 9 centuries
Clive Lee 8 centuries
Russell Pickston 8 centuries
Martin Pinfold 8 centuries
Most Centuries in a season
Andrew Wylie - 5
Andrew Wylie - 4 (Three times)
Martin Pinfold 4
Wayne Law - 3
Fastest Hundred
Martin Calkeld 115 in 34 balls v Hagley 1987

Wicket Keeping
Most dismissals in a season
Martin Calkeld 39. (31 catches and 8 stumpings) 1988

Best Career Figures
Andrew Wylie 1997 - 2004
263 innings, 74 not outs, 12, 941 runs. Ave 68.47.
He also took 191 wickets

Best All - Round Performance
Russell Pickston 5 - 39 and 100 n.o. v Worcester City 3rd XI 1989
Steve Peak 5 - 12 and 93 n.o. v Dudley 3rd XI 1984
Gareth Cornick 2 - 5 and 128 v ? 1st XI 1994

Bowling
Most wickets in a season
Roger Wagg 96 1982 2nd XI
75 wickets or more in a season
Andy Roberts (3 times - 1982,1990,1998 1st XI)
Keith Smith (once - 1991 1st XI)
Steve Jones (once- 1982 2nd XI)
Bob Dyer (once - 1984 1st XI)
Most Wickets in a Match
1st XI Bob Dyer 10 - 51 v Hampton-in-Arden 1984
3rd XI Andy Walters 9 - 34 v Aston Unity 1985
1st XI Bob Dyer 8 - 16 v Hampton-in-Arden 1993
3rd XI Neil Steadman 8 - 23 v Worcester City 1994
1st XI Keith Smith 8 - 26 v Bromsgrove 1991
1st XI Chris DeWit 8 - 26 v Tividale 2002
3rd XI Steve Grosvenor 8 - 34 v Knowle & Dorridge 1984
2nd XI Steve Jones 8 - 46 v Solihull Municipal 1982
Special Performances
1st XI 4 wickets in 4 balls Ross Pearsall v Springdale 1981
1st XI 8 - 3 Including hat trick Andy Roberts v Fordhouses 1980
U.15. 5 - 4 Including hat trick Matt Higgins v Pelsall 1987
Walsall K.O. 6 - 1 Phil Perchard v Pelsall 1995
1st XI 6 - 9 Ian Manwaring v Wishaw 1988
Most Career Wickets
David Franks 1956 - 1980
In 1980 he took his 1000th wicket for Club

Aldridge Cricket Ground Facing SW 2002

Aldridge Cricket Club 1853 - 2003

On Tour

'To any cricket enthusiast, whether he be player or mere "looker-on", who feels the urge for a change from the orthodox seaside or country holiday, the writer can confidently recommend linking up with a party on tour. There one gets good sporting companionship, every variety of environment and scenery, and a full measure of the game he loves.'

So began Jack Matthews' chapter ten on 'Touring' in his 1948 book 'Aldridge Cricket'. His sentiments, perhaps without giving the 'cricket enthusiast' the typical 1940s masculine bias, would seem to apply well to the various excursions undertaken by the Club over the years, often to places that Jack would not have believed possible.

The first recorded short 'tour' by the Club was that of 1882 to Llandudno for the August Bank Holiday weekend and is recorded elsewhere. To say that this was 'only' a weekend and not really a 'tour' fails to take account of the fact that in the early 1880s to mount such a venture was a major logistical project. So major, in fact was the concept of touring that the idea does not seem to have been tried again until 1937.

SCOTLAND 1937 & 1938

'Chiefly because of his association with Scottish cricket in his student days, Dr. Milne had frequently suggested his adopted club arranging a tour in the "Land of the purple heather". This ambitious proposal was thoroughly discussed at several meetings during the 1936 season, and eventually it was decided to go ahead with plans for a week's tour in the August holiday of 1937. Naturally a vast amount of spade work had to be done - invitations to players, arranging fixtures, itinerary, transport, hotel accommodation, expenses and dozens of important details that took months to settle.

Of Aldridge players, only seven were able to fit in their holiday for the specified period, and as at least fourteen would be possibly needed, other invitations were given to prominent players in the district. The coach engaged being a 26 seater, the remaining places were readily accepted by enthusiastic supporters. As all players were members of South Staffordshire clubs, it was agreed that the tourists should style themselves "Staffordshire Knots".

Several of the company were complete strangers one to another when the journey started from Aldridge, but before many miles had been traversed, all were good pals intent on three objectives - a good holiday, good fellowship and good cricket. Though naturally on a tour such as this, capable players are very desirable, this "fellowship" atmosphere is perhaps even more essential. Being in one another's company for a whole week must certainly become very trying and even utterly distasteful if any prove to be "bores" or "wet blankets". On both their tours, the "Knots" were indeed extremely fortunate in the fact that all were thoroughly good "mixers". Never was there a discordant note, except perhaps the one that echoed across the Highland glens when one of the tourists attempted a "skirl" on the bagpipes of a travelling piper.

Starting very early on the Sunday morning, good progress was made; breakfast at Doncaster, then along the great North Road to Darlington for lunch; through Berwick and on to the old seaside town of Dunbar by evening - a very long day's run. A really comfortable hotel satisfied our every need till morning, when we made a short but interesting tour of this quaint and historic Scottish town, after which we moved on to Duns where we played our first match on the really beautiful ground of the Manderston Club. Batting first, we were able to declare with our score at 210 for 4, Jack Haigh of the Y.M.F. Club scoring freely for 103 not out. On taking the field, we discovered that the Scottish custom was for the fielding side to provide its own ball, something quite new to us, but a rule that certainly has much to commend it. Some good bowling and fielding got 8 of the home team wickets down for 80 before stumps were drawn - quite a good start.

Spending the night and till noon next day in Edinburgh, we were able to view many of the wonderful sights of this fine city, including the famous Castle with the

1937. Staffordshire Knots' Scotch Tour (v. Aberdeenshire).

A. Buckley, J. Langford, W. Sidwell, A. Hilditch, S. C. Robson, E. Mortiboy, F. Tibbitts, J. Beards, R. H. White, B. W. Emery, T. Ridgeway, A. Beattie, J. Matthews, A. R. Wootton, F. N. Bower, R. Clare, N. Smets, W. Groves, H. Walton, Dr. Milne, J. Wootton, W. Wootton, H. Crumpton, J. Haigh, H. Ray.

The tourists are 'entertained' in Aberdeen 1937. Some are wearing their 'Staffordshire Knots' badges
A. Beattie,   ? ,   H. Walton,   A. Buckley,   F. N. Bower,   Dr. V. Milne   W. Groves

magnificent Scottish War Shrine crowning its summit - surely one of the most impressive memorials in the world.

Montrose was our next resting place and from here we were due to start next morning for Aberdeen, where our match with the County XI was to take place. Before the game, the County Club entertained the tourists most hospitably to a fine luncheon - gesture highly appreciated by all.

The County had quite a strong side out, including the West Indian professional, Alma Hunt, and Christie, a South African player. Batting first, however, they fared badly against the "Knots" attack, Harry Crumpton taking 6 wickets with his "fast stuff", while Jack Haigh and Bill Emery puzzled most of the batsmen with their cunning "spinners". Smart catches by Bill Wootton at short leg accounted for five batsmen, including Hunt - out for a "duck". The small total of 93 was rather a shock, as the County had been going "great guns" in their previous matches. When the visitors' turn came, they also found they were up against some "hot stuff" from both Hunt and Christie, but the score had crept up to 71 for 5 when the threatening clouds broke, and rain put the closure on a game that would in all probability have had a very exciting finish.

The next day found us at Huntly, where everybody talks and lives cricket. To stengthen the home side, Hunt, the County pro. had accepted a very pressing invitation, and this time he was more fortunate than at Aberdeen and quickly knocked up a vigorous 60 towards a total of 148. The "Knots" replied with 140 for 9 - another very closely drawn game.

Friday was free from cricket, so in the morning, the opportunity was taken to have a good look round Aberdeen itself. One of the chief attractions is the fish market - a truly marvellous sight. Picture an immense stone quay, acres in extent. Here the fish, after first being sorted into their various species and then graded, are laid out in regular rows waiting to be auctioned. Without actually seeing them, one can hardly conceive what fearful and wonderful creatures are brought out of the sea. Some of the more repulsive looking kinds never appear to reach our fish shops.

In the afternoon a long interesting tour of the lovely Dee Valley was made, amongst other fine places visited being Balmoral and Aboyne. At this latter place full advantage was taken of the finely kept bowling green, some of the older members of the party getting their chance to prove that skill is required in this game, as well as in cricket.

Early on Saturday we set off for Montrose again, where we were to fulfil our last fixture. This game also ended in a draw and here the "Knots" certainly had the worst of things, mustering only 75 for 8 against the home team's score of 140. Stumps had to be drawn rather early, as the tourists were due to spend the last night in Perth, ready for the long return journey the next day. We embarked on this last stage very early, and by afternoon had crossed the border at Gretna Green, and following the west route through the lovely English Lake District, reached home late on the Sunday night.

Everywhere we toured in Scotland, we were received with real Scotch hospitality and this, together with the charming and magnificent scenery made the trip one never to be forgotten. All agreed that the tour was a huge success and unanimously voted for a futher venture in the following year.

For the 1938 Tour, the outward journey was made by the West route, and, as the first match was fixed for the August Monday, at Aberdeen, it was decided to start on the Saturday and travel to the Lakes on the first day.

Several changes in personnel were necessary as some who made the first trip found, much to their regret, that business and home ties prevented them accepting the second invitation.

Good headway was made, until after passing Preston, we ran into a prolonged and violent storm. The flooded roads caused a couple of hours' delay - the only occasion on either of the tours that we failed to keep to the scheduled time. Next morning at Keswick the swollen Lake Derwentwater and the inundated countryside gave striking evidence of the torrential rainfall. The day turned out bright however and good progress was made

Aldridge Cricket Club 1853 · 2003

The opposition. Aberdeenshire's professional opening pair, Alma Hunt (West Indies) and Christie (South Africa) walk out to face Harry Crumpton & Jack Haigh. 1937 'Knots' Tour.

and then on to meet the strong Carlton Club. Without Jack Haigh and also Dr Milne, who had stayed behind in his native city, we made a rather feeble show against a team generally considered to be one of the best in that part of Scotland.

All next day was spent on the long homeward journey across the Cheviots and along the Great North Road, and then on through the Midlands, reaching Aldridge late on the Sunday night. Although many invitations were received for further visits, nothing of course has been possible since 1939. Many however are trusting that another tour can be arranged when conditions return more to normal again.

Much of the success of both tours was only made possible by the help and co-operation given by the Coach proprietors and by thier most proficient drivers; by the assistance given by Secretaries and other Officials of Scottish Clubs regarding fixtures and hotels, and most of all by the fine spirit of good fellowship that was shown by all from start to finish.'

Perhaps conditions did not completely return to 'normal' for a further 34 years, for it was not until 1973 that Aldridge again went 'On Tour'.

CORFU 1973

The beautiful Greek Island of Corfu was the destination for the Club Tour of 1973. After touching down in the Dan Air 'Comet 4', (Well the whole excursion did only cost £49.00 all-in) everyone headed for the accommodation at the newly built Messongi Beach Hotel. One pitch, the only one on the island - right in the middle of town, was the exotic venue for three games on the week long excursion. A grass pitch, well almost... surrounded by trees, it was a very pleasant location, particularly after the cars had been moved off the edge before the start of the game. The main civic buildings surrounded the ground, as did the main roads. The sun shone, of course, and the two local teams, which date back to the time when British troops were stationed there, turned out to perform on the interesting surface of a coconut matting covered - concrete wicket.

On Saturday 5th May v. the 'Byron' Club Aldridge blossomed in the sunshine by scoring 139 with the big-hitting Mike Pemberton knocking up an impressive 70 of them. Byron were all dismissed for a poetic 84 with David Franks getting 4 for15. Mike Pemberton thrilled the locals by literally smashing the ball through an ornate lantern light outside of the local cafe to the shouts of 'Pembleton!'... they never did get the name right. On the Sunday it was the turn of 'Gymasticos' to suffer under the bat of 'Pembleton' as he lashed out for 53 of Aldridge's

through the Lowland Country and by evening we once more came in sight of the "Granite City". Next day found us at Mannofield eager for another trial of strength against the County XI. Batting first, the home team were soon in trouble against the bowling of Dr Milne and Jack Haigh. The professional, Hunt, was brilliantly caught by Bob White on the fine leg boundary, after making 13 and the whole side was out for 82.

This low score however proved too much for the "Knots", who failed badly against Hunt's bowling, his 4 for 17 being mainly responsible for the tourists being dismissed for 69. This was a very disappointing start, but better things were hoped for ihn the next game at Forres. This is a delightful little place on the Moray Firth, the furthest north we touched. Unfortunately, several of the Forres team could not manage an early start, and consequently this game ended in a rather tame draw. Reaching Huntly by nightfall, we renewed acquaintance with many of our last year's opponents who had made great preparations for our visit, and for the match on the morrow. Here we had a grand victory, Bob White and Jack Haigh being in grand form with the bat. Unfortunately for him and the team, Jack severely strained his knee during the game, this putting him out of action for the remainder of the tour. Huntly gave us a grand time and we spent a most convivial evening amongst as jovial a crowd of cricket enthusiasts as one could ever wish to meet.

Friday was spent on a long sight-seeing tour of the Highlands, our journey taking us through some of Scotland's most charming and majestic scenery by way of Killiecrankie and Stirling,

100. The island team were all out for 90 with Laurie Butcher taking 4 for 19 and David Franks putting in another excellent performance with 3 for 28. Being in the town centre, the ball frequently found its way on to the main road where on one occasion Bob Riggs, dressed in full flannels of course, found himself chasing it between

Corfu - May 1973

Standing: Colin Brookes (Streetly-Guest umpire), Frank Hastilow, John Burton, David Franks, Mark Biddle, Mike Pemberton, John White, Laurie Butcher (Hendon-Guest player).
Kneeling: Bob Riggs, Keith Buller, Neil Castley, Geoff Walker, Phil Eve

the moving cars, much to the amazement of more conventional tourists, until it eventually lodged under a parked vehicle. The Daily Express Team were also on the island and Monday found Aldridge playing their third tour match against a side which should have been captained by the paper's main cricket writer, Dennis Compton, but unfortunately he was unwell on the day and unable to play. The result, which was not the most significant aspect of the match, was a narrow defeat for Aldridge.

It is a fact of life encoutered with all such tours that all the First XI are rarely available for a week, especially one which is outside of the normal holiday time, and so it was in May 1973. For the Tour, Aldridge were joined by guests Colin Brookes from Streetly who acted as umpire and Laurie Butcher from Hendon Buccaneers. The rest of the team were drawn from all of the Aldridge teams. Geoff Walker accompanied the team as non-playing 'Manager' and of course the ladies came along and enjoyed the

Bob and the Comet

swimming and shopping. Phil Eve, part of the team on this tour is notable for having a famous actor for a brother ... Trevor Eve of 'Shoestring' fame.

Tours are of course primarily social events and with only three days of the week taken up with cricket, there was plenty of time for eating at Mikos, a boat trip to Cavos, with its one Taverna, and lounging around the hotel's excellent facilities.

DEVON 1977-8 1980-1

Britain's own 'exotic' South Devon was the chosen location for four tours. Firstly, in mid June 1977 and then the corresponding week in 1978. After a break in 1979 the tours were resumed in the second week of May 1980 and 1981. All four tours were arranged midweek in order to keep the weekends free for league and cup matches. Naturally the usual problems of availabilty occured but over the four years some 35 players were involved. The fixtures for the first two were Monday: Chelston, Tuesday: Budleigh Salterton, Wednesday: Cullompton, Thursday: Heathcoats (Tiverton) and Friday: Exeter University 2nd XI. In 1980 and 1981 the tours started on Tuesday at Budleigh, continuing as before but finishing with a fixture versus Weston-Super-Mare. In 1979 the Tiverton, Heathcoates side came up to Aldridge.

Primarily social occasions, there are many Devon Tour stories which, as the reader will no doubt be aware, cannot be put into print. However, the consumption of large quantities of alcohol and the inevitable repercussions thereof feature prominently. The holiday atmosphere when with a crowd of mates, encourages cricketers to do things they would not dream of back at home.

Aldridge Cricket Club 1853 - 2003

Above: Scenes from Heathcoats (Tiverton) Devon Tour

In October 1987, the team played three games against the local 'Ex-Pats' Ibiza Cricket Club and won all three. As usual the Aldridge team was augmented by guests from other local teams, on this occasion Mick Tranter from 'Old Wulfs.', and Brian Hodder and Jim Carr from the old Birmingham Municipal Club. The games were played at the delightful sounding 'Es Cana Oval' which, as can be clearly seen from the photograph, was not particularly attractive from a practical cricketing point of view since it almost completely lacked that green component so common on English grounds…grass! The matting wicket was laid on a bright rusty red field of shale which incorporated more than a few rather large pieces of rock, making the ball move in an interesting, sometimes 'lethal' fashion after making contact. Keith Buller reckons that he never managed to get the red stain off his boots.

A certain member will certainly recall lathering up for his shave one morning when suddenly… only half dressed, he walked out of the hotel, down the street into Boots and in front of gobsmacked locals was heard to ask politely … 'Do you sell razor blades?' For some it was not always easy to concentrate upon the game with a 'night before' feeling. Even a 'few' in the bar before the game would cause a bit of a blur in proceedings. According to Bob Dyer at one match versus Cullompton he experienced a blur which was in fact real. The ground was sited in a natural bowl and the sea-mist rolled in, and from where he was fielding it was impossible to see the wicket! … That's his story anyway.

Private cars were used for transport around the various locations in Devon which meant that sometimes the scenic route was taken, but it was not always the one required. Trevor Harvey managed to aquire his title 'B Road' by navigating in this tortuous manner.

As with previous tours the cricket was just a part of a great social occasion for the nineteen Tour members on this popular Mediterranean Island. Football matches were played, as well as cricket and large quantities of sun, sea, and sangria were enjoyed by all.

IBIZA 1987

Standing: **Mike Tranter, Brian 'Bilko' Hodder, Bob Kendall, Tony Clews, Neil Castley, Martin Pinfold, Terry Clews**
Kneeling: **Russell Pickston, Keith Buller, Garry Harris, Ross Pearsall**

Benefit Games

Ron Headley Benefit

Watched by Rachael Heyhoe and other players, Jonathan Franks welcomes Ron Headley to Aldridge

Thursday September 21st 1972 saw Aldridge host its first Benefit Game for a local County player, games which are now almost a regular event every few years. The player concerned, Worcestershire's 'Mr Nice Guy' Ron Headley, selected a team to join him from the following: P. Stimpson, K. Wilkinson, J. Yardley, G. Wilcock, P. Shutt, D. Stewart, I. Khan, A. Kallicharran, P. Pridgeon, Parker, B. D'Oliviera, A. Ormrod & K. Griffiths. On this occasion the home team was a strong 'Aldridge President's XI' comprising: A. J. Franks, G. Nicholls, R. E. Shelton, R. Pickston (all Aldridge), J. McDowell (Warwicks and Sutton), K. Stride (Burton and Staffs), C. Marks (Longton & Staffs), J. Kench (Streetly, P. Bilton (Aston Manor), N. McVicker (Warwicks) and another player.

In a hard fought game affected in the latter stages by appalling light conditions, Aldridge President's XI were defeated by only 12 runs. Headley stated after the match that he was 'absolutely delighted' with the work that had gone on behind the scenes by Aldridge members.

Quite a few people turned out to see the game and support the Club in this new venture, justifying the work which had gone into the preparation and encouraging the Club to host similar events in the future.

Headley opened the innings with David Stewart and they soon got to grips with the bowling and kept the scorers busy. Headley was in magnificent form hitting shots all round the ground even against bowlers such as Warwickshire's Norman McVicer. He reached his 50 with a six at the end of the ninth over, receiving only 45 balls. However, going for another big hit he was out for 71 runs ending a terrific 45 min spell which many will easily remember. Aldridge's Bob Shelton took the wicket breaking the opening stand of 104. Wickets fell quickly as runs became the priority, McVicker doing the damage, notably by taking three in the last over. At the close, Ron Headley's XI had scored 135 for five.

As promised there were 'celebrities' manning the public address system, John Osborne the former Albion Goalkeeper and Jim Cumbes of Aston Villa, who soon announced that Aldridge required nine runs per over to win. Aldridge made an excellent attempt to keep up with the rate, always looking for quick singles and despatch the loose delivery, but found the target too difficult in such poor light. Rachael Heyhoe, the England Ladies Captain, drafted into Ron Headley's side, collected a four wicket haul being on a hat trick at one stage. John Kench of Streetly hammered a quick fire 36 but this was not enough to turn the game.

David Brown Benefit
AUG. 30th 1973

An amazing 318 runs in 50 overs made the spectacle of a David Brown XI v an Aldridge President's side both exiting and enthralling. Besides Walsall born Brown, the visiting side was made up from the likes of Dennis Amiss, Bob Willis and John Jameson, none of them strangers to the Aldridge turf. Amiss was at the crease for just 43 minutes for his 64 runs, scoring 50 in 40 minutes. Jameson, not

David Brown XI & Aldridge President's XI

to be outdone, shot his 50 in a mere 31 minutes going on to score 66. It was Aldridge bowler Bob Shelton who made the break-through, taking the wicket of Amiss with Colin Price of Aston Unity putting his mark on the game by shattering Jameson's stumps. Aldridge, faced with having to knock 200 for victory, were not taking things lying down as Price figured once more by knocking exactly 50 in just 36 minutes before being caught by Jones off the bowling of Amiss. However, Brown, McVicker, Hemmings and Amiss cut through the opposition in a ruthless manner, limiting the President's XI to 119 all out.

Aldridge Cricket Club 1853 - 2003

John Jameson's Benefit 1974

Aldridge President Bill Groves welcomes John Jameson

Warwickshire and former England opening batsman, John Jameson featured stongly in his own benefit match, played at Aldridge on Thursday 15th August, by scoring a whirlwind 103. The County side, as expected delighted the spectators by overwhelming Aldridge in the 30 overs match.

The visitors batted first making 237 - 4, besides Jameson's typically cavalier century Eddie Hemmings hit a masterly 101 not out. Warwickshire didn't get it all their way however being 28 - 2 at one stage after two of the current England test players, Bob Willis and Dennis Amiss were dismissed. Willis in fact made only four and Amiss twelve, their wickets being taken by Mark Biddle who finished with fantastic figures of 2 - 15. Jameson himself was eventually bowled by Les Pullen who had obviously not had pork pies for tea that night! (He was well known for saying *'Never run on a misfield and don't eat pork pies for tea.'*) It was Jameson and Hemmings who really took the Aldridge bowling attack apart hammering 171 in a wonderful third wicket partnership which was destined to take the game beyond what Aldridge could match in the time available.

Against top class bowling, Aldridge in reply could only make 119 - 6 in the alloted overs with Terry Clews 34 , Gary Nicholls 21 and Terry Pendry 21 getting the bulk of the runs. Amiss took 2 - 11 and the former England paceman David Brown 1 - 11.

Over £100 was raised, regarded as a great success. Just for information and perhaps to put the amount into context, admission to the ground was 20p and to park their cars on the ground spectators had to pay an extra 10p.

John Jameson's Benefit, 1974 (RESTRICTED OVERS MATCH)

At Aldridge Cricket Ground (Off High Street) on
THURSDAY, 15th AUGUST, 1974, WICKETS PITCHED 4-30 p.m.

A WARWICKSHIRE X1   from
- J. A. JAMESON   (Warks. & England)   ....
- D. AMISS   (Warks. & England)   ....
- D. BROWN (Warks. & England)   ....
- R. WILLIS (Warks. & England)   ....
- A. KALLICHARAN (Warks. & W. Indies)   ....
- D. MURRAY (Warks. & W. Indies)   ....
- A. C. SMITH   (Warks.)   ....
- W. BLENKIRON (Warks.)   ....
- W. A. BOURNE (Warks.)   ....
- E. HEMMINGS (Warks.)   ....
- S. ROUSE (Warks.)   ....
- N. ABBERLEY   (Warks.)   ....
- B. LANKASTER (B.B.C.)   ....
- J. ROSENTHALL (B.B.C.)   ....

Extras   ....
Total   _____

Umpires: R. B. BIDDLE, G. POPPLE
Scorers: A. NICHOLLS, Mrs. L. PENDRY

AN ALDRIDGE X1
- G. NICHOLLS   ....
- T. CLEWS   ....
- R. PICKSTON   ....
- T. PENDRY   ....
- A. J. FRANKS   ....
- L. PULLEN   ....
- J. FIELDING   ....
- M. REANEY   ....
- K. BULLER   ....
- M. BIDDLE   ....
- P. WILLIAMS   ....

Extras   ....
Total   _____

Refreshments Available   Members Licensed Bar
Admission by Score Card 20p.   (*Children* 10p)
Raffle/Autographed Bat to be Won
Cars Parked on Ground—10p.
All Vehicles and Property Parked or Left entirely at Owner's Risk

Dermot Reeve Benefit Game

Aldridge Cricket Club 1853 - 2003

May 5th 1996

A WARWICKSHIRE XI v ALDRIDGE 1st XI

"... such an overwhelming success"

Billed as the 'Curtain Raiser to the Aldridge Stick & Wicket Club Silver Jubilee Celebrations' over five hundred people turned out to witness an exiting game.

In 1996, Aldridge C.C. were proud to stage a benefit match for the then Warwickshire Captain, Dermot Reeve, who was having his testimonial year. Sunday May 5th turned out to be the only fine day in terms of weather during the whole of that May Day Bank Holiday weekend.

Needless to say, there was eager anticipation from Aldridge. This First XI, only three years before had been in Division Three, but were now up into Division One with a strong team including two high profile former Walsall players, paceman Andy Bryan and one-time Northants batsman Mark Gouldstone. Captained by high class spinner Bob Dyer (Formerly with Staffordshire) & with experienced opening bowler Bob Cattell. Wayne Law, had been the leading non-professional batsman in Division One in 1995.

Shaun Pollock

All-rounder Asif Din and South African Whizz-kid Shaun Pollock were among the XI brought by England International Dermot Reeve. An opening stand of 98 by Mike Burns & Tony Frost paved the way for both Pollock & Reeve to play their shots, but both departed the crease after scoring just 12. Late hitting by Mohammad Shiek (35) and Michael Edmunds (43) took the final Warwickshire total up to 235 for 8 off their allotted 35 overs. Making up for their disappointing batting performances Reeve & Pollock came out to bowl with all guns blazing, and within a few overs Aldridge were reduced to 34 for 7. A late recovery, led by a splendid 44 from Bob Dyer, took the reply to a respectable 149 for 9. It was a comfortable win however, for the Warwickshire side.

Dermot Reeve was no stranger to Aldridge cricket; back in 1982, as part of a Hong Kong side in the ICC Competition, he had played against Aldridge in a warm up for the main event.

Shaun Pollock 'fires' down a quick one.

Aldridge Cricket Club 1853 - 2003

The twenty five sponsors who had helped make the event possible were thanked, the Chairman remarking that:

"The Club has benefited considerably from the day both financially and in the awareness it has promoted throughout the local area."

Sorrows were drowned and victory celebrated with equal enthusiasm after the match in the bar of the Stick & Wicket. Dermot remained at the centre of things, providing more entertainment, this time off the field, when he serenaded all present with his guitar and his brilliant renditions and impersonations of famous cricketing 'greats' such as messrs. Boycott, Benaud, Imran Khan and the like.

Cheque presentation (£2,500) to Dermot Reeve by Club Chairman Russell Pickston

Whilst causing some anxiety for Club Chairman Russ Pickston during the previous weeks, including having to pay out £2000 to insure against bad weather, and the seemingly inconsequential fact that Aldridge lost the match, the day had been an overwhelming success.

Later in the year Dermot was back as Principal Guest at a Sportsman's Dinner arranged by the Club.

Aldridge Cricket Club
Present a
SPORTSMAN'S DINNER
Featuring
DERMOT REEVE
at
McKECHNIE'S BALLROOM
Middlemore Lane, Aldridge
on
FRIDAY, OCTOBER 11th, 1996
7.30 p.m. for 8.00 p.m.
TICKETS: £25.00

The Captains decide and confer

Aldridge Trustee Frank Hastilow presenting the match ball to the umpires, Gordon Popple and Colin Massey

A magic moment as Dermot & Shaun line up with Aldridge Youth Members Ollie Quiney (L) & Joel Edge (R)

Aldridge Cricket Club 1853 - 2003

Nick Knight Benefit Game
May 16th 2004

Warwickshire XI : 266 - 7   **Aldridge XI : 227 - 9**

Warkwickshire won by 39 runs

An exciting first match in the Nick Knight Benefit year programme brought a star-filled Warwickshire International XI to The Green. In the glorious sunshine which must have reminded him of home, South African Dewald Pretorious knocked a rapid 78. Aldridge stalwarts Neil Steadman and Howard Shippey showed their mettle with the ball but Chris De Wit took 3 - 69 as well as taking the all important catch to dismiss Nick Knight who had ambled gracefully to his half - century. Ian Bell (38) and Jonathan Trott (36) figured in Warwick's entertaining innings. Jay Bradburn stopped Aldridge's decline with a fine 51 whilst Andy Wylie performed his usual magic with a cracking 39 including putting one on to the pavilion roof. Young Inderdeep Singh added 31 toward the home team's creditable total.

Warwickshire

Nick Knight (Capt)
Dougie Brown
Tony Frost (W/K)
Ian Bell
Neil Carter
Jonathan Trott
Dewald Pretorious
Ian Westwood
Ian Clifford
Trevor Penney
Graham Wagg

Aldridge

Andy Wylie (Capt)
John Rowley
Jay Bradburn
Andy Bowers
Ali Lawrie (W/K)
Ross Shelton
Chris De Wit
Howard Shippey
Neil Steadman
Alan Walters
Josh Prior
David Banks
Inderdeep Singh
James Whittock

Aldridge Cricket Club 1853 - 2003

The Davies Family

Those observing the landscape of Aldridge in the late 19th century witnessed a great change in the nature of the village and its surroundings. Two distinct areas were emerging, the picturesque sleepy rural idyl unchanged for centuries, and a vibrant heavy industrial landscape grossly polluted by noise, smoke and dust. Whilst the Cricket Club was, and still is, very much in the rural part of the village, surrounded by trees and fields, many of its members worked in the collieries, brickworks and other factories. It was this rise of industry which led to a rapid expansion of Aldridge attracting many hundreds of workers from all over the country. One thing which united the two parts of the village at this time was a love of cricket.

Around 1881, Jim Davies, a young man in his early 20s living in Pear Tree Cottage, Sandbach Cheshire, attracted by the thought of a relativley well paid job in the expanding South Staffordshire village of Aldridge packed his bags and travelled south. The attraction was the newly opened Leighswood Colliery. He soon managed to obtain a job which eventually put him in charge of the Slack - Washer, an important part of the pithead works. Like many young men of his day he was a keen cricketer and was soon enrolling as a playing member of Aldridge C.C.

Jim was soon playing regular cricket, certainly by 1883, with fellow members of his team with such family names as Myring, Crumpton, Whitehouse, James, Lote, Hastilow, Hopley, Sales, Cook, Millington and Simmons; names which turn up frequently in the annals of the Club and the village. He was playing against teams such as Walsall 2nd XI, Walsall Locomotive, Wednesfield, Aston Lower Grounds, Sutton Coldfield, Erdington, Little Aston, Gt. Barr, and Chasetown. Well over 80 yrs old, he was still around when Jack Matthews wrote his book 'Aldridge Cricket' in 1948. Jack new him quite well and reports him as saying that he witnessed the laying of the present pitch, this would have been during his first few years at the Club, around 1884. When he died, in October 1957, Jim was the Club's oldest member.

Living in a bungalow in Whetstone Lane, next to the railway Jim had four sons, John T, Ralph, Jim and Sam. The boys grew up in Aldridge and like dad enjoyed a game of cricket. By 1911 at least three of them, Jack (John) T, Ralph and Sam were all part of Aldridge C. C. However, it was to be events far outside the village of Aldridge which would shape the family for years to come. The Davies family was destined to be torn apart by the tragic events on the grisly battlefields of the Great War hundreds of miles away.

The eldest boy Jack ('J. T.'), tall like his father, had enjoyed some success as a batsman in the 2nd XI and was a keen cyclist. Like many of his generation he responded to the

Jim Davies (Senior) batting for Aldridge c.1890

call to fight for King and Country. However, he was wounded in action at Le Sars and returned from the conflict with only one leg. No more would Jack go cycling around the leafy lanes of Aldridge. Showing stubborn determination typical of the family, no doubt born of necessity, like his father he got himself a job at Leighswood Colliery working as a blacksmith. He had two sons, Ron and Leonard. Until 1926 he lived in Walsall before returning to Aldridge and renewing his association with the Club in the important role of Umpire. Working as Caretaker at Cooper and Jordan School from around 1930 and living in School Cottages, he was conveniently close to the ground as well as the school, as those such as Jim Bevan who would follow in his footsteps years in the future would testify. A popular figure at the Club, in May 1937 he was elected to the position of 'Pavilion Manager' and was the recipient of a Testimonial Match in 1948. Jack continued with his umpiring until March 1949 when he officially retired, being presented with a clock, still in the posession of his son Ron. After 1949 J. T. continued to be a familiar sight at matches recording the games as official scorer.

Ralph, the second son, shortest and it could be said luckiest of the four brothers, batted in the 2nd XI from 1911, survived his time in the Great War and took up with the team when it re-started after the conflict in 1919. He continued playing until 1922.

Jim junior had five boys of his own, Tommy, Jack, Reg, Jim and Ralph (Jim & Ralph being twins). He had much to return home for but Sadly, Jim did not return from his expedition to France. On the 18th November 1916 like thousands of others he died in the bloody massacre that was the Somme battlefield leaving the five lads to grow up without their dad.

Ralph and Jack 'J.T.' Davies ouside the new Eagle Scoreboard sometime around 1958

Sam Davies in 1912

Keith 'Beef' Davies in 1970

Sam, the youngest of the brothers, was a good all - round cricketer who played for the 1st and 2nd XI's between 1911 and 1914. He was, by all accounts also a very good soldier, a Sergeant marksman who had excelled at the famous Bisley firing range. His shooting skills however, put him right in the front line where he too was killed in action on 11th March 1917.

Of the four Davies boys only two had returned from the war and one had lost a leg. They were typical of a whole generation who as fit young men went willingly to fight for their country but either failed to return or came back physically or mentally disabled.

The next generation of the Davies family were not as fully involved with the Club as their parents had been. Of Jack's two sons, Leonard and Ron, only Ron played in a team, mainly in the 2nd XI as an all-rounder between 1933 and 1938. Jim's five sons didn't play either, but Ralph (Jnr), one of the twins did help Jim Bevan as Assistant Groundsman in 1958.

Ralph's son, Keith, was a regular all-rounder in both the 1st and 2nd XI's from the 1950s right through into the 1980s. Keith, a well-built left handed bat has always been known as 'Beef' Davies to distinguish him from another regular team member also called 'Keith Davies', (no relation), referred to as 'Ticker' Davies. Keith on one famous occasion, in a game versus Knowle & Dorridge, went for a 'skyer' and clashed with the one person you would not wish to run into...Mike Pemberton. The result was quite interesting, a bit like the irresistible force meeting the immovable object. Keith carried on fielding but suffered concussion whilst Mike left the field in agony!

The story of the Davies family's involvement with Aldridge C.C. is far from being unique. It is perhaps typical of many whose lives have been inextricably tied up with the Club through the generations, as they participated in a friendly sporting recreation which provided, and still provides, a counter-balance to what can be a harsh and unfriendly everyday world.

Aldridge Cricket Club 1853 - 2003 'Colts' & Juniors

Aldridge cricket Club has always encouraged its young cricketers - the players of the future. Even back in the 19th century young players such as Alf Buckley were given the chance to play in a 'Junior Team'. Quite often however, there was no formal team put out. Sometimes for the young aspirant players it was a matter of turning up at a game and waiting to see whether or not everyone in the team was present. Occasionally, there was an unforseen absence and one of the lucky 'young uns' was given a game. Arthur Pheasant, Frank Hastilow and Sam Harvey can all remember waiting hopefully in this way, to get on the pitch. Encouraged by Jack Matthews to attend each week, and it was difficult to avoid him at school or at the youth club, it was sometimes possible to get a session in the nets with a regular player. Another method of gaining access was to be 'Scorer'- you got to know the players, were there for the games and hopefully occupied any spare time with bat and ball. Many quite well known Aldridge players over the years have trodden this path to success, from Charlie Holland to John Burton. The problem was that the whole thing was so informal, lacking any kind of structure, progressive training or development.

From the mid 19th century it was the schools that really provided a structured approach to teaching the game with regular coaching and matches being arranged. Some quite small Aldridge Schools managed to field sides but they were no match for the likes of Queen Mary's Grammar in Walsall which would regularly take on some of the Club sides, including Aldridge. Connections between Aldridge C.C. and the Boys School were very good since its Headmaster and staff were often regular playing members of the Club, in the early years notably, Sam Cashmore, Frank Stephens, and of course Jack Matthews. The school certainly had its own playing field and perhaps even its own cricket pitch in those days. Junior equipment was obtainable from shops in Walsall if you had the cash available, many youngsters did not.

Starting after the 2nd World War and with the population of Aldridge expanding during the 1950s and 60s, Juniors were given one night per week for a practice session under the guidance of a senior player. This was an opportunity for boys, and only boys in those days of course, to have a chance to be taught the skills required from the experienced cricketers. They would be allowed to borrow and use real cricket equipment, regarded as a priviledge for few could afford to buy it themselves ... Arthur Pheasant recalls Jack Matthews letting him use a set of Junior 'Club' pads which he eventually used for most of his playing career and was still wearing for a veterans match more than 50 yrs later!

The exploits of the almost legendary junior team of 1962 which took on all the works teams of Aldridge in the knockout competition and won, are described elsewhere. Consequently, it was now clearer than ever that Junior cricket must be encouraged.

After April 1966 the Juniors became known as 'Colts', at their own request it seems. In 1971, for the first time the fixtures and membership card had 'Senior Player in Charge of Colts A. W. Pheasant'. The structure which had been lacking when Arthur was a lad was now starting to appear and it was Arthur who had the responsibility. Naturally enough, because just as he had looked up to the experienced players of his youth, such as Howard Walton, Victor Milne, Ray Clare and the like, the youngsters of the early seventies were able to follow Arthur's lead. Later the coaching staff was increased to include Steve Randall and Bob Riggs, Tony Warwood, Keith Davies, Phil Butler and of course Don White. In 1975 with the arrival of R. W. O. 'Don' White, an extra coaching night was introduced for 'selected Colts' and the first Colts Fixtures appeared in the printed card with games against Rugeley, Bloxwich and Wednesbury. By the end of the 1970s Gordon Popple, Terry Pendry and John Heming were also involved as the 'Coaching and Youth Committee'.

Colts 1975 v Wednesbury

Standing
**Gordon Popple   Arthur Pheasant   Mark Foden   Andy Cashmore   Clive Dancey
P. Evans   Tim Joiner   Ian Stanley   Don White.**
Front Row sitting:
Bob Dyer   Frank Fitzpatrick   Mark Groves   Mick Cook
Front centre sitting: **Bryan Popple**

Aldridge Cricket Club 1853 - 2003

Under 16s 1980 at Moseley

Standing: L-R Andrew Foster   Lincoln Barrett   Adrian Cooper   Michael Edge   Adrian Turner
Ian Manwaring (Capt)   Andy Roberts   Gordon Popple
Kneeling: L-R
Nigel Beck   Gary Harris   Mark Rasmin   Paul Godwin   Bob Barnes   Keith Woodhall

From around 1976 the under 16 team played in the Alpine Soft Drinks League and Knockout. In 1980 they reached the semi-finals at Moseley. The Juniors were then participating in two Junior Cricket competitions, the Alpine under 16 which took the lads to Alrewas, Milford Hall, and Lichfield and the Manders under 19 League Group B, against sides from Walsall, Old Hill Smethwick and Brierley Hill. By 1981 there were under 15 fixtures as well as the Alpine and Manders Competitions. The Manders League in 1983 was not regarded as 'Junior Cricket' any more and there was the Alpine under 16 League, Under 15 Sportsland Trophy, Under 13 Sportsland Trophy (8-a-side) and under 13 Midshires One Day Knockout also 8-a-side. The Junior Leagues continued throughout the eighties with most having a name change virtually every year. So many were the fixtures by 1989 that even the Fixture card itself needed to be greatly enlarged, featuring West Midlands Youth Cricket Association Leagues and Knockouts as well as Staffordshire Cricket Association and Alpine Knockouts. The name 'Colts' had been abandoned before the end of the 1980s.

The West Midland Youth Cricket Association Under 13, Under 15, and Under 18 Leagues and Cup Competitions as well as the Alpine Under 16 League and the Staffordshire Cricket Association Under 13 and Under 15 Knockouts all had teams of Aldridge youngsters by 1990. From 1995 an Under 11's side was participating. In 1998 the Under 18 League changed to be Under '17'. It is a tribute to the high esteem of Youth Cricket at Aldridge that Gordon Popple has now been the Chairman of the Midland Youth Cricket Association for more than ten years.

Starting in August 1995 there was a series of matches arranged for the 'Ron Biddle Memorial Cup' played by Aldridge U 16s against Weston Super Mare. The Cup, in memory of Ron, who died in November 1994, was played against Weston because that is where Ron's son Mark, an Aldridge player from 1965 - 1975, was now an active cricketer. Dad had been, naturally, particularly proud of Mark's cricketing success. Ron had been an integral part of Aldridge C.C. and the Stick & Wicket for nearly 30 years serving on Committees, Umpiring for some 25 years, being affectionately dubbed 'Fingers Ron', and for several years being at the very centre of things as Club Secretary.

Throughout the 1990s and into the new Millennium there have been many representative Youth games hosted at Aldridge such as Staffs v Northants U 13s, Midland Combined Counties U 19 v Staffordshire U 19.

Ron Biddle Trophy Match
Aldridge under 16s v Weston-Super-Mare under 16s 1995

In centre at back Mrs Sheila Biddle, Mark Biddle & Gordon Popple

Aldridge Cricket Club 1853 - 2003

The Youth Academy

Lloyd Taylor, writing in the Club Commemmorative Brochure produced in 2003, explains that at the end of the 1999 season he was asked by John Westwood to attend a meeting of the youth section of the Club to advise on a coaching structure. By the end of September 1999 the first meeting of Aldridge Cricket Club Youth Academy was held. Within three months a structure was in place, a constitution formalised, officers appointed and a summer coaching programme drawn up. A five year plan was constructed to bind it all together and provide a focus.

The season begins in October with indoor sessions at Edgbaston allowing the youngsters to get quality indoor net practice. Running parallel to this are sessions at Aldridge School. Squad sessions for each group take place before Easter, after which they move outdoors with Tuesday as a set training night. A bowling machine has been purchased, along with ball trainers and mats for catching and keepers' practice. Equipment levels have been improved and a range of kit introduced to give the Academy a clear identity. The aim is to provide the opportunity for players, some of them girls, to develop to their maximum. The production of players who can enter into the senior sides has already begun and this will provide strength in depth for the Club over the next few years. In 2001 the Academy had no fewer than twelve county representatives across the whole age range.

In August 2001, Aldridge Youth Cricket went full-circle inasmuch as there was a return to working with schools. Firstly, the Youth Academy organised a 'Primary Schools Cricket Festival' in which the local Cooper & Jordan School, Hydesville Towers and Whitehall Schools took part. Teams of 8 played a version of the game called

Under 10s v Bronze 1996

'Pairs'. Every member of each squad got to bat resulting in an excellent day being had by all. Cooper & Jordan School, virtually next door to the Club, won the competition. Secondly, later the same month, a successful Under 15, 11 - a - side Cricket Festival was organised in conjunction with Aldridge School. The 35 over games were played over four days from 23rd July at Aldridge School and Aldridge Cricket Club. Teams from Aldridge, Old Hill, Bloxwich, Brewood, Walsall, Aston Manor, Beacon and Lichfield competed for a place in the final, played at Aldridge C.C.. The event continued in 2002 with Aldridge youngsters making the final that year. As a direct result of initiatives from Aldridge C.C., an Under 10s League team was started in 2001 which the Aldridge team won in its inaugural year. Officers of the Academy in 2003 are: President: A. G. Popple, Chairman: L. J. Taylor, Secretary: Mrs. C. L. Whittock, Treasurer L. J. Taylor. Coaches: A. Chew, M. James, A. Lee, T. Pettitt, L. Taylor, I. Whittock, A. Wylie & T. Robothan.

Youth Academy members 2000

Staff *Left to right* Chairman Gordon Popple, Coaches Mike Hunt, Alan Waldron. LLoyd Taylor, Ian Whittock and Mike James

The Social Side

Aldridge Cricket Club 1853 - 2003

Social activities of the Club have always reflected the trends of the day. It is not the place of this volume to provide a social history of Aldridge, since that is what it would need to be, certainly to record all the events prior to 1900. The Cricket Club, with its associated activities and events, was a major player in village life... an integral part of the fabric of the place.

Entertainment has usually gone hand in hand with the 'official' occasion; presentations, formal dinners and the like. Perhaps this pattern has been much more the case in the years since World War II when just organising an event for its own sake has not been so popular. Fund raising functions were pioneered in the 1880s when Mr George Gibbon Potter opened his hall, later known as the 'Assembly Rooms', the first event to be held there in 1884, the first of many, was a fund raising concert for Aldridge C.C.. The 'Assembly Rooms' was to become a 'second home' for the Club for many years. The Club 'Headquarters' was of course, the appropriate place for the annual "Do" so the old Elms, and then the Swan for much of the 1920s and 30s being the favoured venue. After the Assembly rooms were restored the Club was soon back in residence but had to move to the new Elms when the Assembly rooms were demolished in the late 1960s.

Jack Matthews, writing about 'Social Functions' in his book 'Aldridge Cricket' put pen to paper in the late 1940s, a time when he could personally recall his own early days with the Club, now more than a century ago. The publication year of 1948, was in the middle of a post-war period, of severe austerity - there were shortages of virtually everything. Food rationing, in particular, was still in force and the sheer indulgence of those lavish pre-war social occasions was looked back upon with a certain envious longing and relish only years of 'making do' could engender.

'The Club is far from dormant during the winter months, and every year Whist Drives and Dances are held, which, besides providing pleasant social entertainment for their numerous patrons, have been the means of materially augmenting the Club funds.

In these modern days, Whist Drives are so numerous in the village, it is hardly possible to believe that such forms of entertainment were almost unknown before the 1914 war. In fact, the Cricket Club was one of the first village organisations to "run" them. The writer well remembers approaching a dear old lady of his aquaintance regarding the purchase of a ticket for one of these early Whist Drives. "Drive", said she, "Oh no! you see, my rheumatism is very bad just at present, and, though I should much enjoy a nice drive in the summer time, I couldn't possibly stand it while the weather is so cold."

Before the Assembly Rooms were renovated, the old Institute in Leighswood Road was used for these events. Here, everything was far from ideal - an upper storey room, dimly lighted by smoky, smelly paraffin lamps - tables, chairs, crocks, etc., all had to be borrowed and collected from many different places. It was a work of some magnitude "getting up" a Whist Drive under such conditions. But still it was done, and very welcome was the money raised by these efforts.

The Cricket Whist Drives are now widely known, and are generally agreed to be among the most popular in the district. The high standard set at the beggining has been well maintained even in these difficult austere times.

In the early years of the century, the great social event of the village was the Annual Cricket Ball, which was billed in good time to allow the ladies every opportunity of obtaining a smart "creation", and Miss Selina Reynolds at the Paper Shop was soon sold out of the latest fashion books.

To give the old Hall (the present Assembly Rooms) a festive appearance, but also to cover up the then many defects in the walls and ceiling, a lavish display was made of muslin and bunting. Piano, violin and sometimes harp provided the music, rather a contrast to the present day blare of trumpet, saxophone, drums, and other kinds of queer "music".

The M.C. with his white rosette, and the Stewards (red rosettes), were waiting punctually, to welcome the dancers and arrange introductions. The dinky little programmes with their dainty coloured pencils and tassels were soon being exchanged and names entered thereon. As you may be sure, the more attractive ladies were not long in getting their programmes full, so the special task of the Stewards was to see that the "Wallflowers" got a fair share of dances.

Which of us whilst listening to the popular wireless feature "Those were the days!" cannot help but recall the Cricket Balls of those times?

A study of an old programme is fascinating. There we find the Polka, the Schottische, Barn Dance, the stately Quadrilles, the dreamy Waltz, the bustling Lancers, and several other real old timers.

Yes, one certainly needed a "cooler" after a rollicking set of Lancers, and the ladies' ornamental fans were very much in evidence.

And the Interval Dance - one had to be very discreet in choosing one's partner for this, as of course it determined whom one escorted in to supper. Wouldn't present day mortals welcome such a "spread" as was then provided. One's mouth waters to think of it all.

After the Interval, the gay business started all over again, and the pace was kept up till the early hours. The final "Galop" and the rendering of "Auld lang syne" brought another Cricket Ball to a close. Yes! those were the days indeed!

Another function always eagerly looked forward to was the "Annual Dinner", held at the Club headquarters. A neat little card indicated one's place - food amounting to a present month's ration disappeared in a short time - speeches extolling the merits and virtues of all and sundry were made, and toasts were drunk with enthusiasm.

Aldridge Cricket Club 1853 - 2003

This was the occasion too, when the company were wont to hear little anecdotes, often highly coloured, concerning well-known village characters. At one gathering, we heard the dramatic story of a determined assault on the well-known Village Sexton and gravedigger. It appeared that one dark and dismal winter's night, with the rain descending in torrents, he was winding his homeward way feeling all merry and bright, and loudly proclaiming the fact that he was the undisputed "King of Whetstone Lane". Little did he think that a jealous rival was at large. With difficulty, he negotiated the pits and puddles of this then neglected by-way, until, after crossing the railway bridge, he received a terrific bump in the rear, which sent him sprawling. Recovering slowly from this sudden and unexpected onslaught and brandishing his stout and trusty holly stick, he prepared for battle, but the unseen foe relentlessly attacked again and again until the poor fellow, buffeted in front and behind, was forced to call for help. The mysterious assailant was found to be none other than Jack Parkes' ancient goat, which evidently strongly resented his vociferous claims to sovereignty. The word "goat" was a "red rag" to the fallen monarch for many months afterwards.

Then there was Jack Aston's perennial story concerning the nocturtnal stalking and subsequent "bagging" of the feathered phenomenon in the grounds adjoining the Moot House. As to the bird's real identity, we were yearly left in doubt, as at one telling it was a flashy cock "pheasant", whilst at another it was a highly plumaged "parrot". Maybe it was neither, but the story was well told, and though perhaps nothing to do with cricket, it always provided much hilarity.

The best raconteur of all, however, was Howard Walton, almost as good a storyteller as he was cricketer. Many of the village "worthies" and even "unworthies" were caricatured in his witty rhymes and stories.

Perhaps his outstanding masterpiece was the screamingly funny epic poem giving a most vivid account of the grand ceremonial parade of the illustrious Mayor and Corporation through the beflagged village streets, amidst the acclamations and plaudits of the assembled crowds.

The Chairman of the now defunct Parish Council was the late Mr Joseph Marriott, one of our highly respected Vice-Presidents, and he was present on this particular occasion. During the opening lines, he was duly invested with a Chain of Office (surreptitiously purloined from a very intimate chamber adjoining), thereby making part atonement for the Authority's failure to furnish such a distinguished citizen with this important item of regalia.

The succeeding verses graphically pictured the auspicious event. Little Johnny Dunton, complete with shining leggings and flowing scarf and perched precariously on Mr Bonner's grey mare headed the cavalcade.

Weird strains from Jess Watson's rhythmically swaying concertina set a dignified pace for "Winkle", the Council Mace-bearer, who, frequently emitting cries of "Argus!", preceded the stately Mayor, resplendent in full regalia. Next came the brightly robed Councillors and State officials, followed by the sombre apparelled citizens making humble obeisance to their elected overlords. As a final tableau, came Joe Ditchfield's "Yellow Peril", belching out volumes of poisonous fumes, its owner almost engulfed in the cockbit, and honk-honking it along on its noisy and erratic course.

It was all well done. No offence was meant, nor yet taken, and everyone enjoyed the fun. Well merited applause greeted the musical interludes by the various artistes, while the ever popular humorists enlivened the proceedings with their songs and jokes. No such "do" was considered complete without the rendering of the ever popular duet "Watchman, what of the night?" and the old favourite "The Village Pump".

War and austerity have called a halt to such enjoyable functions, but doubtless they will return.'

And return they did, with the Assembly Rooms filled with Aldridge C.C. folk old-time dancing to the sounds of such bands as 'Vic Moseley and his Knights of Gladness' or 'Madame Bruce and the Spiders'. The floor was always liberally covered with chalk to facilitate a lightness of foot but this became positively dangerous on the very dry areas adjacent to the floor standing gas heaters. Sometimes there would be a smutty comedian who would leave certain distinguished ladies sitting po-faced and not amused! The Annual Dinner was soon resumed as a feature of the Club year. For many years this has been the occasion when trophies and awards were distributed although more recently the award-distribution has been made the subject of a separate occasion. Although the 1950s venue was the Assembly Rooms and later the 'Elms', other local facilities have also proved popular. Druid's Heath Golf Club, Walsall Football Club, Masonic Hall, and the Fairlawns Hotel, have all been used. Traditionally, a Cricket celebrity has been invited as principal Guest, a speech being made usually on some pertinent cricketing topic of the day which was then duly reported in the 'Walsall Observer'. Such guests have included, Dermott Reeve, Graham Gooch, George Pope, David Brown, Norman McVicker, Alan Smith etc. Some of the newspaper headlines which followed the events, provide a flavour of the speeches. Sometimes, like the one which read: 'Game of Cricket has deteriorated says Pope' - they require a second look!

With the modern facilities of the 'Stick & Wicket' being available virtually every day of the year for more than thirty years, it's perhaps hard to envisage the role unofficially assigned, in the past, to some individual Club members as they provided harmless 'recreation' after a game bashing out a tune on the old piano in the pavilion. This home spun fun was personified by the likes of Jim Bevan and his unique rendering of 'Cock - Robin' still remembered by many today. The 'Ladies Committee', when functioning, was frequently involved in organising social occasions and raising some much needed cash. (See page 60)

Fund - Raising is always required. Even though the social facilities at Aldridge are first-class, there is always a cost to keeping them up and running. On the playing side too, equipment, coaching, administration, ground-maintenance and countless other requirements mean that the Cricket team of today is constantly seeking to generate an income just to remain in business.

Aldridge Cricket Club 1853 - 2003

Annual Dinner 1937
The Swan - High Street

Billy Groves · Howard Walton · T. H. Partridge · Alf Buckley

Playing members are standing.

Future bright for Aldridge cricket club

Bring youth into cricket, says League president

Game of cricket has deteriorated says Pope

Bad wickets – complacency ar...

UNIVERSITIES ROB ALDRIDGE OF PLAYERS

TEST FAILURE IS REFLECTED ADVERSELY

CRICKET NEEDS 'CHARACTERS' SAYS ALAN SMITH

Enterprise praised

THE SPORTING SPIRIT OF CLUB CRICKET

Annual Dinner 1956
Assembly Rooms
Rookery Lane

Howard Walton · Dr. Victor Milne · Mr McCarthy · Harry Crumpton · David Partridge · Mrs Crumpton · Mrs Partridge · Alan Collins · Mrs Whitehouse ? · Billy Bunn · Geoff Whitehouse · Mrs Whitehouse · Stan Whitehouse · Mrs Davies · Keith Davies · Mr Davies · Vince Edgar · Mrs Edgar · Mrs Newsome · Jack Newsome

The Social Side — Page 103

Aldridge Cricket Club 1853 - 2003

ALDRIDGE CRICKET CLUB

CENTENARY
1853 — 1953
DINNER

At the
ASSEMBLY ROOMS
on
Monday, March 9th 1953

Toasts

Toast — "THE QUEEN"
The Chairman (H. Walton Esq.)

Toast — "THE CLUB"
B. Burrell Davis Esq.
Response H. Walton Esq.

Toast — "THE PRESIDENT and VICE-PRESIDENTS"
Ald. Sir J. Cliff Tibbits J.P.
Response Mrs. Buckley
Dr. V. E. Milne

Toast — "THE ..."
W. Groves Esq.
Response ...

Toast — "THE ..."
F. P. Stephens Esq.

Aldridge C.C. congratulated on policy

ALDRIDGE CRICKET CLUB

ANNUAL DINNER
ASSEMBLY ROOMS, ALDRIDGE
MONDAY, MARCH 10th, 1958

ALDRIDGE CRICKET CLUB
ANNUAL DINNER AND DANCE
HELD AT
THE ELMS HOTEL, ALDRIDGE
ON
MONDAY, JANUARY 30th, 1961

GUEST OF HONOUR:
H. W. HOMER, ESQ.
President of Old Hill C.C.
Chairman Warwickshire County Cricket Club Committee

ALDRIDGE CRICKET CLUB
Cricketers Dinner
on
THURSDAY, 21st APRIL, 1977
held at
DRUIDS HEATH GOLF CLUB

ALDRIDGE CRICKET CLUB
Cricketers' Dinner
at
FAIRLAWNS HOTEL, ALDRIDGE
...DAY, 13th NOVEMBER, 1987

Cricket Club's important part in Aldridge life

Perhaps the

CRICKET'S LOW EBB DISCUSSED

Annual Dinner 1970 — The Elms

Pictured: Bill Baker, Mrs Baker, Helen Franks, Mrs V. Milne, Jenny Milne, Russ Pickston, Brian Crabtree, Jean ..., Sheila Brown, Mearns Milne, Geoff Walker, Ken Brown, Sheila Hastilow, Jonathan Franks, Frank Hastilow, Geoff Whitehouse, David Franks, Stan Wycherley, Bill Groves, Christine Franks

Page 104 — The Social Side

Aldridge Cricket Club 1853 - 2003

A Cricket Club Wedding in the 1960s
L to R
Martin Tyas, Martin Baker, Russell Pickston.
The happy couple - Mick & Sheila Hall
Jack Newsome, ? , Frank Hastilow

largest, and certainly the most famous fund-raising social events in the Club's history were organised in the late 1960s. Cash was needed to re-fit the pavilion and turn it into a facility which would, hopefully, meet modern requirements. Much of the cash for the modernisation, including some to spare, was raised by holding 'Ox-Roasts'. On August Bank Holiday Monday, 1967 the first of these great fund-raising and social events was held. David Franks, who had suggested a 'barbecue' some three years before, was the driving force behind this bold project. Stalls and sideshows were set up around the perimeter of the field with a cricket match in progress. Thousands of visitors turned up with over £500 being raised - an absolutely fantastic total. The event was repeated by the Cricket Club over the next two years with similar results. In 1970 the Ox-Roast became a combined operation with the Hockey Club under the new banner of the 'Stick & Wicket'. Again, a social success it was a very good way of building bridges between the two Clubs.

With the opening of the 'Stick & Wicket' many social functions were organised via that committee rather than being simply cricket affairs. In 1978 the minutes of Aldridge C.C. recorded that... *'the Sports Section is being subsidised by the Social Side.'* The generation of funds for the Cricket Club continues to happen through the auspices of the 'Stick & Wicket' as well as from separate events.

Special cricket matches have always attracted visitors and this is where the purely social and cricketing sides of the Club can work together. A particular celebrity or 'Benefit' match can be transfomed into a great social occasion where some extra cash can be raised. Fund raising events which use the field such as 'Fun Days' have also been supported by the playing of a cricket match.

In the 150th Anniversary Year, 2003 there has been a number of special events some of which are described on the following page. A lavishly illustrated 'Official Commemorative Brochure' was produced by the Club to mark the year containing goodwill messages from friends and supporters in the local community. Richard Shepherd MP, Member of Parliament for Aldridge-Brownhills, wrote that *'... community is fortunate to have a club that provides such a wonderful opportunity to us all'*. The Mayor of Walsall, Cllr. Roger Collins, stated that *'... Aldridge Cricket Club has distinguished itself as an institution dedicated to promoting the spirit of sportsmanship...'* Dennis Amiss, Chief Executive, Warwickshire County Cricket Club commented that the Club was *'...superbly run, with a charming ground and excellent facilities...'* Alan Neal, Chairman of the Midlands Club Cricket Conference recalled his first game at Aldridge whilst playing for Burton 2nd XI. He recorded his first half-century in senior cricket that day as part of a century making opening partnership. The match, which finished in torrential rain, was won by Aldridge but continued in a nearby pub ... probably the Elms. Neal said that it was *'...amazing to think that this match took place 45 years ago...'*.

At The First Ox Roast 1967

A well-balanced young lady tries her hand at removing the ring without upsetting the "boat" at Aldridge Cricket Club's ox roast and fete at the club ground on Monday.

Can you spot Mike Pemberton, Greg Pendry, Kent Kirby and Sylvia Langford?

Aldridge Cricket Club 1853 - 2003

Family Fun Day and Under 11 Tournament
May 5th

150 Not out

2003 - 150th Anniversary Year

Aldridge Veterans v Invitation Veterans
July 11th
Evening match

Standing L- R: Gordon Popple (Umpire) John Carter (Rugeley) Jim Hartley (Aldridge) Micky Dawson (Rugeley) Brian Boyd (Highcroft/Gt. Barr Unity) Keith Buller (Aldridge) Neil Castley (Aldridge) Bill Newbold (Highcroft/Gt. Barr Unity) Alan Waldron (Aldridge) Mick Dufty (Aldridge) Steve Dean (Aldridge) Ray Edge (Aldridge) Ray Cutler (Aldridge) David Edge (Aldridge) Ron Chew (Aldridge) Peter Williams (Aldridge)

Seated L- R: Stirling Hamman (Cannock & Rugeley) Les West (Cannock & Rugeley) Alan Russell (Bloxwich) Sam Harvey (Aldridge) Russ Pickston (Aldridge) Bill Tranter (Old Wulfs.) Brian Cornick (Aldridge) Ian Whittock (Aldridge)
Front: Inderdeep Singh (Aldridge)

ALDRIDGE CRICKET CLUB

2003

150th Anniversary Year

Fixtures and Membership Card

Founded 1853

Affiliated to the
Midland Club Cricket Conference

Registered Office:
THE STICK AND WICKET PAVILLION
Telephone: 01922 451400

Meetings:
STICK AND WICKET CLUB

www.aldridgecricketclub.co.uk

BATTING ORDER

Reception
7.30 - 8.00
Please be seated by 8.00 p.m.

Grace
A. G. Popple Esq. Aldridge Cricket C.C.

Dinner
Guests are requested to refrain from smoking
at the tables until after the Royal toast

The Queen
Proposed by: A. J. Franks Esq. President Aldridge C.C.

150 Years of Aldridge Cricket
Proposed by: Andrew Wylie, Boland C.C., S. Africa and
Aldridge C. C.

Response - A. J. Franks Esq.

Umpire - R. E. Pickston - Secretary Aldridge C. C.

Dancing & Entertainment by
Garry Allcock & The Allstars

Celebration Dinner at Bescot Stadium Walsall
September 26th

ALDRIDGE CRICKET CLUB
150 ANNIVERSARY
CELEBRATION DINNER

FRIDAY 26th SEPTEMBER 2003
The Priory Room - Bonsor Suite
Bescot Stadium
7.30 p.m. for 8.00 p.m.

Dancing & Entertainment by the
Garry Allcock & The Allstars

Bar extension until midnight   Sponsored by Bank's

At 8pm on the last Thursday of each month between May - Aug there was a social gathering for current and former players. Many stories were exchanged over a pint or two.